Fascism

Modern Ideologies

FASCISM

Noël O'Sullivan
*Senior Lecturer in Politics,
University of Hull*

J.M. Dent & Sons Ltd
London and Melbourne

First published 1983
© Noël O'Sullivan, 1983

All rights reserved
This book is set in 11/12½pt VIP Plantin by
Inforum Ltd, Portsmouth
Made in Great Britain by
Biddles Ltd, Guildford, Surrey for
J.M. Dent & Sons Ltd
Aldine House, 33 Welbeck Street, London W1M 8LX

British Library Cataloguing in Publication Data

O'Sullivan, Noel
 Fascism.—(Modern ideologies series)
 1. Fascism
 I. Title
 335.6   JC481

 ISBN 0-460-10428-4
 ISBN 0-460-11428-X Pbk

Preface

The immediate subject of this book is fascism, but in a broader perspective it is also about the emergence in the modern world of a revolutionary new style of politics of which fascism is only one manifestation.

To find a word which would describe the new style accurately has been difficult. The word 'total' has the attraction of diametrical opposition to the older, 'limited' style of politics which the new style aims to supersede, but I have rejected it because total politics need not be activist: Plato, for example, advocated total politics, but was completely opposed to any kind of activism. In the end, the word activism seemed the most suitable because it conveys most adequately the main characteristic of all modern radical ideologies, which is the assertion that no government can be legitimate unless it offers scope for active participation in politics by 'the people', however defined. It was particularly important to stress the activist impulse in the present context because the most striking feature of fascism, which is the ideal of permanent revolution, is only fully intelligible when it is related to this.

It is perhaps unnecessary to add that what I describe as the new activist style of politics ultimately owes much to two long-established and deeply rooted western political phenomena which have tended to converge in communist and fascist visions of utopia. One of these phenomena is the tradition of millennial speculation and apocalyptic hopes which has an almost uninterrupted history, extending back to the ancient world, in spite of persistent attempts at suppression by the established authorities. I have referred briefly to this tradition in so far as it is directly related to the study of facism, but without attempting to do full justice to the suggestive pattern of symbols explored in the work of scholars such as Norman Cohn and Eric Voegelin.

The other phenomenon is the tradition known in contemporary literature as 'civic humanism'. The point at which the civic humanist tradition became 'activist' in the sense adopted here may be identified as the time when it merged with the doctrine of popular sovereignty. Since this occurred only at the end of the eighteenth century, to have traced the civic humanist theme back over earlier centuries would have been a distraction from the main purpose of this study. No proper understanding of either the activist style at large, however, or of fascism in particular, is possible without reference to J.G.A. Pocock's exemplary studies of this subject.

A brief sketch of what is meant by 'limited' and 'activist' politics appeared earlier, in an edited collection of essays for Wheatsheaf Press on the theme of revolution in the modern world, but without any attempt to bring the analysis to bear specifically on fascism.

Finally, it remains to be noticed that one of the most interesting and important documents of twentieth-century political life has not only been frequently neglected but is also relatively inaccessible. This is the Constitution of the Province of Carnaro (better known, more briefly, as the Constitution of Fiume). The document is important for the light it throws on the theory and practice of Italian Fascism, but it is even more important for the insight it provides (in a microcosmic setting) into the structure of the new activist style at large. A translation of this document is printed here as an Appendix to the volume.

Hull, May 1983   N.K. O'S.

Acknowledgments

I am grateful to David George for the patience with which he discussed every aspect of my work with me.

I am also grateful to Jocelyn Burton for her meticulous attention to the entire manuscript, and for constructive suggestions which invariably improved it.

Contents

For

M. O. and E. K.

Introduction

The flow of new books on fascism now threatens to become a deluge. It is therefore desirable to indicate briefly the reason for adding yet another work to a subject which already gives every indication of becoming the academic growth industry of the next decade.

The study of fascism poses six crucial questions. The most remarkable feature of contemporary political science is the fact that, some sixty years after Mussolini's march on Rome, and in spite of the constant flow of new works at the present day, scholars are still in doubt about the answers to all of them.

The first question arises as soon as one casts even the most superficial glance at the extensive literature now devoted to the subject. Why, the reader will inevitably ask, does this literature reveal so much radical disagreement about what fascism actually was, even though more than thirty years have elapsed since the Italian and German regimes were destroyed? By way of reply to this question it is suggested (in the first chapter) that the prevailing intellectual mood of our age has inevitably made fascism incomprehensible to us. It has made fascism incomprehensible because, according to the ideological assumptions implicit in that mood, fascism was not supposed to happen at all. It is this dangerously optimistic conviction which explains not only the present inadequacy of our intellectual theories, but also the failure of statesmen to recognize clearly the destructive implications of fascism during the inter-war period itself. To liberal, socialist and conservative politicians alike, the notion that a modern ideology might be wilfully destructive came as a complete surprise.

This almost universal sense of surprise, it must be stressed, is not a thing of the past. It persists, on the contrary, right down to the present day. The assumptions about life, morality and politics which account for it, however, remain as effectively

1

concealed from our own generation as they did from the inter-war generation by the increasingly elaborate theories into which the old ideological prejudices which originally made fascism unthinkable have been refined in the meantime. Of these theories Marxism continues to be the most influential, but in different forms the same surprise and incomprehension permeate not only liberal theories of fascism, but also the large body of purportedly 'empirical' work on the subject produced by sociologists, political scientists and socio-psychologists. The upshot is that the greater part of the current literature on fascism continues to offer little more than an elaborate series of conspiracy theories.

The weakness of all these theories is that each of them necessarily entails a highly oversimplified reading of modern European intellectual and political history, since each is in-tended to explain why something which was not supposed to happen nevertheless occurred. Within this framework of thought, the conventional analyses of fascism proceed upon the assumption that the modern age can be analysed in terms of a conflict between tendencies regarded as 'progressive', on the one hand, and countervailing tendencies regarded as 'reaction-ary' or 'regressive', on the other. Fascism, of course, is treated as the product of the regressive tendencies. Surprise, then, generates conspiracy theories, and conspiracy theories produce historical oversimplification. They require, that is, that the complexities of history should be abandoned in favour of a retrospective search for nice and nasty ideas, thinkers and tendencies, in a world which is polarized into saints and sinners, 'left' and 'right', good and evil, or light and darkness.

The second question arises from the first. If current inter-pretations of fascism are unsatisfactory because they are rooted in the historical oversimplification produced by ideological prejudice, then it is necessary to reconsider the true character of the relationship in which fascism stands to the cultural and political life of the modern European world. This is the subject of the second chapter. Instead of engaging in the usual quest for the 'origins' of fascism, the analysis offered there deals with this problem by fixing instead upon what is at once the most striking, and yet also the most elusive, feature of our age. This is the fundamental ambiguity and consequent instability of our most treasured moral and political ideals.

The ambiguity and instability, it will be suggested in that chapter, can only be understood in the light of the impact of a new style of politics which first appeared at the end of the eighteenth century, at the time of the French Revolution, and has spread in the meantime throughout the western world. This new style of politics may be described as an activist style of politics, in contrast with the older limited style of politics which had previously been regarded in Europe as the supreme achievement of civilized societies. The nature of these two styles will be described more fully in due course; for the moment it must suffice to note that it is the impact of the new activist style of politics upon the older limited style which has rendered the modern European political tradition unstable. The result is that all our political ideas have been left exposed to extremist interpretations, each of which may claim – with every semblance of plausibility – that it is the only 'true' interpretation. Of the variety of possible extremist interpretations, fascism is the most dramatic and in many respects also (unpalatable though the fact may be) the most consistent and plausible.

The third question relates to the vexed problem of whether it is permissible to use fascism in a 'generic' sense, to include both the Italian and the German regimes. Both the structure and the ideology of these regimes differed in vital respects. Likewise, the intellectual, social and political traditions from which they arose were also extremely different. Although most contemporary scholarship is now fully sensitive to these divergences, an uncritical acquiescence in the abstractions of Marxist theory has often served to obscure them by treating both as instances of exploitation by desperate capitalists. Once the Marxist interpretation is set to one side, however, the difficulty of establishing a plausible basis for continuing to subsume the two disparate regimes under the single label of 'fascism' becomes especially acute. The justification offered in the present analysis for doing so is implied in what has just been said. They are linked, that is, by the fact that the ideological premises upon which both relied were rooted in the new activist style of politics; and they are united, more specifically, by their com-

3

mon endeavour to weld the intellectual ingredients which comprise that style into a *Weltanschauung** which speciously purported to provide a dynamic, extra-constitutional fusion of the two great revolutionary movements of the modern age, viz. nationalism and socialism. It is worth recalling, in this connection, Elizabeth Wiskemann's pertinent remark, that 'many who called themselves Nazis . . . were rather Fascist than Nazis'.[1] In other words, the fanatical idea of physically annihilating the Jews which is the most obvious distinguishing feature of Nazism was the concern of only a small proportion of Nazi supporters; few of those who supported Hitler, it must be remembered, did so for racialist reasons of this extreme nature.

The fourth question, like the third one, can only properly be answered by a full consideration of the intellectual premises, the logical structure, and the practical political implications of what is referred to as the new activist style of politics. This question concerns the relationship between fascism and its great ideological rival, communism. According to their own professions, these two ideologies are mortal foes. Yet fascism, in spite of its professed hostility to Marxism, claimed to be a form of socialism – 'national socialism'. Unfortunately, as one scholar remarks, 'the socialist aspects of fascism are those most commonly ignored',[2] since to stress them conflicts with the prevailing (and totally misleading) intellectual identification of fascism as a right-wing movement. Communism, likewise, has in practice become an increasingly nationalist ideology, in spite of its claim to be an internationalist creed. Communist ideologues, needless to say, would deny this; but since Stalin proclaimed the doctrine of 'socialism in one country', the dividing line between Marxism and National Socialism has become even more difficult to discern. This does not mean, it should be stressed, that Marxism itself is 'really' a form of fascism; what is suggested in the present work is rather that the overt opposition between these two ideologies merely serves to conceal a more basic

---

* Sir Ernest Barker's definition of this term remains the most useful: 'a general set of social and political ideas which covers and colours the whole of life, and is in that sense total, but is yet, and at the same time, exclusive and peculiar to [a party]' (*Reflections on Government*, p. 88–9).

4

underlying affinity between them. The nature of the affinity, however, can no more be brought out by treating fascism as a deviant form of Marxism (as A.J. Gregor, for example, has recently maintained) than by treating twentieth-century Marxism as a form of fascism. The analysis offered here approaches the controversial question of their relationship in a different fashion: instead of trying to present one ideology as a variant on the other, both are presented as two variations of that broader and distinctively modern style of politics which is described, for want of a better term, as an activist style.

The fifth question concerns the nature of fascism itself. Was fascism an ideology, or was it – as the fascists themselves often claimed – an anti-ideology in which a cult of action took the place of any doctrinal commitment? Or was it, as others have maintained, merely an emotional affair, 'essentially a romantic adventure, a kind of . . . emotional fling'?[3] In France, for example, Brasillach spoke of fascism as a 'poetry' and was fascinated, as one scholar reminds us, 'by poetic images, images of young men camping around fires at night, of mass meetings, of heroic exploits of the past'.[4] To deal with this question, a more extended consideration of the intellectual structure of the new activist style of politics already mentioned is necessary, in order to determine more precisely the character of the specifically fascist version of that style.

This is the subject of chapters three, four and five. The main point that emerges in the course of considering this problem is that fascist ideology introduced no novel or unique idea or principle into western political experience. The significance of fascism is to be found, on the contrary, not in its novelty, but in the fact that it made explicit implications of the new activist style which other versions of activism (such as communism) have endeavoured to conceal. The most important of these implications is that the natural tendency of the new activist style of politics is towards three things: a condition of permanent revolution, a cult of despotic leadership trapped out in democratic guise, and a highly theatrical form of state-worship that culminates in an ideal of self-sufficiency which makes a programme of conquest and expansion integral to the fascist philosophy.

The sixth and last question concerns the significance fascism possesses for the future of the West, and indeed for the world at large. Are we to take seriously the claim originally made by Mussolini, but now commonly advanced by contemporary political scientists, that ours will be the 'century of fascism'? Or are we to regard the significance of fascism as confined to the inter-war era, or even more narrowly, to Italian and German history? The answer to this complicated question must be postponed until the final chapter, in which an attempt will also be made to indicate how fascism is related to contemporary terrorist movements.

It will be clear that none of the six questions outlined above can be adequately dealt with by culling new facts from the archives. What they require is, instead, an analytic and interpretative approach, of a kind which the vast body of existing literature on fascism has for the most part thus far failed to provide. It is in this light that the present essay is to be viewed; as an attempt, that is, not to chart altogether unknown territory, but to sketch the contours of a map whose landmarks are familiar, but whose outline still eludes the eye. In this way it may help to make the meaning and significance of fascism within modern European history more intelligible.

1 A Bolt from the Blue

The word 'fascism' enjoys the distinction of being the most novel term in the vocabulary of twentieth-century political thought.[1] From almost its first appearance there, however, it has also enjoyed the further distinction of being the most controversial and elusive term in that vocabulary, in both popular and academic usage. Even in academic quarters, no agreement has yet been reached about its nature and significance, although five decades of research and reflection now lie behind us. In this situation, it would be useless to begin by adding yet one more definition to the existing plethora, since that would merely confuse matters still further. Before a definition can profitably be attempted, the ground must first be prepared by determining why the existing position is so unsatisfactory. Why, in a word, has fascism proved to be such an elusive concept?

The answer, in fact, is not far to seek. Stated briefly, and very baldly, it is that fascism appeared like a bolt from the blue. The advent of fascism in the present century, that is to say, took nearly everybody by surprise; and surprise, of course, is at once the parent and the child of theoretical incomprehension. In every case, the great ideologies of our century left no room for a phenomenon of this kind. Marxists, after all, had been dreaming of a proletarian revolution; socialists had hoped for a more peaceful transition to the workers' utopia; liberals had hoped that, after the shock of the Great War, the world would resume its way towards democracy, enlightenment and moderation; and conservatives, with a nostalgic eye on the past, had not suspected that a movement which purported to be anti-socialist might also be radically anti-conservative.

What will be suggested in the present chapter is that this unsatisfactory response is explained, as was remarked in the introduction, by the naive optimism which has been the most marked characteristic of modern western cultural and political

7

life. This optimism became the basis of western intellectual orthodoxy during the eighteenth century, when men ceased to believe that evil is an integral part of the human condition, as the old Christian doctrine of the Fall had taught, and came to believe, instead, that evil originated in the structure of society. Evil, it followed, could therefore be eliminated by changing the order of society. In a perfectly organized society, consequently, there would be no more evil, no more oppression, no more 'alienation', and no more conflict. Human nature, in short, would finally achieve completely free and harmonious self-expression. In a more or less attenuated form, the belief in human perfectibility which replaced the old belief in the ineliminable character of evil has survived down to the present day. Our great ideologies, our political theory and our political science all continue to rest upon this assumption, even if, after two world wars, the dream of human perfectibility has now lost some of its plausibility. And it is precisely because our scholarly apparatus, as well as our day-to-day beliefs, are infected with this optimism that the prevailing theories of fascism – especially the Marxist and the liberal ones – are all so unsatisfactory.

But how, it will naturally be asked, does the surprise born of this surviving Enlightenment optimism reveal itself in academic theories of fascism? It is, after all, one thing to recognize in a general way that fascism took the present century by surprise, but quite another to be able to identify the persuasive and insidious forms which this surprise assumes in the elaborate theories of fascism which confront us. The most convenient way of illustrating how the element of surprise penetrates and vitiates academic theories of fascism is to begin by considering the form it assumes in some of the simpler and more familiar approaches adopted by liberal thinkers.

In the simplest form of all, liberal optimism rests upon a reading of western history which treats fascism as the outcome of an 'irrationalist' revolt against the western tradition of reason and moderation. Here, surprise is transparent in, for example, Hans Kohn's assertion that, 'The outlook on life of those who have adopted fascism or communism has nothing in common with the western tradition of reason.'[2] Similar sentiments inspired the Oxford philosopher R. G. Collingwood, when he identified fascism as the 'new barbarism'.[3] A final example is Hannah Arendt's conviction that the advent of totalitarian regimes constitutes such a radical break with all our traditions that it has completely exploded our categories of political thought and our standards for moral judgment.[4] Even more dramatically, totalitarianism is said to originate in forces which are so entirely alien to the western political tradition that they 'can no longer be deduced from humanly comprehensible motives'.[5]

When surprise and moral outrage reach these heights, there is an obvious danger that liberal hostility to fascism may make it totally inexplicable. If the totalitarian experience is absolutely unique, that is, and lacks any connection with the western tradition, or any 'humanly comprehensible motives', then how are we to escape the conclusion that theoretical interpretation must inevitably fail altogether, leaving only the spectacle of fascism as the beast emerging from the abyss?

In the end, the liberal intellectual cannot escape this conclusion, but there are various strategies by which the weaknesses of his theoretical position are concealed both from himself and his reader. Of these strategies, four are sufficiently familiar to be worth noticing.

The first consists of confining the study of fascism to individual portraits of the Führer, the Duce, and the individuals surrounding them, with every detail of their lives meticulously documented. We now know, for example, 'the secret of the seventeen-year-old Hitler's hopeless passion for the beautiful and unapproachable Stephanie, the daughter of well-to-do parents, with whom he never succeeded in exchanging a word'.[6] But what is to be learned about the nature of fascism, in the last resort, from these more or less massive biographies? They only serve, if anything, to make fascism still more incomprehensible, since by its very nature the detail of personal biography distracts from the broader patterns of cultural and political life. The present intention is not, of course, to deny or disparage the value of detailed historical research on the fascist leadership, but only to point out the serious intellectual limitations which arise from failure to situate this work within the broader context of European political life which gave rise to

9

fascism. The same failure is reflected in two further ways of dealing with fascism, both of which encourage complacency by obscuring its intimate connection with the modern European liberal democratic tradition.

One of these strategies – the second of the four to be considered – consists of explaining fascism by constructing a rogues' gallery composed of all those thinkers who are regarded as having encouraged reactionary or irrational tendencies in an age otherwise inspired by progressive, humanitarian and idealistic goals. The most notable rogues' gallery venture in recent years was the publication of a series of volumes entitled *Roots of the Right*.[7] In that series, thinkers as disparate as Max Stirner, José Antonio Primo de Rivera, Gobineau, Hippolyte Taine, Charles Maurras and Alfred Rosenberg were conscripted into a series of 'black books' in whose pages, the editorial preface claimed, were to be found the origins of the 'return to barbarism' which our age has witnessed. (There is no reason, of course, why the selection of rogues should be limited to those named; Schopenhauer, Nietzsche, Bergson and H. S. Chamberlain are favourite candidates for inclusion in enterprises of this kind.) The extraordinary intellectual incoherence involved in bringing together such totally disparate figures, linked neither by class, nor interest, nor doctrine, is not the only problem involved in identifying 'the right' which is supposed to be the unifying subject of the series. No less problematic is the historical anachronism inherent in works like Karl Popper's *The Open Society and Its Enemies*, which is only the best-known of many works that trace the rogues as far back as Plato in the ancient world – often fixing upon the much-maligned Machiavelli as a particularly important transitional rogue en route from Plato to Hitler. The rogues' gallery approach, it is hardly necessary to add, is not peculiar to liberal intellectual historians; Lukacs' study of the origins of fascism, in his *The Destruction of Reason* (1954), is obviously a parallel treatment, albeit one which issues from a different stable. The purpose of Lukacs' book was 'to bring to light all the intellectual spadework done on behalf of "the National Socialist outlook" ' by tracing the line running from Schelling to Hitler.[8]

The criticism being made at present, it should perhaps be

stressed, has nothing to do with whether the favourite candidates for the rogues' gallery of 'right-wing' villains constructed by liberal and socialist scholars were really villains or not; to pursue an issue of that kind would not take us beyond moralizing. The criticism, rather, is that the rogues' gallery procedure disregards the possibility that the modern liberal democratic tradition may itself contain potential sources of instability and extremism. This suggestion is hardly novel, since it is to be found in nineteenth-century thinkers like Constant, de Tocqueville and Burckhardt; yet latter-day writers, ignoring the caveats of these earlier thinkers, have been content to attribute the origins of political extremism to the periphery of modern European intellectual and political life, by ascribing them to a line of thinkers who are presented as enemies of freedom, reason and moderation.

In somewhat different form, a similar oversimplified and complacent interpretation of fascism occurs when the liberal historian concludes that because fascism was primarily an Italian and German phenomenon, it therefore has no broader significance for modern European politics. Nazism, in particular, is prone to be dismissed in this way. To A. J. P. Taylor, for instance, the Third Reich was the kind of political bungle one might expect from Germans once they tried to do anything for themselves, since the only genuinely creative elements in German political history have always come from outside Germany. The old empire 'had been imposed by the armies of Austria and France; the German Confederation by the armies of Russia and Prussia, the Weimar Republic by the victories of the Allies, but the "Third Reich" rested solely on German force and German impulse, it owed nothing to alien forces. It was a tyranny imposed upon the German people by themselves.'[9]

Finally, there is a fourth liberal strategy for preserving an optimistic attitude towards the sources of political extremism to be found in modern western political life. This is the most dangerously complacent strategy of all. It consists of dismissing Hitler and Mussolini as madmen and branding fascism as a phenomenon which appeals only to the psychologically disturbed, or to stupid masses who blindly follow a leader endowed with some mysterious quality called 'charisma'. The result is

11

that fascism becomes a sort of Murder Incorporated, as Joachim Fest recently put it,[10] which is intelligible, in the last resort, only as a species of insane demonism.

It may well be objected at this point that the existing literature on fascism is being dismissed in a way which is far too high-handed to do it full justice. This objection can most easily be countered by considering in some detail the most ambitious study of fascism that has appeared during the past two decades. This is Ernst Nolte's major work, *Three Faces of Fascism* (1963),[11] which provides excellent illustrations of the main methodological weaknesses that have just been said to characterize a great deal of the contemporary literature on fascism.

Nolte's thesis is quite simple. Fascism, he maintains, is a phenomenon peculiar to one epoch in modern history – viz. the inter-war epoch. Being peculiar to that epoch, for reasons which will be considered shortly, it naturally disappeared from the world at the end of the Second World War, when the two great fascist regimes were finally destroyed. It is true, Nolte says, that some manifestations of fascism have lingered on into the post-war period, but these, he writes, do not contradict the 'epochal' character of fascism since they do not possess what he describes as 'world significance'.[12]

Nolte begins, then, by assigning to fascism only an epochal and not a world significance. The implication of this assertion, clearly enough, is that fascism is in some sense an aberration in what might otherwise have been expected to be the 'natural' course of modern historical development. What Nolte considers to be the natural course of the modern age is evident from his assertion that what he calls 'the great trends of the age' are most truly reflected in Marxism and liberalism, rather than in fascism. It is these two great 'progressive' ideologies, he believes, which have not only shaped the basic structure of European society since the French Revolution, but will also 'always be present in what is to come'. It is for this reason, according to Nolte, that Lenin and Woodrow Wilson both possess 'world significance', as men who embody the great enduring ideals of our age. Hitler, by contrast, possesses only 'epochal significance'. Hitler's significance, that is to say, is confined purely to the inter-war epoch, and does not transcend his age, as that of Lenin and Wilson apparently does.[13] Since Nolte regards Hitler in this way, it is no surprise to find that throughout his book he clearly regards fascism as somehow 'untypical' of our age; as something, that is, which is definitely an aberration or deviation from the essential nature or main tendency of modernity, which is assumed to be basically progressive. This is especially evident when he writes, for example, that 'in the overall relationships of the age, fascism . . . will have to be regarded as primarily a reaction'.[14] But if that is so, then obviously fascism can only be interpreted in terms of a more or less elaborate conspiracy theory designed to explain how this reactionary triumph occurred, and the remainder of Nolte's analysis accordingly endeavours to provide one. It is instructive to examine the three principal ways in which he goes about this task.

In the first place, since fascism is not rooted in the 'great trends' of the age (i.e. Marxism and liberalism), it must arise, Nolte assumes, from the survival of regressive ideals into a progressive era in which those ideals can only play an alien and destructive part. Accordingly, Nolte casts his eye about for these surviving regressive elements, and seizes upon the French reactionary tradition as the antiquated vehicle within which the fascist germ cell was carried for over a century, before it finally festered and erupted in the inter-war years. Fascism, that is to say, is an extension of the French counter-revolutionary tradition. Taken in conjunction with the reactionary tradition, fascism thus reflects 'the despair of the feudal section of bourgeois society for its traditions, and the bourgeois element's betrayal of its own revolution . . .'[15] Nolte's first attempt to construct a conspiracy theory, then, identifies the conspirators as the French reactionary thinkers. Yet this explanation of the origins of fascism is of course absurd.

It is absurd because reactionary ideology, unlike fascism, was never an activist ideology; the last thing it ever aimed at, that is, was mobilizing the masses. The whole philosophy of will behind the fascist ideal, with its corresponding cult of action, is quite alien to the reactionary tradition, in which the part which

13

man's will plays in shaping his destiny is reduced to the barest minimum. What is more, there is of course no evidence at all to indicate that Hitler and Mussolini were ever influenced, let alone inspired, by thinkers like de Maistre and Maurras, to whom Nolte nevertheless devotes one-third of his book. Finally, if the 'great trends' of today are indeed Marxism and liberalism, then it is impossible to understand how reactionary ideas, which are assumed to be alien to the present age, ever became the basis of mass movements. Mass movements, given the logic of political parties, could only arise by drawing upon the 'great trends' of the age. Other trends, being archaic survivals of reactionary sentiment, could never win the support of the masses, since they are by definition an affair of minorities.

There is, however, a second line of thought to be found in Nolte's work, more especially in his treatment of Nazism, and it is therefore necessary to consider whether it enables him to deal with the difficulty just indicated. In order to explain how the Nazi movement won mass support, Nolte concentrates his analysis upon the person of Hitler. Hitler is presented as a near psychopath, a man 'on the border of sickness, driven by pathological fears'.[16] But the problem, in that case, is to understand how a mass movement could arise, with only a psychopath to explain its existence. Nolte's answer is to represent Hitler's hold over his followers as deriving from a kind of hypnosis, which deprived its victims of all responsibility for their actions. Thus the unlucky Germans became, Nolte believes, 'the victims of the more logically consistent mind', being quite unable to recognize the demonic character of that mind.[17] But how a psychopath ever came to be so logically consistent, or to exercise such an hypnotic influence remains a mystery. One extraordinary implication of this contention must, however, immediately be noticed. It follows that once the hypnotist disappears, the victims become their normal, decent selves once again. It is in this way that Nolte arrives at the strange conclusion that, 'After the Führer's death the core of leadership of the National Socialist state snapped back, like a steel spring wound up too long, to its original position, and became [once more] a body of well-meaning and cultured Central Europeans.'[18] This is obviously a consoling conclusion for a liberal and patriotic German writer to draw, but equally obviously it leaves all the important questions unanswered.

Finally, a close scrutiny of Nolte's work reveals that he relies to some extent on yet another way of explaining the appeal of fascism. This third way, which has frequently baffled his critics and defenders alike, involves nothing less than transposing the conspiracy theory of fascism to a cosmic setting. What we need in order to understand fascism, he insists, is a new method of study, which he describes as a 'transcendental sociology'.[19] In terms of this method, fascism is to be treated in the overall context of man's search for 'wholeness', which Nolte describes as his quest for transcendence. In this perspective, fascism is defined as the endeavour to prevent the achievement of transcendence, whilst liberalism and Marxism, in different ways, facilitate this most basic of human desires. Fascism, that is to say, is ultimately interpreted by this ambitious new methodology as a cosmic, extra-historical struggle between the forces of transcendence and the forces of immanence. This seems to be what Nolte means, for example, when he describes fascism as a perverse attempt to resolve the tension between the finite and the eternal.[20] It is significant that Nolte explicitly connects the new methodology he is advocating to theological categories.[21] And this is precisely why Nolte's new method is so disastrous: the very fact that it is rooted in theological conviction rather than in sociological or historical insight precludes it from ever explaining how fascism came to power in an age in which (according to Nolte) liberal and socialist movements should be in the ascendant. The theological conviction which inspires the new methodology is useless, in other words, because the 'transcendental' perspective which Nolte seeks does not explain fascism but only serves, on the contrary, to leave it hanging in an intellectual vacuum, suspended completely outside the complexities of modern European history.

Nolte's interpretation fails, then, because it never succeeds in establishing a plausible connection between fascism and the course of modern European intellectual and political history. On the contrary, it succeeds only in disconnecting fascism from modernity. The disconnection occurs because Nolte's whole analysis ultimately rests upon the belief that the modern period

15

may be polarized into 'progressive' and 'regressive' tendencies. The main objection to such an analysis is that it grossly distorts and oversimplifies the complexities of modern European history by presenting the modern world as essentially a struggle between the opposing forces of 'the left' and 'the right'. Usually, this simplistic left/right dichotomizing of history takes the sociological form of a class-based analysis, but Nolte himself rejects that manner of thought. The left/right dichotomy, however, creeps back into his own analysis in an intellectualist form, as a tension between the finite and the eternal, or between the forces of transcendence and immanence.

In Nolte's case, as in the case of others who share his simple interpretation of modern history as a struggle between progressive and regressive tendencies, the left/right dichotomy makes it totally impossible to deal adequately with one absolutely crucial problem. This is the problem of accounting for the affinity between fascism and Marxism. Both ideologies, after all, obviously share the same radical, dynamic character which is associated with 'movement' ideologies, and both aim at creating a utopia in which, by violent and fanatical methods, the powers of darkness and the forces of evil will be eliminated from the world. Yet their affinity remains inexplicable within the conventional polarization of history upon which thinkers like Nolte rely, since according to this view of modern history Marxism belongs to 'the left', whilst fascism is located on the extreme 'right'. The result is that in much of the literature on fascism its socialist aspects tend to be conveniently ignored. The crude identification of fascism as a right-wing movement accords very well with Russian official propaganda, of course, but it hardly makes for intellectual clarity. The best that Nolte can do is merely to acknowledge the problem, whilst simultaneously evading the task of dealing with it. Thus he insists, on the one hand, that an adequate definition of fascism must stress the anti-communist aspect of fascist ideology, whilst also insisting, on the other, that 'fascism should never be said to exist in the absence of at least the rudiments of an organization and propaganda comparable to those of Marxism'. We are left, in the end, with the problem of the precise relationship between the two ideologies unresolved, simply being told that fascism stands to Marxism as 'a radically opposed and yet related ideology'.[22]

In order to deal satisfactorily with the relationship between fascism and Marxism, it is necessary to abandon the kind of historical oversimplification entailed by Nolte's analysis. Before rejecting the left/right spectrum analysis of history altogether, however, we must look more carefully at the Marxist theory of fascism itself.

The Marxist analysis began with the definition of fascism laid down by Stalin's Comintern in 1933. According to Comintern doctrine, 'Fascism is the open, terrorist dictatorship of the most reactionary, most chauvinist and most imperialist elements of finance capital.'[23] Fascism, in other words, is the tool of capitalism in its most advanced phase. During the past half-century this crude doctrine has been increasingly refined in ways which allow that neither Mussolini nor Hitler can plausibly be regarded as the mere stooge of capitalist manipulation, but the subtleties of recent Marxist thought must be passed over* in order to concentrate attention upon the two aspects

---

* Marxist doctrine is still sufficiently influential in academic quarters to make one reluctant to follow Henry Turner Jr's tempting example and dismiss it out of hand (*Reappraisals of Fascism*, 1975, pp. x-xi). I will merely note here, however, that the best efforts of Marxist scholars to refine on the original Comintern doctrine seem to amount in the end to no more than a list of generalizations about the supposed socio-economic conditions under which fascism occurred, of the kind with which Martin Kitchen concludes his recent book, *Fascism* (1976). But a list of such conditions, no matter how long, does not amount to a coherent Marxist theory of fascism; it is, on the contrary, merely an abridged and inadequate account of the complex course of German and Italian history. More generally, the Marxist concept of 'capitalism' has had to be so refined, in order to deal with fascism, that it ends in an abstract structuralism which deprives that concept of what little intellectual precision it may be felt to have once possessed as an instrument for intellectual analysis. This is especially true of Nicos Poulantzas' *Fascism and Dictatorship* (1974). Indeed, as an English Marxist (Ralph Miliband) has pointed out, it may well be that the new, refined analysis of fascism merely recreates (albeit in a different form) the disastrous situation in which the Comintern found itself in 1933. 'The political danger of structural super-determinism', Miliband wrote in an exchange with Poulantzas, 'would seem to me to be obvious. For if the state elite is as totally imprisoned in objective structures as Poulantzas suggests, it follows that there is *really* no difference between a state ruled, say, by bourgeois

of fascist ideology which always defy analysis by Marxist categories. The most obvious of these aspects is the importance of nationalist sentiment in explaining the appeal of fascism, but scarcely less obvious is the importance of youth in the theory and practice of fascism. Since both nationalist sentiment and the support from youth cut across the left/right class interpretation of modern society, Marxist theory naturally finds it impossible to explain either.

The problem which nationalism posed for Marxist theory first became acute in 1914; in the year, that is, when the proletariat deserted the Second International and the cause of world revolution and rallied, instead, behind the various national governments. The year 1914, in short, demonstrated that nationalism was a more potent ideological force than socialism. The first socialist to learn this lesson – Mussolini – made, as we know, notable use of the discovery. Thereafter, the story of Marxist theory, taken as it was by surprise by the power of its nationalist rival, is basically a story of various attempts to meet the nationalist challenge by a theory of conspiracy, according to which the triumph of fascism is to be explained in terms of how the masses were hoodwinked by capitalists who feared an imminent communist revolution. The masses, that is, were victims of 'false-consciousness' or mistaken class-interest. No matter how elaborate and ingenious the Marxist model becomes, however, it always encounters two intellectual difficulties. On the one hand, the intimate connection which Marxism postulates between fascism and capitalism makes it impossible to explain why extremist movements based on nationalist sentiment have appeared in non-capitalist or economically backward societies such as Italy, Hungary, Poland and Roumania, for example. On the other hand, a theory which accounts for the appearance of fascism in an

constitutionalists, whether conservative or social-democrats, and one ruled by, say, Fascists. It was the same approach', he notes, 'which led the Comintern . . . fatally to underestimate what the victory of the Nazis would mean for the German working-class movement.' (In *Ideology in Social Science*, ed. R. Blackburn, Glasgow, 1972, p. 259; his italics.) So far as the revision and development of the Marxist theory of fascism is concerned, then, it is tempting to conclude, *plus ça change* . . .

advanced industrial society like Germany cannot explain why it did not also occur in Britain and the U.S.A.

The second inescapable difficulty presented by Marxism is its inability to account for the fact that fascism, like modern radicalism at large, is connected more closely with age than with economic class. Thus National Socialism, as the historian Walter Laqueur remarks, came to power, not as the party of the middle class, but as the party of youth; and the sociologist Hans Gerth reminds us, likewise, that the Nazi party 'could truthfully boast of being a "young party" '. The statistics, in this case, are especially interesting. According to the Reich's census of 1933, those between the ages of eighteen and thirty constituted nearly one-third (31.1%) of the German population as a whole. 'The proportion of National Socialist party members of this age group rose from 37.6 per cent in 1931 to 42.2 per cent a year later, on the eve of power . . . By contrast, the Social Democratic party, second in size and the strongest democratic force in German politics, had only 19.3 per cent of its members in the eighteen to thirty age group in 1931. In 1930 the Social Democrats reported that less than 8 per cent of their membership was under twenty-five, and less than half was under forty.'[24]

In the end, the main result of attempts to make Marxist theory fit fascism has been to render the concept of fascism itself useless by depriving it of any connection with its original western context, in a way which leaves it available for polemical application anywhere that any degree of industrialization has occurred, no matter how different the indigenous cultural tradition may be. It is no surprise to find, for example, that the Japanese Marxist scholar, Masao Maruyama, has been able to document the development of 'fascism' in Japan between 1919 and 1945 in his *Thought and Behaviour in Modern Japanese Politics* (1963). It is no surprise, again, to find that as long ago as 1925 the Soviet historian V. M. Purishkevich had taken advantage of the confusions of Marxist theory in order to describe a member of an intransigent Russian political party which appeared in 1905 (the 'Union of Russian People') as a 'fascist' who had set the style for fascism ten years before it arose as a political movement in Italy.[25] The fact that the Russians of 1905

19

had no word for fascism did not, of course, matter to him: since there was some slight industrial development it followed that Russia must, by definition, have been prone to fascism. Finally, it is no surprise to find that a theory which makes it possible to speak of fascism in Russia in 1905, and in Japan between the wars, naturally finds it much easier to establish the 'fascist' character of countries such as Britain and the United States. Harold Laski was amongst the early proponents of this idea, which presented Roosevelt's New Deal policies as conclusive evidence of the rise of fascism in America.[26] In every country there is always someone who feels more at home in jackboots than in Hush-Puppies, and America accordingly has had its George Rockwell (1918–67). But men of that kind, belonging as they do to eccentric fringe groups, do not justify the vague and useless concept of fascism upon which thinkers like Laski rely.

The Marxist theory of fascism, then, must be set to one side, mainly on the ground that economic materialism dangerously oversimplifies the sources of instability in modern western society upon which fascism was able to feed. What must now be noticed is that this criticism is not confined to Marxist theory; on the contrary, an almost identical one may be made about the principal interpretations of fascism devised by contemporary non-Marxist political science. Amongst these, developmental theory has the main claim to attention.

The starting-point for this kind of theory is the assumption that the movement from an agricultural to an industrial social order is possible only via limited and well-established paths, to each of which there corresponds an appropriate set of political institutions. Each of these paths, however, involves passing through a definite number of stages, as a society moves from agricultural childhood to industrial maturity. Ignoring the difficulties presented by the arbitrary teleology involved, the claim made on behalf of developmental theory is that it deepens the analysis of fascism by accepting the importance of the socio-economic elements stressed by Marxist theory, whilst also acknowledging the historical relevance of many other factors or 'variables', such as religion, culture, and age. Dictatorship of the fascist type, in this perspective, is especially likely to occur in societies which are modernizing by using 'mass-mobilization' ideologies. To this class of ideologies belong, we are told, not only Italian Fascism, but also 'Marxist-Leninism, Shintoism, Kemalism, Gandhism, the current Egyptian Philosophy of the Revolution, Sun Yat-Sen's Three Principles of the People, the Indonesian Pantjasila, and many others'.[27] Unfortunately the attempt to compare these vastly disparate movements by relating political to socio-economic change has one obvious defect, which is that it completely fails to explain why Nazism occurred in a modern industrialized society, instead of in a situation of 'delayed industrialization', as the theory would seem to require. Nazism is therefore set to one side as an inexplicable 'special case'. Once special cases are admitted, however, the whole of developmental theory is brought crashing to the ground since to acknowledge such cases is to try to save the theory at the expense of arbitrarily narrowing down the very subject-matter which it originally set out to explain.

The difficulty presented by the Nazi phenomenon points, more generally, to the weakness which lies at the heart of developmental theory as a whole. This is the assumption that political and economic development are closely connected with one another. Unfortunately, there is no evidence to justify this assumption. The emergence of nationalist doctrine in Europe, for example, occurred at a time when western industrialization was still in its infancy. It occurred, more precisely, in response to the French Revolution and the Napoleonic Wars, and not in response to industrialization. It is true, of course, that economic backwardness (or 'delayed industrialization') may breed discontent, and that this may facilitate the spread of nationalist sentiment; but in human affairs, a host of factors other than poverty may produce the same effect. The rise of nationalism in Japan between the wars, for example, occurred at a time when that country was not 'underdeveloped'. Nothing could be more absurd, once again, than to regard Gandhism, for instance, as an ideology functionally related to the requirements of industrialization, since nothing was further from Gandhi's mind than the encouragement of an industrial revolution. What is more, even if the proposition is put the other way round, as in W. W. Rostow's contention that it is nationalism which generates economic growth, the evidence still yields no indication of any clear connection between nationalism and the requirements of economic growth. On the contrary, we are reminded, nationalist ideology 'may require the disruption of successful economic activity'.[28] Nazi Germany is, of course, a case in point.

The kind of difficulty Nazism presents for developmental theory is well illustrated by A. F. Organski's endeavour to deal with it in his study of *The Stages of Political Development*.[29] According to Organski, political extremism tends to occur only in the course of the modernization process, and not at the stage when the process is complete. Advanced industrial development, or 'modernization', he assumes, automatically brings with it welfare policies, political stability, and social integration. In its Italian form, Organski therefore finds fascism intelligible, since Italy was still only embarking upon the industrialization process at the time of the March on Rome. In its German form, however, fascism is inexplicable, since Germany was a fully modernized society at the time when Nazism came to power. Organski can find only one way of dealing with this unpalatable fact: in effect he simply legislates Nazism out of existence, by branding it as an historical aberration detached (as Nolte detached it) from any connection with the main course of European history. His sole justification for this arbitrary procedure is that Nazism does not conform to his dogmatic presuppositions about what should happen at each of the so-called stages of political development.

Organski's conviction that Italian Fascism can be seen as a developmental regime even though Nazism cannot, is sufficiently widespread amongst contemporary political scientists to require a moment's further consideration. The American scholar A.J. Gregor, for example, is quite explicit in maintaining that Italian Fascism 'was a mass-mobilizing developmental dictatorship committed to the modernization of Italy's economy'.[30] Between 1920 and 1938, Gregor claims, 'Fascist Italy had become (both in terms of industrial growth and the modernization of agriculture) an economically mature society.'[31] The evidence, however, suggests that the overall economic performance under Fascism was considerably less impressive than the rate of growth achieved in the liberal period before the First World War. According to one estimate, for example, the annual rate of incręase in national income was of the order of 2.49% between 1894 and 1913, falling to 1.82% between 1920 and 1939.[32] If we turn from growth in national income to technological change as an index of modernizing tendencies, then this adverse verdict on the Fascist economic achievement is again confirmed. Over the period from 1911 to 1951, Hildebrand found that traditional industries contributed as much to industrial employment as the new manufacturing ones: 'In short,' he concludes, 'no tendency is evident for employment to concentrate within the technically more progressive branches of industry. This indicates the relatively slow pace of industrialization down to 1951.'[33] So far as the 'corporate state' is concerned, it will be seen later that in reality this was merely a sham, 'a façade behind which the labour interest was suppressed, while organized industry and the bureaucracy established a new intimacy of relationship'.[34] It may be added that favourable retrospective interest in the Fascist corporate state has sometimes been influenced by the fact that the Industrial Reconstruction Institute (I.R.I.), which was credited with facilitating the post-war 'economic miracle', was originally created in the Fascist era. The I.R.I., however, was not a product of the corporate state structure, and was never regarded in the Fascist period as an instrument of development and modernization.[35]

The main problems with developmental theory, then, are clear enough: on the one hand, it is at odds with the economic facts, and on the other, it relies on an uncritical belief in the ultimately beneficial implications of economic growth. As a result of this belief its adherents are unable to take seriously the oldest and most familiar of all political phenomena – the phenomenon, that is, of political fanaticism. The dangers created by this wilful blindness become even more apparent if we now complete this survey of the main theories of fascism by considering briefly a mixed bag of alternative ones which suggest that fascism, far from being caused by socio-economic factors, is caused instead by religious, cultural and psychological ones which have produced a general spiritual malaise in the modern western world. The precise nature of this malaise is diagnosed in different ways by different thinkers, but three types of diagnosis appear to exhaust the principal possibilities.

One diagnosis, favoured by some Christian and conservative critics of fascism, is in terms of the decline of religion, or the 'death of God' in the modern world. The best example of this manner of thinking is the philosophy of Jacques Maritain, to whom modern politics presents itself as a cosmic struggle between good and evil. Good, for Maritain, is identified with Christianity, and evil with what he regards as the 'Pagan Empire'. The Pagan Empire, as we might expect, is most fully exemplified in Nazism, in which Maritain sees a 'demonic pantheism' – a challenge, that is, aimed at God himself.[36] What is puzzling about this view is the fact that countries like Britain and America, which presumably fall within the Pagan Empire, have not mounted a fascist (i.e. a 'demonic pantheistic') attack upon God, whilst Italy, which would seem to be a more Christian land, joined with the Nazis in launching such an attack. More generally, however, it may suffice to note that surprise and moral outrage, for thinkers of this kind, derive from the conviction that God certainly would not approve of fascism. Yet God himself, after all, gave Job such a dreadful time of it that even in a Hitler He may perhaps have found some instrument of His purpose. The trouble is, of course, that we still lack definite guidance about His purpose, or about His specific political prejudices, so that speculations of Maritain's kind must necessarily remain inconclusive. Further consideration of theological interpretations of fascism may properly be postponed until the life hereafter.

A second, purely secular diagnosis has been inspired by romantic yearnings and by the development of psychoanalysis. According to this second diagnosis, which owes much to the work of Freud in particular, fascism is an extreme response to centuries of emotional deprivation and sexual repression. Fascism, on this view, is the final blind and desperate revolt of twentieth-century man against the cruel civilization which has left him standing – albeit ithyphallic, if he is lucky – in a desert of dead passions.

Literature of this second kind, then, endeavours to explain fascism by presenting it as an appeal to the murky irrational part of the psyche which has been suppressed by the cold, impersonal and rationalist structure of modern civilization. From this point of view, fascism is a pathological eruption of, 'Forces that had been too long suppressed by the superficial layer of good manners and the domination of an artificial Ego . . .'[37] It is, in other words, due to a 'character neurosis' arising from what the writer, W. Reich, regards as 'the destruction of man's vital function that had taken place over thousands of years'. Everywhere, today, man's 'vital function' is threatened by 'our authoritarian machine civilization and its mechanistic . . . conception of life'.[38] The difficulty in this case, of course, is to understand why fascism is not a ubiquitous phenomenon, since the 'authoritarian machine civilization' is found everywhere in the western world.

An influential variant of the psychological approach which requires separate attention reveals the influence of Marxist class analysis. In this version, attention is concentrated upon the lower middle class, which is said to be the most repressed section of modern society, and hence the most prone to support fascism. Members of this class suffer from feelings of insecurity, induced by the fear of 'massification', or else from feelings of anomie, loneliness, insignificance, and powerlessness, all of which combine to produce sadistic and masochistic tendencies.[39] Taken together, these tendencies constitute the basis of the 'authoritarian personality' which is supposed to be the distinguishing trait of the lower middle class.[40] The possessor of this personality is a wretched creature, overwhelmed inwardly by sexual deprivation and afflicted outwardly by the ruthless economic order of capitalism, constantly liable to panic under the burden of a freedom for which he really has no use, since it leaves him feeling cold and miserable. In a desperate endeavour to escape from his misery, he welcomes political extremism. He craves, in particular, for the false sense of security produced by complete submission to a strong leader; and he welcomes a destructive political programme, satisfying as it does his sadistic tendencies, provided that it promises to eliminate all the sources of his anxiety. He thus gravitates naturally towards an 'automatic conformity'.[41] Subsequent research, however, has exposed a difficulty about the authoritarian personality which, it might well seem, was obvious enough without the need for academic studies to reveal it to us. It is that the psychological characteristics ascribed to this type of personality are not peculiar to the lower middle class, but are even more pronounced amongst the working class.[42] Apart from this setback for the psychological interpretation of fascism, however, it must be remarked once more that theories of this kind make it impossible to explain why fascism did not become a mass movement in countries such as Britain and the United States, since the authoritarian personality was, of course, just as endemic in those countries as in Germany and Italy.

One further variant on the psychological interpretation of fascism is of sufficient interest to deserve brief mention. In this case, the interpretation has emerged from the field of so-called 'generational theory', which stresses the discontinuity in the transmission of cultural and political values from one generation to the next caused, in particular, by the Great War. The fascist führer, according to the version in question, satisfied 'oedipal longings [which] were heightened for the sons left alone with their mothers during years of war'.[43] Thus 'a direct relation', it is suggested, 'existed between the deprivation German children experienced in World War I and the response of these children and adolescents to the anxieties aroused by the Great Depression of the early 1930s. This relationship is psychodynamic: the war generation had weakened egos and superegos, meaning that the members of this generation turned readily to programmes based on facile solutions and violence when they met new frustrations during the Depression. They then reverted to earlier phase-specific fixations in their child development marked by rage, sadism, and the defensive idealization of their absent parents, especially the father. These elements made this age cohort particularly susceptible to the appeal of a mass movement utilizing the crudest devices of projection and displacement in its ideology. Above all it prepared the young voters of Germany for submission to a total, charismatic leader.' Ironically, the writer concludes, 'instead of finding the idealized father they, with Hitler as their leader, plunged Germany and Europe headlong into a series of deprivations many times worse than those of World War I'. In like fashion, Martin Wangh maintains that the Nazi movement's deification of the Führer and its infernalization of the Jew relieved homosexual tensions through submission to an all-powerful leader, through turning women into 'breeders' of children, and by presenting Jews as 'incestuous criminals' and 'defilers of the race'.[44]

The problem with all such analyses, as already mentioned, is that they do not explain why other nations whose children were left fatherless in the First World War did not produce successful führers and Nazi-type mass movements. In other words, they explain everything, and therefore tell us nothing. In the present context, however, the main thing to be noticed is that the element of surprise which has provided the theme of the present chapter is, as it were, built into these theories in the form of an assumption that any well-balanced, emotionally sane, properly brought up person could not possibly be a fascist. They rest, that is, upon the hidden ideological postulate that any right-minded person must necessarily be a liberal or a socialist. Once this hidden postulate is granted, it naturally follows that those who dislike parliamentary institutions, respond to nationalistic appeals, and show a taste for heroism and self-sacrifice, are the victims of some psychological disorder. This is obviously a consoling thought for the liberal and socialist psychologists who entertain it. It is also, however, a dangerously complacent thought, since it merely explains fascism away by pushing it out of sight into a psychiatric ward. In order to understand fascism, it would be necessary to restore the complex historical context which the psychologists either neglect or overemphasize – the context, that is, of European intellectual and political development since 1789.

During the past six decades, then, a wide variety of different disciplines has been brought to bear on the study of fascism. The final outcome, however, is so disappointing that one author recently began a study of the subject by declaring, in a note of mild despair, that in his book no definition of fascism would even be attempted, since, 'Fascism is one of those "isms" for which every person will find his own definition'.[45] In an even more pessimistic mood, the American political scientist, A. J. Gregor, ended his comprehensive survey of the various theories with the observation that there is little prospect that the near future will bring any improvement. The one slight hope he could hold out was that, whilst everybody would continue to offer different theories of fascism and to pursue different approaches to the subject, in some mysterious way these myriad streams might nevertheless finally converge in one big eclectic theory of fascism, blending together the work of historians, psychologists, sociologists and political sociologists.[46] A sceptic might be forgiven for feeling that in this fashion we might indeed construct a massive encyclopaedia on fascism, but nothing which amounted to a coherent interpretation of it.

In this chapter, it has been suggested that the prevailing confusion about fascism derives from a far deeper source than is apparent from a superficial glance at the conflicting academic methods and models which confront students of the subject. The nature of this source becomes evident as soon as one notices the common mood or spirit which pervades all these different methods and models. On closer scrutiny, this spirit quickly reveals its continuity with the eighteenth-century Age of Enlightenment. In spite of our various disillusionments, that is to say, our political theory nevertheless continues to display pronounced traces of the sentiments which Wordsworth expressed as he contemplated the French Revolution and came to believe, with the revolutionaries themselves, that

> . . . the whole earth
> The beauty wore of promise.

The result of this optimistic sense of 'promise' is that the various interpretations of fascism have failed to pay due regard to that darker, less attractive side of modern idealism of which a contemporary of Wordsworth, Mary Shelley, tried to remind the modern world, in a simple and instructive fable. The western world, she saw, had followed the example of Wordsworth by taking Rousseau and the belief in human perfectibility to heart; so much so, she felt – drawing in particular upon a close study of her husband, in whom the new optimism found one of its purest expressions[47] – that the world had quite ignored the possibility that the perfect man might turn out to be a Frankensteinian monster rather than an Emile.

Since Mary Shelley's day, it is true, a few thinkers have occasionally broken through the complacent shell of western optimism and reminded us that political extremism of the fascist kind might not really be so alien to the modern liberal-democratic world as we have generally chosen to believe. In 1940, for example, George Orwell published a short but thoughtful review of *Mein Kampf*. The response of western democracies to fascism, he noted, has leaned heavily upon the tacit assumption 'that human beings desire nothing beyond ease, security and avoidance of pain'. Those who make this assumption, however, are precluded (Orwell continued) from any comprehension of the fact that fascism might have a deep-rooted and potentially universal appeal to the modern spirit: an appeal, that is, which is not confined to some particular section and class of society, or to some particular nation. However unsound fascist political and economic ideas may be, he insisted, 'Fascism and Nazism are psychologically far sounder than any hedonistic conception of life . . . Whereas Socialism, and even Capitalism, in a more grudging way, have said to people, "I offer you a good time," Hitler has said to them, "I offer you struggle, danger and death," and as a result a whole nation flings itself at his feet.' This does not mean, Orwell emphasized, that the majority in every modern state are constantly ready to respond to an appeal to nationalistic and military values: after a few years of slaughter and starvation, the populace rapidly appreciates the advantages of ease and order. But in times of disappointed expectations and of social, economic and political confusion, the masses are tempted to abandon the notions of a 'normal' and 'healthy' life which underlie the optimistic and complacent materialism of liberal and socialist ideology.[48] Those who cannot appreciate this, he concluded, forget that it is possible to be 'too sane to understand the modern world' – too sane, that is, to appreciate that there is no reason at all to be surprised about the appeal to the modern world of an anti-hedonistic ethic of power and military 'glory', of nationalism, of religious and racial bigotry, of feudal 'loyalty' and heroic 'honour'.[49]

A century before Orwell, an isolated thinker, the great Swiss historian Jacob Burckhardt, had warned his contemporaries about the dangers inherent in the doctrinaire republican, nationalist and socialist ideologies which were beginning to take possession of the European world. In a letter of 1849, for example, Burckhardt wrote that, 'I am of the opinion that democrats and proletarians, even though they make most furious efforts, will have to yield to an increasingly violent despotism, for our charming century is made for anything rather than genuine democracy.'[50] Over thirty years later, in 1881, he had found no reason to modify his opinion. In another letter written in that year he observed that, 'In the last few days, Radicalism has lurched another step forward all over Switzerland, and unless everything deceives me, there is a European movement at the back of it, and [Germany] will soon experience something of the kind. I feel deep down inside me,' he continued, 'that something is going to burst out in the West, once Russia has been reduced to confusion by acts of violence. That will be the beginning of the period when every stage of confusion will have to be gone through, until finally a real Power emerges based upon sheer, unlimited violence, and it will take precious little account of the right to vote, the sovereignty of the people, material prosperity, industry, etc.'[51] The democratic ideal of the age tends, as he summarized his view one year later, in 1882, to terminate in 'supposedly republican Military Commands'.

Burckhardt did not, however, expect anyone to pay attention to these gloomy but accurate predictions because, as he remarked, 'people do not like to imagine a world whose rulers utterly ignore laws, prosperity, enriching work, and industry, credit, etc., and who would rule with utter brutality'.[52] In this respect, he anticipated the response of the twentieth century to fascism very well. Where Burckhardt identified a marked tendency towards political extremism as the predominant characteristic of modern European history, thinkers of our own time have generally begun from the opposite assumption, regarding extremism as a baffling historical aberration.

30

Most of what has been said in the present chapter follows from this. It is that the outraged optimism of the twentieth century has been reflected, in theoretical terms, in a variety of oversimplified interpretations of modern western history. Drawing together the material reviewed above, three principal kinds of oversimplification may be distinguished, amounting, in effect, to three strategies which can be deployed, with appropriate modifications, for liberal, Marxist or conservative ideological ends.

The first kind of oversimplification consists of a naive vision of modernity as a struggle between progressive and regressive tendencies, interpreted in a variety of ways – most commonly, perhaps, as a struggle between 'the left' and 'the right', conceived either in class terms, or else in terms of a more abstract intellectual tension between progressive and regressive (or 'reactionary') ideas of the kind found, for example, in Nolte. The second form consists of an alternative view of modernity as a conflict between God's will and the powers of darkness. This form, of course, can overlap with the other two, as they may with it, in turn. Thus Marxism, for example, partially falls into this category, in so far as 'God's will' is identified with the proletarian cause, and the powers of darkness with the capitalist cause. The third form consists of a vision of modern history as a conflict between the principles of reason, sanity and moderation, on the one hand, and those of pathological disorder, on the other.

In all three cases, as has been seen, the overly simple theories of fascism thus produced are unsatisfactory for a specific reason. This is that the urge to rescue some fragments of the optimism which has for two centuries provided the main impulse of western thought reduces the theories, in the last resort, to conspiracy theories. The conspiracy in question may be conceived of in more or less sophisticated ways, and the theory based upon it may well be genuinely illuminating, although only within narrow limits – there is, that is to say, obviously something to be learned from each of the approaches to fascism which have been mentioned. In the end, however, any conspiracy theory necessarily terminates in mystery and intellectual opacity, since its main function is not really to explain fascism at all, but to salvage ideological optimism (whether it is of a liberal, Marxist or other variety) by concealing the more deep-rooted sources of political instability and extremism characteristic of modernity. Yet it is precisely these which a satisfactory theory of fascism must bring to light.

Clearly, the next step is to consider these deeper sources of political extremism. What will be suggested is that they arise from the fact that the modern European liberal-democratic tradition has been marked, ever since 1789, by a radical ambiguity which not only leaves it intrinsically vulnerable to extremist interpretations but actually encourages them. In the next chapter the origin of this ambiguity will be traced to a fundamental conflict in the modern period between 'states' and 'movements' – a conflict which may alternatively be described as one between an older, limited style of politics which the western world once favoured and a newer, activist style which is incompatible with limited politics but is now nonetheless much in favour. It is the existence of this ambiguity that fascism was able to exloit for its own ends, in a way which enabled it to pose as a respectable and credible interpreter of the liberal-democratic tradition, rather than as its destroyer. We must now turn, then, to consider in detail the nature of the ambiguity referred to.

2 Fascism and the New Activist Style of Politics

The greatest ideal of the western political tradition, from the time of the Renaissance until the time of the First World War, was the creation of what may be termed a limited style of politics. Fascism may be defined as an ideology which explicitly rejects this ideal in favour of a new and entirely opposed political style, which may be described as an activist style of politics. The new activist style has assumed several forms in the modern world, but in its specifically fascist form it may be defined as a style which conceives of the highest good for man as a life of endless self-sacrifice spent in total and highly militant devotion to the nation-state, the claims of which are held to embrace and override every other object of human attachment and to require unconditional allegiance to a fascist 'leader', whose arbitrary personal decree is the sole final determinant of right and wrong in every sphere of national life.

Fascism, thus defined, is inevitably destructive of the conditions of civilized social life as they have traditionally been understood in the West. It is destructive, because the spiritually unified nation-state with which fascism identifies the highest good for man is always conceived of in extra-constitutional terms. The unity at which fascism aims, that is to say, is a 'unity without legality'. This is why fascism, which sometimes appears noble and even politically constructive in its more plausible forms, amounts in practice to nothing more than a barbaric demand for servile obedience to anyone who holds the reins of government, regardless either of how he acquired power or of how he uses it. The only restriction which fascism imposes upon this 'leader' is that he must indulge in a certain amount of rhetorical cant, of the kind indicated in the definition just given, and that he must, above all, succeed in acquiring and retaining power. Since in practice this amounts to no constitutional restriction at all, fascism is therefore a complete negation of the

33

traditional limited style of politics.

Since no definition ever represents more than a point of departure, it is obviously necessary to elaborate upon what has just been said, and in particular to explain what is meant by a 'limited' style of politics, by contrast with an 'activist' one. The meaning of these terms becomes fully intelligible only when the definition is situated within the context of a revolutionary transformation which has occurred in the political order of the European world during the past two centuries. Some states, of course, have offered notable resistance to this transformation, although none has remained unaffected by it. Such matters of detail, however, must be passed over here in order to highlight the general nature of the revolution itself.

Put briefly, this revolution consists of the widespread transformation of the European political order from one based upon 'states', which were the supreme creation of a limited style of politics, into one consisting of 'movements', which are the relatively amorphous entities thrown up in our own century by the new activist style of politics. 'Fascism' is the term which will be used in the present study to refer to the specific form which the ideas and institutions associated with this revolutionary transformation assumed in Italy and Germany in the inter-war period.* Before turning to consider fascism in detail, however, the broader context within which it should be viewed must first be clarified by a brief sketch of the character of the overall transformation in western political life of which fascism is only one particular aspect.

From a Limited to an Activist Style of Politics

The ideal of a limited style of politics, to which western

---

* Since every European country witnessed the growth of a fascist movement in this period it is perhaps necessary to explain why attention is concentrated upon the Italian and German movements. The justification for this restriction is that the other inter-war movements were either copies of the two main ones, or else stooge regimes created by them. In neither case would a detailed consideration of these movements add significantly (so far as the study of ideology is concerned) to what may be learned from the main ones.

liberal-democracies still display a half-hearted commitment, is intimately connected with the development of the concept of the state. The first recognizably modern delineation of this concept appeared at the end of the feudal period, in the pages of Machiavelli. During the following centuries, ambitious princes and governments gradually made the state the typical form of European political life, although in some countries, such as Germany and Italy, the political unity entailed by state organization was only established at a relatively late stage, whilst in others, such as those of eastern Europe, it never amounted to more than a precarious construction. The complex histories of individual states, however, are not relevant here; what matters is the long tradition of theorizing, from Machiavelli through Bodin, Hobbes and Locke, down to thinkers like Hume, Burke and de Tocqueville, in which the concept of the state was elucidated. Overriding their different concerns and disputes, a broad area of agreement may be discerned about four characteristics of the state, which together provide the elements of what has been referred to as a limited style of politics. Since the simplest way of understanding the new activist style of politics is by contrasting its component ideas with these elements, it is necessary to consider each of them in turn.

The first element consists of the idea of law as the bond of community. Within this style of politics, that is to say, a community was believed to be held together, not by some shared purpose – such as the religious purpose of getting to heaven, or the secular one of increasing national prosperity, or working for the triumph of the proletariat, or for the purification of the Aryan race – but by the formal bond of law. Within the new activist style of politics, by contrast, it is a shared purpose which is the basis of community, and not the idea of law. This shared purpose is expressed in what we have come to call an ideology, which is a more or less carefully articulated vision of the ideal social order which it is the purpose of activist politics to realize. In the activist political style, then, ideology takes the place of law as the bond of community.

Secondly, a limited style of politics is one in which a distinction is made between public and private life, or between

35

state and society. The state, that is to say, is not conceived of as an all-embracing or 'total' organization, but only as the highest (or 'sovereign', as it is usually called) authority to which men are subject. In practice, this limited conception of the place of the state in human affairs owed much to the Christian tradition which tempered political power by its conception of human destiny as, in the last resort, a matter for the individual. Within the activist political style, by contrast, human destiny is always thought of as a collective destiny: the individual cannot, and should not, attempt to go it alone. The activist style, in a word, replaces an individualistic conception of life with a collectivist one, within which politics becomes a total activity.

Thirdly, within a limited style of politics power is always regarded as an object of suspicion, and great stress is laid upon the need to create institutional safeguards in order to restrict the possibility of its abuse. Thus from Machiavelli's *Discourses* down to de Tocqueville's *Democracy in America*, the classic question asked about power is not, 'How should it be used?' but, 'How can power be limited, irrespective of how it is used, or of who wields it?' Within the new activist style of politics, by contrast, power is no longer thought of as intrinsically suspect. This is because so long as those who hold it claim to be using it in order to implement one or other of the ideologies upon which the various forms of activism rely, they may do pretty much as they please. From this point of view, institutional safeguards against the abuse of power are completely ignored. In particular, matters of a procedural kind, involving compliance with the rule of law and the observance of settled constitutional rules, are totally disregarded. In theory, of course, proponents of activism may profess a deep regard for legality and for constitutional forms, but in practice these are allowed to remain in existence only so long as they serve to foster the impression that the ideology and the methods associated with the activist regime have overwhelming popular support. The support may of course be a reality, but the main point is that institutions which were once associated with the preservation of limited government can now be used instead to legitimate any policy the activist regime cares to pursue, no matter how brutal or aggressive it may be.

Fourthly, the state, within the framework of a limited style of politics, was generally (but not invariably) regarded as a specific territorial unit. This territorial unit was recognized as essentially the outcome of history. The state was thought of, in other words, as the artificial product of tradition, war, dynastic alliances and diplomacy. Within the activist style, however, the idea of the state as linked to a particular territory, whose frontiers are the artificial outcome of history, is at most an incidental one. It is incidental because a community is thought of instead as held together primarily by an ideology, a 'mission', or a shared purpose. In practice, what this means is that there is no reason, in principle at least, why an activist regime should regard existing historical frontiers as more than an unfortunate obstacle to its aspirations. The unsettling implications of the activist style of politics for the international order are obvious, since within this style diplomacy no longer has any connection with the preservation of an established balance of power but relates instead solely to whatever ideological fantasies the activist regime may care to entertain. What is more, because the activist style tends to determine frontiers by reference to ideological considerations rather than historical ones, it necessarily imbues international disputes with an inflexible and uncompromising element of fanaticism.

A limited style of politics, then, is marked by its regard for law as the bond of community; by the regard it shows for the individual in distinguishing between state and society; by its regard for constitutional forms of government; and by the relatively limited and specific character of its territorial aspirations. An activist style of politics, by contrast, substitutes ideology for law; subordinates individuals to an all-embracing political order; has no intrinsic respect for constitutional forms; and rejects the existence of historic frontiers as a relevant determinant of its scope. The result of this new style has been the creation during the present century of what must be regarded, from a constitutional point of view, as the most primitive form of political association which the West has yet known. This is the 'movement regime', exemplified most notably by fascist and communist dictatorships.

It is the new activist style of politics which has now come to dominate the modern world, then, that provides the overall context within which the advent of fascism must be situated; and unless this context is borne firmly in mind, neither the novelty nor the significance of the fascist phenomenon is easily discernible. Consider, for example, the most central and persistent of the problems associated with the study of fascism. This is the problem of determining whether fascism was really a revolutionary movement at all. The Nazis themselves were in no doubt about the answer: in 1933 they had secured, without bloodshed, the triumph of an entirely new philosophy of life (or *Weltanschauung*). This, they said, was what a true revolution meant, since only a new *Weltanschauung* could transform the nature of man and of society, initially in Germany, and subsequently throughout the world. The other so-called revolutions of the modern world – those of 1789, 1848, 1905 and 1917, for example – were not genuine revolutions in their eyes, since each had concentrated upon changing the political and social order instead of effecting that total change in spiritual values which only a new *Weltanschauung* could bring about.

As soon as the views of their various critics and opponents are considered, however, the Nazi view of the fascist revolution encounters difficulties. Thus Marxists, for example, deny that fascism was a revolutionary movement on the ground that it did not question the sanctity of private property or aim at the wholesale abolition of capitalism. Liberal scholars also tend to be sceptical about the propriety of describing fascism as a revolution, although for different reasons. Both Nazism and Italian Fascism, they suggest, are merely the old phenomenon of despotism dressed up in new clothes, and in this they find nothing that is particularly novel or revolutionary. Conservative thinkers, by contrast, often regard fascism as a revolution, but disagree about what kind of revolution it was. This confusion is further increased by the writings of sociologists and students of comparative government. These generally grant that fascism was indeed a revolution, but disagree about whether it was a political or a social revolution. The confusion thus created about the nature of fascism is intensified, of course, by the fact that observations which appear to fit Italian experience fail to accord with German experience, and vice versa. We seem to be reduced, then, to the kind of vague conclusion at which Schneider arrived after examining the details of the march on Rome, in an early work on Italian Fascism. 'It is a metaphysical question', he observed, 'whether there was a revolution at all. Some say the event was little more than a parade to celebrate a cabinet crisis, others regard it as comparable to the French Revolution.'[1] When applied to fascism, in short, the notion of revolution would appear to be in danger of evaporating altogether into a haze of intellectual uncertainty and ideological disagreement.

The present mode of analysis, by contrast with those just mentioned, makes it possible not only to identify fascism as a truly revolutionary development in western political experience, but also to provide a precise, non-ideological specification of what the vague word revolution means in this connection. Fascism was a revolutionary development, in the sense that it deliberately and explicitly set out to destroy the state concept upon which the western style of limited politics had been based for the previous five centuries and to replace it with something very different, viz. a 'movement'. In this respect Mussolini and Hitler were alike. Both adopted and implemented a style of politics in which there was no intrinsic regard for legality; in which state and society were to be submerged in one all-pervasive movement; in which all constitutional restraints upon power were excluded, in principle at least; and in which the nation, as conceived of by fascism, was an essentially fluid entity whose territorial limits were to be determined solely by the ideological fanaticism of the fascist leaders.

Fascism, then, constitutes a revolutionary break with the western style of limited politics. But in this respect, of course, the fascist revolution is by no means a unique phenomenon. Communism, for example, also constitutes a revolutionary break with the western tradition of limited politics. It is necessary, therefore, to refine the analysis by endeavouring to discern what marks off the fascist revolution from other revolutionary movements produced by the new activist style of politics.

What, then, are the distinguishing marks of fascist ideology? The four ideas which are usually fixed upon in this connection are nationalism, racialism, corporatism and irrationalism. None of these ideas, however, offers a satisfactory way of characterizing fascism, since none of them is peculiar to it. Thus extreme nationalism, for example, is a characteristic of reactionary groups like the *Action Française*, which was in no sense a fascist movement.[2] Racialism, again, was a prominent feature of Nazi ideology, but one which played a relatively minor part in Italian Fascism. Racialist doctrine, moreover, was not a fascist invention, nor was it peculiar to fascist ideology. It was not even a doctrine to which all who supported Nazism subscribed. Concentration upon it, indeed, is positively misleading, not only because it distracts attention from the structural connection of Nazism with the new activist style of politics at large, but also because it is impossible to explain in this way why thirteen million people voted for National Socialism in 1932. Turning to the corporatist ideal, this, like racialist doctrine, is not peculiar to fascism. In one form, it extends back to the political thought of early nineteenth-century romantic thinkers; in another form, it is a vital element in the Catholic tradition of political thought, which has been especially influential in Austria and Portugal; in a different form, it belongs to the tradition of syndicalist thought; and in yet another sense, corporatism may be said to be a general tendency of advanced industrial society at large. Finally, 'irrationalism' is not peculiar to fascism, and certainly has no necessary connection with it. It is doubtful, in any case, whether the word can be made sufficiently precise to meet the requirements of serious intellectual inquiry.

Nationalism, racialism, corporatism and irrationalism, then, fail to yield a tool adequate for the purpose of the present analysis. They are of course important for an understanding of fascism, but in order to interpret their position and meaning within it, it is necessary to abandon the abstract search for unique institutional and doctrinal characteristics. It is necessary, in particular, to jettison the familiar procedure of first arbitrarily elevating either the Italian or German experience of fascism to paradigmatic stature and then focusing a quest for the 'essence of fascism' upon whichever movement is felt to embody this essence most completely. A method of this kind inevitably ends with results which are as arbitrary as the point from which it began, even leading, for example, to the conclusion that Mussolini's Italy was not really fascist at all.

Setting these unsatisfactory intellectual techniques to one side, it will be more useful to begin by recognizing at the outset that fascism offered no new idea or theme of its own. What it did was to draw together, and then pursue to extreme lengths, a pattern of ideas which had worked, for well over a century before fascism seized upon this pattern, to bring about the destruction of the older western style of limited politics and its replacement by the new activist style. The sole distinction of fascist ideology lies in the fact that it may be regarded as the most extreme, ruthless and comprehensive expression of this new style of politics. The only adequate way of understanding the nature of fascism, in consequence, is by examining more closely the pattern of ideas which gave rise to the new activist style. What then were the ideas and ideals which led the European order to abandon the state concept in favour of a manner of thinking about politics which impelled it, albeit often unwittingly, towards a world of movement regimes?

The Origins of the New Activist Style of Politics

From an intellectual standpoint, the origins of the new activist style may be determined with precision. Specifically, the shift from a limited to an activist style of politics occurred under the impact of four new ideas which gradually won credence in the European world during the latter part of the eighteenth century, although their practical implications were not fully disclosed until our own time.

The first idea was a novel theory about the origin and nature of evil. The second was a new theory of political legitimacy, in the form of the doctrine of popular sovereignty. The third was a new concept of freedom. The fourth was a manner of thinking about politics which conferred an unprecedented potency upon the power of human will to transform the entire social and

41

political order in ways which would make it conform more closely to whatever dreams human fancy might suggest.

Taken in conjunction with one another, these four ideas constitute the basic prerequisites of fascist ideology. They are basic to it, however, in a dual sense. On the one hand, they provided the framework of ideas which fascists were able to exploit for their own ends. On the other, they facilitated the fascist cause in a more general and more disturbing way which even now is insufficiently understood. They did this by depriving the modern European political tradition of significant powers of resistance to utopian political interpretations. To those insensitive to this endemic weakness of the tradition, fascism will naturally continue to appear as an unequivocal negation of the long tradition of moral and political idealism upon which men have prided themselves ever since the end of the eighteenth century. To those who view this idealism in a more sceptical light, however, fascism will appear instead as the mirror in which the inescapable ambivalence which activist zeal had brought to the European world from the outset was finally revealed. Although the four ideas upon which fascism fed are intimately connected with one another, the precise way in which they have facilitated the fascist cause can best be illustrated by considering them separately.

1. Evil: politics as an activist crusade   The new theory of evil first found mature intellectual expression during the eighteenth century, in the moral and political thought of Jean-Jacques Rousseau, and ever since that time it has constituted the basis of activist thought. During the two thousand years of western moral and intellectual reflection before Rousseau, men had generally been content to regard evil as an intrinsic and ineliminable part of the human condition. Since Rousseau, however, they have come to believe instead that evil is not intrinsic in the human condition but derives from the structure of society. Man, Rousseau maintained, is innocent and free, and yet is everywhere found enslaved and degraded by the social order under which he lives. It was this new theory which imparted to European political thought an activist impulse which had hitherto been lacking. What the theory implied was that the primary task of politics must henceforth lie in arousing the masses to an awareness of the oppressive social order under which they lived. If the masses could be awakened from their apathy and brought to remove the villains who exploited them, then the implied assumption was that they would in due course be able to achieve a form of social unity under which power would never again be abused.

The immediate consequence of this ideal of social unity was to endow the activist style of politics with the fanatical character of a religious crusade. Within this style of politics, that is to say, the object of governments was no longer the relatively modest one of securing for their subjects the benefits of order, prosperity, and security from external aggression. It was, instead, the far more ambitious one of unifying the social order by purging it of all traces of evil. Politics, in a word, became a matter of ensuring the triumph of light over darkness, in a world which was seen no longer in shades of grey, but solely in terms of black and white.

Conceived of in this way, politics now acquired a disturbing similarity to a long tradition of millenarian fanaticism in which dreams of a future golden age had inspired intermittent outbursts of religious frenzy which may be traced back through the medieval to the ancient world. In particular, three of the symbols which Rousseau used in developing the new theory of evil displayed a disquieting parallel to those which had constantly recurred in the millenarian tradition during the preceding two thousand years of western history. There was, most notably, his belief in man's natural innocence and his concomitant faith in human perfectibility, with its implied rejection of the orthodox Christian doctrine of original sin. There was, secondly, his belief in a possible salvation in this world, rather than in the next, to be achieved by the elimination of the moral distortion brought about by social inequality. What Rousseau visualized, although he did not use the word himself, was the end of the 'alienation' (or inner division) which has hitherto characterized human history, and whose origins he portrayed in mythical form in the *Second Discourse*. There was, finally, his belief that the coming salvation would have a collective rather than an individual character, requiring as it did a total surrender on the part of individuals to the general will.

These three symbols – belief, that is, in man's natural innocence, in a coming golden age, and in the collective character of the salvation which this would entail – have subsequently become as integral to the structure of the activist style of politics as they formerly were to the messianic religious fanaticism which had occasionally threatened to overturn the established authorities of the European world. At the most general level, it is this secularized religiosity, expressed in the conception of politics as a crusade to eliminate evil from the world, which was eventually to find its purest expression in fascism. An instructive illustration is to be found in the role assigned by Codreanu, the Roumanian fascist leader, to the Legion of the Archangel Michael. The Legion, Codreanu said, 'shall be fundamentally different from all other political organizations. . . . All [these] believe that the country is dying for lack of good programmes. And so they put together some perfectly congenial programme and they take off with it to gather more. That is why people ask: "What programme have you got?" ' When Codreanu paused to explain what was to take the place of politics and programmes, his answer was characteristic of fascism at large in its presentation of the world as the scene of a cosmic conflict between good and evil. He wanted, he said, a sovereign, unified people, living in 'a new atmosphere' of perfect spirituality, entirely free from 'the power of evil', and led by, 'The finest souls that our minds can conceive, the proudest, tallest, straightest, strongest, cleverest, bravest and most hard-working that our race can produce.'[3] In conformity with the same spirit of a religious crusade, article five of the Verona Manifesto* described the Italian Fascist Party as 'an order of fighters and believers' whose task is to become 'an organism of absolute political purity, worthy of being the custodian of the Revolutionary Idea'. Fascism itself, Gentile (in common with other fascists) insisted, 'is a religion . . . therefore it has re-established a love of martyrdom for the idea of our country; and therefore it stands invincible in the field whilst its

---

* This Manifesto was the basis of the Salo Republic, the fascist rump state which Mussolini created in 1943, after the Allied occupation of southern Italy.

unfit and base adversaries abuse it. . . .'.[4]

It is the pseudo-religious character of the activist style of politics which explains, in particular, the way in which Hitler regarded the Jews. In *Mein Kampf*, as elsewhere, he wrote of them in accents which are most readily intelligible when they are recognized as those in which a medieval religious fanatic, like John of Leyden, who took over the town of Münster in 1534, would have spoken about Anti-Christ. 'If our people . . . fall victims to those Jewish tyrants of the nation with their lust for blood and gold', he ranted, 'the whole earth will sink down, entangled in this polypus; if Germany forces itself from this embrace, the greatest of dangers for the people will be regarded as vanquished from all the earth. . . The Jew goes his baleful way until the day when another power comes to oppose him and in a mighty struggle casts him, the stormer of the heavens, back to Lucifer.'[5] Fanatical utterances of this kind are not, of course, peculiar to Nazi anti-semitism; they are typical, on the contrary, of the way in which an activist crusade regards any group which is identified as a major obstacle to the triumph of good over evil. Lenin, for example, spoke in a similar way about the extermination of the Kulaks. At this stage, however, we are concerned with the general style of politics to which fascism belongs, rather than with its ideological peculiarities.

Extremism of this kind is not to be found in the pages of Rousseau himself; yet without the new theory of evil which he propounded, the activist conception of politics as a crusade to purge society of evil would have lacked the secular philosophical foundation upon which it has continued to rest down to the present day. But how, it will naturally be asked, was the crusading fervour which marks this style imparted to the world of European politics at large? How, in other words, was the new theory of evil carried from the purely speculative writings of Rousseau into the political arena itself?

2. Democracy and the 'out-group'   The answer is provided by the French Revolution. It lies, more especially, in the doctrine of popular sovereignty enunciated by the French revolutionaries in 1789, in the declaration of the Rights of Man and Citizen. It was with this Declaration that the new activist style first acquired practical significance in the European world. 'The principle of sovereignty', the Declaration announced, 'resides essentially in the Nation; no body of men, no individual, can exercise authority that does not emanate from it.' Here, then, is the second idea which has underpinned the new activist style of politics. Henceforth, the doctrine of popular sovereignty implied, good government was to be identified with democratic or republican government, upon which the doctrine conferred a monopoly of political legitimacy.

The extraordinary significance which the doctrine of popular sovereignty now lent to the modern democratic ideal will not be appreciated unless it is recalled that the period before 1789 had been notable for its flexible and tolerant attitude towards constitutions of every kind. Absolute monarchy in France, Spain and Prussia, for example; constitutional monarchy in England; a wide variety of republics in Italy and in the free cities of Germany; autocracy in Russia, despotism at Constantinople, and theocracy in the states of the Church – all were regarded as equally legitimate. Democracy, in short, had no more legitimacy than any other form of government.

Consider, for example, the responses of European states to the execution of Charles I by a people in revolt. One might have expected that European monarchs would have rallied to defend royal rights, in the face of the threat presented by the republican principle, and that other republics would have welcomed the new English one into their company. In practice, however, one of the most indignant critics of the parliamentary cause was Holland, which was itself a fellow republic, whilst the monarchs of Spain and France, after only a token protest against the fate of the English king, both hastened to recognize the Commonwealth.

The reflections of Cardinal Mazarin upon this incident indicate that, in the face of conflicting principles of legitimacy, it was to prudence, rather than to ideological considerations, that a statesman would resort. 'It would seem', Mazarin wrote to the Regent, Anne of Austria, 'that . . . the King [Louis XIV] could do nothing more prejudicial to his reputation than to desert the cause of the legitimate king, his near relative, neighbour and ally, and nothing more unjust than to recognize usurpers who have dipped their hands in the blood of their sovereign. But', Mazarin continued, 'a prolonged refusal to recognize the Commonwealth would do nothing to augment or to confirm the rights of the king . . . Besides, there is reason to fear that if the Spaniards are once closely linked with the English, they may prevent them from entering into good relations with us, and may get them, if not to make open war on us, at least to give Spain powerful assistance against us. There remains therefore no doubt', he concluded, 'that we should without delay enter into negotiations with the English republic, and give it such title as it may desire.' In accordance with Mazarin's advice Louis XIV recognized the legitimacy of the English Commonwealth, and in due course every state in Europe followed his example.[6]

After 1789, pragmatic sentiments such as those of Mazarin were to disappear almost entirely from the consideration of constitutional forms, for henceforth only democratic government was to be recognized as legitimate government. This change, it was believed, marked a definite advance in European political thought, since only when peoples ruled themselves (it was assumed) would the rights of individuals be secured, and peace between states be adequately guaranteed. In practice, however, the new democratic dogmatism contributed neither to liberty nor to international harmony. It was unable to do either, because the word 'democracy' now no longer referred to a specific form of government, but to a vague dream about how politics might become instead the vehicle for realizing the central fantasy of the new activist style.

This fantasy was aptly described not long after the promulgation of the doctrine of popular sovereignty in 1789. 'By sending us as deputies here,' Danton announced to the Convention of 1792, 'the French nation has brought into being a grand committee for the general insurrection of the peoples.'[7] It is this vision – a vision of 'the general insurrection of the peoples' – which continues to inspire the activist style of politics. A century and a half later, a euphoric French fascist, Robert Brasillach, contemplated the spread of the activist flame first lit in 1789 and indicated how little it had to do with either individual liberty or international peace. Reviewing its progress during the twentieth century, he wrote that 'we watched as the fire began to kindle in every direction, burning here with a feeble flame, there with a higher one. We saw how the old world, little by little, became menaced.' Throughout the whole of Europe, he said, 'a lost bell rang out beginning a long night of turmoil and sleeplessness. Everywhere peoples could be heard singing, each in their own way, "Nation, Awake! Arise!" ' At last, 'The world was ablaze, the world sang and gathered together, the world toiled.'[8] 'Turmoil and sleeplessness', then, rather than liberty and peace, were the most obvious fruits of the new style of politics.

What inspired this fervour, it will be recalled, was nothing more substantial than the naive democratic conviction that a people can never have any interest in ruling itself badly. Only rulers who have a sectional interest of their own, distinct from that of the people as a whole, the democratic doctrine holds, can ever have any wish to oppress the people; a self-governing people has nothing to gain by abusing power. In practice, this doctrine has meant that any government which claims to be republican or democratic – in the vague sense of deriving its power 'from below' – may now claim to be legitimate, no matter how badly it rules. Conversely, no government may any longer claim to be a legitimate government, regardless of how well it rules, unless it claims to derive its power directly from the people. Where this faith in popular sovereignty has been moderated by a long-established commitment to representative government, as in Britain and the United States, the dogmatic and imprudent attitude towards government which it otherwise encourages has also been moderated. In countries such as Italy and Germany, however, where representative institutions were grafted onto the modern democratic faith only at a late stage, the unquestioning belief in the identity of self-government with good government provided instead the solvent by which the revolutionary transformation of states into movements was set under way.

Why this should be so can most readily be appreciated by considering the chief result of the doctrine of popular sovereignty. This was to direct attention away from the problem of how the abuse of power was to be avoided and concentrate it instead upon the origin of power. The main question now became, in short, 'Who possesses legitimate power?' About this question, however, the doctrine of popular sovereignty was, as we shall see, inescapably ambiguous; and it is upon this ambiguity that the activist style has traded from 1789 down to the present day. The outcome has been the reduction of modern European politics, under the impact of the new activist style, to a deadly game without which fascism would have been inconceivable. It is the nature of this game which must now be considered briefly.

The point of the game is very simple: it is to decide which group in society may exclude, and even exterminate, other groups by the use of state power. Within the game's framework, in other words, politics becomes a matter of identifying an 'in-group', on the one hand, and an 'out-group' which is to be exterminated by it, or at any rate expelled from the social order, on the other. In the event, three versions of the game have proved especially popular during the past two centuries, and have provided the foundation for the great movement regimes of the present century. Of these three, one is based on the idea of class, another on the idea of the nation, and a third on the idea of race. Both the nature of this game and its relation to fascism will quickly become apparent if we now return for a moment to the difficulties presented by attempts to define the concept of the sovereign (or 'true') people.

For the democrats of 1789, the concept of the people was relatively unproblematic: it meant the Third Estate, or middle class. From this standpoint, all those not included in the Third Estate constituted an out-group deemed to be composed of traitors, or at best obstructionists. One of the revolutionaries explained how members of the out-group might expect to be treated: 'Those who are not of my species are not my fellow men'; he observed, adding that 'a noble is not of my species; he is a wolf and I shoot'.[9] It is noteworthy that members of the out-group did not actually have to oppose the new republic in order to be guilty of a crime: they needed only to fail to display sufficient activist zeal. 'Even the indifferent are to be punished,' said St Just, 'all who are *passive* in the Republic.'[10] It was in this spirit, for example, that the Convention passed a decree (on

10 March 1793) to suppress the out-group by taking cognizance (in the words of the decree) 'of every counter-revolutionary enterprise, of all offences against the liberty, equality, unity and indivisibility of the Republic, and the interior and exterior security of the State; and of all plots tending to re-establish the monarchy'. In order to enforce the decree special courts were created in which the judge could stop the trial at any point if the jury professed that they were already convinced, and in which the prisoners were ultimately deprived of counsel and then condemned in batches, in order to speed up the proceedings. Since the concept of a crime used by the courts was wholly indeterminate, they were in effect emancipated from the rule of law and were able to impose the death sentence for whatever they chose to regard as an offence. In Paris alone, the numbers condemned and guillotined were as follows: between 15 April and 1 October 1793, sixty-six, or an average of three a week; between 1 October 1793 and 9 June 1794, 1,165, or an average of over 32 a week; between 10 June and 27 July 1794, 1,376, or an average of over 196 a week.[11] By twentieth-century standards these figures seem in retrospect to be modest ones, but they indicate that the game of 'define the true people' begun by democrats in 1789 would inevitably give a murderous character to modern European political life.

During the first half of the nineteenth century, the democratic identification of the people with the middle class continued to provide the underlying premise of activist ideology. Even before the turn of the century, however, it had become clear that the democratic revolutionaries were mistaken to assume that their definition would be readily accepted by the whole of society. The most vulnerable point in their position was their assumption that the right to property, which Article 17 of the Declaration of Rights had declared to be 'inviolable and sacred', would remain unchallenged by still more radical exponents of the new activist style. In April 1796, the appearance of Sylvain Maréchal's 'Manifesto of the Equals' indicated that the day was not far off when legal and social reforms would no longer be considered sufficient, and the concept of the people would be redefined by socialists in terms of wealth and property ownership. 'For a long time now, for too long a time,' the Manifesto said, 'less than a million individuals have had at their disposal what belongs to more than twenty millions of their fellows, of equals. Let it come to an end at last, this great scandal that our posterity will never believe! Disappear at last, revolting distinctions between rich and poor, great and small, masters and servants, governors and governed.' In place of the inequality entailed by the democratic commitment to private property, the Manifesto wanted to put a socialist society in which the only differences between individuals would be those of age and sex, and in which 'there should be a common education and a common supply of food'.[12]

In spite of the warning note sounded by Maréchal, however, it was not until 1848 that the democratic version of the activist game began to be effectively challenged by a socialist one. In that year a new wave of revolutionary fervour spread through the capitals of Europe. The most notable feature of the events which occurred at that time was the part played in them by the urban proletariat, and it was this fact – the advent, that is, of the proletariat upon the political scene – which signalled the start of a new phase in the activist style. From 1848 onwards a long line of activist ideologues claimed that the concept of the people, properly understood, referred, not to the middle class, but to the working class. Amongst these ideologues, Marx was especially influential in refining the structure of the activist game in order to establish that the parasitic members of society (that is, the out-group), originally identified by the democrats of 1789 with priests and aristocrats, should now be redefined as the capitalist class.

In spite of Marx's belief that his redefinition of the 'true people' as the proletariat represented a scientific and therefore final stage in activist strategy, the subsequent course of twentieth-century intellectual history revealed that his own position was as unstable as the one which he had attacked. Consider, for example, the doctrine advocated by Sultan Galiev in 1919, in an article entitled 'Social Revolution and the East'. Galiev was a Marxist, in the sense that he followed Marx in identifying the true people with the proletariat. He differed from Marx, however, in his definition of the proletariat itself. The trouble with western socialism, Galiev wrote, is that 'the

East, with its population of a milliard and a half human beings, oppressed by the West European bourgeoisie, was almost entirely forgotten. The current of the international class war bypassed the East and the problem of revolution in the East existed only in the minds of a few scattered individuals.'[13] For Galiev, the true proletariat now became the Muslim, Hindu and Chinese masses of the East, and the Marxist class struggle was accordingly transformed into one between the white and the coloured races. Other non-European socialists rapidly took up this theme. For example, in 1920 Li Ta-chao, one of the founders of the Chinese Communist Party, defined class-struggle as racial conflict 'between the lower-class coloured races and the upper-class white race'. In this struggle, 'China really stands in the position of the world proletariat.'[14] In Japan, Ikki Kita also pursued the racial method of defining the true people as the populace of the third world, maintaining (in his *Outline for the Reconstruction of the Japanese State*, 1919) that, 'There are self-contradictions in the fundamental thought of those European and American socialists who approve of proletarian class-struggle within a country but who consider international proletarian war as chauvinism and militarism.'[15] In recent decades, Frantz Fanon has been the best-known exponent of this particular variant of the new activist style of politics.

It hardly needs to be said that anyone who grasps the simple structure of the political game just illustrated will have no difficulty in redefining the true people – and with it, the corresponding out-group – in a way which can be made to serve any ideological purpose at all. Reviewing the ideological arsenal available to contemporary feminists, for example, Simone de Beauvoir remarked that, 'The proletariat can propose to massacre the ruling class, and a sufficiently fanatical Jew or Negro might dream of getting sole possession of the atomic bomb and making humanity wholly Jewish or black; but woman cannot even dream of exterminating the males.'[16] Bearing in mind the infinitely flexible logic of the game of 'define the true people', however, her conclusion seems overly cautious since within the framework of that game there is no reason why the male as such, rather than the aristocrat or the capitalist, should not be branded as a parasite and treated accordingly. In fact this step was taken quite recently, when a Feminist Manifesto published in *Medusa* (subtitled the Journal of the Bradford Lesbian Feminist Surrealist Group) proclaimed that 'woman is the only sex. Men are a lower form of animal.'[17]

It has seemed worth outlining in some detail the history, structure and implications of the familiar and well-established political game into which modern European political life has constantly tended to degenerate because it is only against the background which it provides that the emergence of fascism is fully intelligible. In order to understand the fascist form of the game, however, it is necessary to look more closely at a version which has so far only been lightly touched upon. This is the nationalist version. Instead of being defined in democratic or in socialist terms, the sovereign people might be defined as 'the nation', understood as an entity which welded together all the different groups in society. On the Continent, the nationalist version of the activist game has in fact been intimately and inextricably connected with the democratic one from the very beginning. The democratic principles proclaimed by the French revolutionaries, it is true, were abstract and universal. At first sight, the idealism of the French revolution, appealing as it did to the rights of man, had no obvious connection with nationalist ideology. In this respect the overt ideology of the revolution seemed rather to look back to the cosmopolitanism of the Enlightenment than forward to the age of antagonistic nationalist creeds. Barely concealed beneath the universal language of the new democratic ideology, however, it is possible to discern the contours of a nationalist ideology which rapidly revealed that it had none of the pacific character to which the democrats now laid claim. In practice, as two distinguished historians remark, 'Humanity, which had been the ideal of 1789, was identified with France, the spread of French ideas with that of French power, and liberation with French conquest.'[18]

The immediate result of the fusion of democratic with nationalist sentiment was to give the new activist style a militant and aggressive tendency which its proponents disclaimed in theory but pursued ruthlessly in practice. Article VI of the Constitution of 1790 declared: 'The French nation renounces all wars of conquest, and will never employ her forces against the freedom of any people.' Only two years later, however, 'a decree of the Convention declared that the French nation, while it would not embark on a war against another nation, deemed it right to defend a free people against the unjust aggression of a king, and a later decree directed the executive power to give help to people struggling in the cause of liberty'.[19] With the aid of nothing more than a little verbal juggling, then, war and aggression might now be concealed as a quest for world peace through the reorganization of the international order in accordance with the interests of any nation that claimed it stood for freedom and justice. It was this technique with which Hitler was to bemuse the world so successfully in the years after 1933. In that respect, however, he showed no originality; the technique had for long been part of the stock-in-trade of the new activist style of politics inaugurated by the doctrine of popular sovereignty.

In the hands of the Nazis, the militant implications of the new activist style of politics proved decidedly unpalatable to the western world. What is too easily forgotten, however, is that this intrinsically ambiguous style, when deployed by other hands, had for long been a matter for profound admiration. It is this style of politics, for example, which permeates the history of Italian republicanism and facilitated the unification of Italy. Consider, in this connection, the career of Garibaldi, who adopted the French 'liberation' strategy long before Hitler used it for more ambitious purposes. In 1860, in an exploit which won him fame and approval throughout Europe, Garibaldi invaded Sicily with only one thousand men at his command. In his own eyes and in the eyes of the world, this act of aggression was a spectacular example of the triumph of the mixture of democratic and nationalist sentiment which together comprise the Continental republican tradition. The invasion, that is to say, was inspired and justified by the new activist mythology, according to which the Sicilian people were assumed to be eagerly awaiting their 'liberation'. One of those who accompanied Garibaldi, the novelist Ippolito Nievo, records the disappointment which awaited this band of intrepid activists when they landed. 'It was on the rumour of a Sicilian revolution', he wrote, 'that we had risked death and drowning to arrive at Marsala, yet on arrival we found nothing.' There were, he records, 'only some minor demonstrations in the towns and unrest among certain armed bands in the countryside'.[20]

In a land which for over twenty-five centuries had borne the weight of many heterogeneous civilizations – 'all from outside, none made by ourselves, none that we could call our own', as a native Sicilian writer recently remarked[21] – this was hardly surprising. The Sicilians, after all, had long been familiar with the incursions of Byzantine tax-gatherers, Berber Emirs, and Spanish Viceroys; to them, one more invasion was consequently neither here nor there. When Garibaldi subsequently went on to invade the mainland of southern Italy, however, the problem presented by his conduct became even more acute: was it to be described as a straightforward programme of conquest on behalf of the northern Kingdom of Piedmont, or was it a programme of 'liberation', in the style favoured by Danton and the French revolutionary armies? Garibaldi himself, of course, was never in any doubt. On one occasion, for example, he had to correct a Swiss journalist who said that he had 'conquered' the Italian provinces. Garibaldi duly reminded the journalist that he had merely helped them to deliver themselves.[22] Those sympathetic towards Garibaldi's aims will naturally describe him, as Vergilio Titone recently did, as a 'realist', by comparison with Mazzini and others. For, Titone insists, 'Garibaldi was the only one who understood the real situation and acted consistently. He alone was capable of giving to those thousands (thousands rather than millions) who formed the "real Italy" a positive creed and an unhoped-for power . . . This happened in Sicily, and again afterwards at Naples.'[23] The identification of the 'real Italy' with a few thousand men is curious, yet the new democratic creed had from the outset sanctioned the identification without a qualm. After Garibaldi's conquest of Sicily and southern Italy, for example, poems were written in his honour by Tennyson, Elizabeth Barrett Browning and George Meredith, among others, and at a banquet in London in 1864 he was lionized by the English establishment. The present purpose, however, is not to pass judgment on this admiration, but only to indicate that it should not obscure the main point of relevance.

55

This is that the activist style of politics has always sanctioned ideological acts of aggression which have made the requirements of international order indistinguishable from romantic fantasy.

But what, it must be asked, was the character of the democratic republic which the new activist style was expected to create? Consider again Garibaldi, as a respected and successful activist practitioner. In 1903 Garibaldi was described by the English liberal thinker, John Morley, as 'the soldier who bore the sword for human freedom'. In those days, Morley added, 'there were ideals; democracy was conscious of common interest and common brotherhood; and liberal Europe was then a force and not a dream'.[24] What then was the object of this democratic idealism? The answer may be gleaned from the address which Garibaldi delivered to the constituent assembly at Rome on 5 February 1849. 'Not only the people of Rome but those of all Italy are looking to us to choose a new form of government,' he declared, 'and I therefore propose that we should not leave this hall before we have reached agreement.'

Now this might seem to be a grave and complex matter, but the significant point is the casual way in which Garibaldi swept the complexities of government to one side. 'Let us not bother', he urged those present, 'about mere forms and practices.'[25] An obituary in *The Times* (5 June 1882) took an indulgent view of Garibaldi's career, declaring that 'with a heart like Garibaldi's a man can afford to allow his brain to go a wool-gathering'. Unfortunately, however, the vagueness given to Garibaldi's objectives by his indifference to constitutional forms was not the mark of some intellectual woolliness peculiar to himself. On the contrary, the whole character of the activist style was such as to encourage a conception of democracy in which extra-constitutional action completely usurped the place of parliamentary institutions and constitutional procedures.

Consider, from this point of view, the criticism which an equally famous republican activist, Giuseppe Mazzini, made of Garibaldi in 1867, at a time when Garibaldi was longing to start a movement to acquire Rome for Italy. 'He loves Rome,' Mazzini wrote, 'but does not make this love a real *religion*. . . . He ought to be a real believer, but is not. He looks at the matter more from a *materialistic* than from a moral point of view, thinking more of the body of Italy than of its real soul.'[26] How then should a 'real believer' in the sovereignty of the people behave? In 1831, Mazzini had founded Young Italy, one of the myriad secret societies which proliferated in Europe in the post-Napoleonic era with the aim of promoting the activist cause. It was for this society that he provided a tract entitled *Instructions for the Members of Young Italy*. The instructions are interesting. 'Insurrection – by means of guerilla bands – is the true method of warfare for all nations desirous of emancipating themselves from a foreign yoke,' was the political message they conveyed. Insurrection by such terrorist methods, Mazzini continued, 'forms the military character of the people, and consecrates every foot of the native soil by the meaning of some warlike deed'. As a further contribution to this extra-constitutional manner of pursuing political objectives, Mazzini wrote a tract entitled *Rules for the Conduct of Guerilla Bands*. 'Guerilla warfare', he explained there, 'opens a field of activity for every local capacity; forces the enemy into an unaccustomed method of battle; avoids the evil consequences of a great defeat; secures the national war from the role of treason, and has the advantage of not confining it within any defined and determinate basis of operations. It is invincible, indestructible.'

The fusion of nationalist with democratic ideology in 1789, then, produced a style of politics in which both international aggression and terrorism might readily find an ideological sanction. Indeed, within the new activist style which was fuelled by this combination of nationalist and democratic doctrine, violent and extra-constitutional methods of political action tended from the outset to appear more desirable, because more 'heroic', than parliamentary and constitutional ones. Yet the full extent of the extremist potential with which nationalism endowed the deadly game inaugurated by the democratic doctrine of popular sovereignty in 1789 still remains to be indicated.

The 'nation' upon which the democratic doctrine had, in effect, conferred sovereignty was, then, obviously just as ambiguous an entity as was the abstract idea of 'the people' originally invoked by the French revolutionaries. It might

57

therefore be defined in a variety of ways. In practice, cultural and linguistic criteria were subsequently to find most favour, but in principle there was nothing to preclude a genetic or racialist criterion of the kind which Nazism adopted. Regardless of the criterion of nationhood adopted, moreover, the nationalist version necessarily resulted – as did every other version of the game, of course – in the creation of an outgroup or 'enemy' which had to be eliminated in order to bring about the perfect social unity to which the game was supposed to lead. The Jews were often cast by nationalist thinkers as eminently suitable candidates for this part, in place of the aristocrats favoured by the democratic version of the game and the capitalists selected for Marx's communist version.

It was basically the nationalist version of the activist game which both Mussolini and Hitler were to play. They played it, however, in a way which gave it a venomous twist that no previous player had foreseen. What they did was to take it to its logical conclusion by making clear that there were in fact no rules for playing it, except the entirely arbitrary ones made by the fascist leader. It is instructive, from this point of view, to recall an occasion at the Party headquarters at Villa Cavallero on which Mussolini asked rhetorically, 'What is Fascism?' 'It can only be answered in one way,' Mussolini reflected, 'Fascism is Mussolinism. Let us not delude ourselves.'[27] Here then was the fascist answer to the question, 'Who is the sovereign people?' The people, the fascist replied, is whatever the leader says it is. On this point, the Nazi theorist Carl Schmitt was quite explicit. The primary idea of Nazism, Schmitt insisted, was that of 'the immediate fact and real presence' of the leader. On this view, it is therefore the leader who defines and creates racial unity, with the result that even race became in effect whatever Hitler said it was.[28]

It was in this way that fascism finally stood the democratic idealism of 1789 on its head. The sad thing, of course, is that it required such little ingenuity to do so; but then, ever since 1789 the new activist political style fostered by this idealism has infected the European political vocabulary with such profound ambiguity that men need only to mention democracy, freedom or national unity in order to be able to get away (quite literally) with murder. Earlier proponents of activism were a bit too old-fashioned, or a bit too naive, to notice the grease on the pole they were climbing. The fascists welcomed it. It will be evident, for instance, that there was nothing in the modern democratic tradition to prevent the Belgian Rex movement from declaring in all good faith that 'we are the true democrats'.[29] Likewise, there was nothing to prevent Mussolini from defining fascism, quite plausibly, as 'organized, concentrated, authoritarian democracy on a national basis'. Again, there was no absurdity (although much that was disastrous) in Hitler's repeated assertions of the democratic character of the Third Reich. In a long speech to the Reichstag on 30 June 1934, for example, he declared that, 'it will always be a first care of the National Socialist Government of the Reich to ascertain anew how far the will of the nation is incorporated in its Government. And in this sense we "savages" are really the better democrats.'[30] Hitler, it should now be clear, was not merely playing with words; he was exploiting a genuine incoherence which lies at the heart of the modern European democratic tradition, as it has been shaped and moulded by the new activist style of politics. It is this incoherence which explains, in particular, why it is wrong – as Franz Neumann remarked – 'to assume that during the twenties and early thirties National Socialism simply set out to prove democracy worthless or to propose a substitute: monarchy or dictatorship or anything else. Quite the contrary,' Neumann continues, 'it paraded as the salvation of democracy.'[31] We have already seen why that parade was all too easy.

Whilst the new theory of evil has imparted a fanatical, crusading character to the activist style of politics, the doctrine of popular sovereignty has opened the way to a despotic interpretation of the modern democratic ideal which was adopted by the European world in the period after 1789. It is now necessary to turn to a third, equally fatal, source of instability which entered the western political vocabulary at the end of the eighteenth century, and subsequently proved no less vital for the phenomenon we call fascism. This was the appearance of a new concept of freedom.

59

3. Freedom as struggle and terror Freedom, as that term was used by the early defenders of a limited style of politics like Locke, referred to an external relationship between different subjects, or between subjects and their governments. The new concept which emerged at the end of the eighteenth century, and has since become generally accepted throughout the western world, however, has an entirely different meaning. Instead of referring to an external relationship, it came henceforth to refer to an inner condition of the individual psyche. It came, more generally, to refer to what we would now term 'self-realization'. The result has been that the word freedom, referring as it now does to an inner condition and not to an external relationship, has long since lost all connection with any specific form of constitution. It is in this way that there arose, right at the heart of the modern European political vocabulary, another source of vulnerability which fascism duly exploited to the full. The nature and extent of this vulnerability can most easily be illustrated from the writings of the great German philosopher, Immanuel Kant, who provided the first systematic philosophic formulation of the new concept of freedom.

The greatest good for man, Kant wrote in his *Lectures on Ethics*, 'is freedom in accordance with a will which is not determined to action'. By 'a will which is not determined to action', Kant meant a will which remains uninfluenced by any external considerations. So long, that is to say, as the will is not affected by historical, social, religious, physical or other external factors, the man who wills it is completely free. In this new usage of the term freedom, then, a man may still think of himself as free even if he is imprisoned in a dungeon. Conversely, he may plausibly deny that he is free even if he lives in a liberal-democratic order, under a constitutional government. Merely by asserting that his will is in some way conditioned or moulded by the liberal social order, for example, he becomes entitled to regard his 'real' condition as one of servitude, in spite of the external security for his person and property provided by liberal political institutions.

It was in this way, then, that the new inner conception of freedom united with the democratic doctrine of popular sovereignty to deprive the modern European liberal-democratic tradition of any necessary connection with a limited style of politics. Just as the doctrine of popular sovereignty enabled even a despotic government to claim that it was legitimated by the will of the people, so the new concept of liberty enabled it to claim, in addition, that everything it did contributed to the 'true' freedom of its subjects. It was this ambiguity which eventually made it possible for fascists to claim that they themselves were the defenders of 'true' liberty, just as they were able to claim that they were the true democrats.

Consider, for example, the ease with which the Italian philosopher Gentile was able to defend the 'liberal' character of what Italian Fascists liked to regard as their 'ethical' ideal of the state. 'There is', he wrote, 'nothing really private . . . and there are no limits to State-action.' This doctrine, he admitted, 'appears to make the State swallow the individual', yet on closer inspection, he assured his readers, 'one might say just the opposite: for in this conception [of liberty] the State is the will of the individual himself in its universal and absolute aspect, and thus the individual swallows the State; and since legitimate authority cannot extend beyond the actual will of the individual, authority is resolved completely in liberty. Lo and behold,' this delighted fascist concluded, 'absolutism is overturned and appears to have changed into its opposite; and the true absolute democracy is not that which seeks a limited State, but which seeks no limits to the State that develops in the inmost heart of the individual, conferring on his will the absolutely universal force of law.'[32]

The confused reasoning by which freedom becomes indistinguishable from the 'absolute democracy' of Gentile and his fellow fascists will be evident from what has already been said. Since the new conception of freedom did not refer to *civil* liberty, but only to liberty understood in the inner sense of 'self-realization', little ingenuity was required in order to link it to the cause of despotism. Self-realization, after all, can mean anything, according to the taste of the ideologue who defines it.

This ambiguity first became apparent at the moment when Rousseau (who was primarily concerned, like Kant, with inner freedom) distinguished between a 'real' and an 'actual' self, and then proceeded to identify the real self with the general will or common good. The result was to shift the individual's centre of gravity away from his private concerns, and re-establish it on a collectivist basis. Thereafter, German romantic philosophers, like Fichte and Adam Müller, rapidly devised a muddled metaphysic which reinforced the new collectivist meaning which freedom had now acquired. The individual who concerned himself with civil liberty, this metaphysic maintained, was making a great mistake. He was mistaken, because concern with the external conditions of liberty committed him (so it was said) to a vulgar, divisive and materialistic ideal of liberty which ignored the spiritual (or inner) aspect of freedom and thus brought about the destruction of national unity. Since there are no barriers within the inner world of pure spirit in which true liberty was now located by these philosophers, it followed that there was no need to concern oneself any longer with the external institutional barriers against the abuse of power required by civil liberty.

Treading in the footsteps of Rousseau and the German romantic thinkers, Marx later proceeded to claim that men possess a 'species-being' (that is, a real or true self) which should lead them to pursue universal (i.e. collectivist) ends, in place of the allegedly selfish and purely personal ones which they pursue under capitalism. Unless they conform to their species-being men are unfree, or 'alienated', as Marxist jargon has it. Subsequently, the English liberal tradition, as restated by T. H. Green and Bosanquet, perpetuated this muddle by completely ignoring the conditions necessary for pursuing civil liberty in order to concentrate instead upon liberty understood once more as self-realization. Imbued as their idea of self-realization was with a desire for social reform, liberty came in this way to be identified once again with a self-sacrificing life of service to a mythical communal whole into which the individual was to be absorbed.

During the nineteenth century, it is true, isolated voices were occasionally to be heard protesting against the spread of this doctrine and warning of its dangers. Amongst them were those, for example, of Benjamin Constant and Alexis de Tocqueville. In an age of democratic optimism and collectivist fervour, however, even those who listened to these voices were often all too ready to subordinate liberty to a moral idealism which obscured the conditions necessary for the maintenance of a limited style of politics. Such was the case, for example, with the thought of de Tocqueville's English admirer, John Stuart Mill, for whom liberty was primarily an instrument for realizing the moral progress of society. Even in England, then, the new inner concept of freedom produced relative indifference to the conditions for civil, or 'external', liberty.

By the end of the nineteenth century, in short, the concept of freedom as self-realization introduced by Rousseau and Kant, and popularized thereafter by both socialist and liberal thinkers, had become the foundation of all the great modern radical ideologies. Long before fascism took over the word for its own purposes, in other words, freedom had become an ideal which was so thoroughly detached from any clear connection with constitutional government, and so deeply wedded to a nebulous collectivist ideal, that there was little difficulty in adapting it to suit the purposes of an entirely authoritarian ideology. In order to make freedom and fascism entirely compatible with one another, all that fascist ideologues needed to do was to accept the long tradition of thought which identified liberty with self-realization through service to society or the nation, whilst adding that the good of the nation must be identified with the mission of the fascist leader. Once this last step had been taken, 'true freedom' naturally meant unconditional obedience to the fascist regime.

Even this step, however, added no novel dimension to a way of thinking about liberty which had already been prefigured in the decades before the French Revolution. When it is recalled that Rousseau had argued that true freedom might require unconditional submission to the dictates of a supra-human Legislator, who alone was competent to express the general will, then the fascist conception of freedom as submission to a leader appears as no more than the plausible outcome of a European libertarian tradition which had already emasculated the word 'liberty' by stripping it of the social and political institutions required to give political substance to the word.

From this point of view, there is much that is persuasive in

Hallowell's contention that liberalism was not murdered by fascism, but committed suicide.[33] Where an older, pre-revolutionary liberal tradition continued to tie the liberal ideal to representative institutions, as in England and America, the constitutionally ambiguous implications of the new inner concept of freedom were held in check, even when an increasing gap opened up between the muddled ideas of liberal philosophers who identified liberty with social reform, on the one hand, and the prosaic requirements of limited government, on the other. Where no such pre-revolutionary liberal tradition existed, however, as in Italy and Germany, there was little to halt the unstable course upon which the new concept of freedom had placed the European liberal tradition after 1789. In view of this, it is misleading to maintain, as Eugen Weber has done, that, 'Twentieth-century fascism is a by-product of disintegrating liberal democracy'.[34] From the outset, the modern liberal-democratic tradition was vulnerable to extremist interpretations, and the advent of fascism, in consequence, cannot be said to have marked its 'disintegration'. It marked, rather, the final disclosure of ambiguities which had been present from the beginning.

This disquieting fact will become still more evident if we now notice an aspect of the modern concept of liberty which did more than any other to promote activist extremism, especially in its fascist forms. This is the highly intransigent, uncompromising and militant attitude towards the external world which the new ideal of inner liberty tended to encourage. Since it was this which rapidly came to provide the ethical basis of the activist style of politics at large, it is necessary to consider briefly how the redefinition of freedom as self-realization converted liberty from a word synonymous with moderation into one which pointed instead towards wanton terrorism, of the kind perpetrated under the fascist regimes.

The essence of inner or spiritual freedom, as Kant had made clear, is that it is incompatible with any external restrictions upon the will. From this position, it is only a small step to the conclusion that freedom is only achieved in the course of an endless struggle to master the moral challenge presented to the will by the existence of an external world which forever appears to threaten the will's autonomy. In this way, then, struggle or conflict, regarded now as the index of moral vigour, became intimately connected with the new ideal of inner freedom. It is hardly to be expected that an individual who adopts this ideal should pay much attention to the external freedom of other individuals, when that threatens to restrict what he considers to be the requirements of his spiritual life.

When Mussolini wrote (in *The Doctrine of Fascism*) that the fascist ethic 'looks at life as duty, ascent, conquest', he was not adding anything to this tradition of moral theorizing. Any man who took virtue seriously, Kant had made clear long before, would certainly see life as 'duty, ascent, conquest', in the sense that he would accept and welcome the need for endless moral struggle. 'The being endowed with freedom', Kant wrote in *The Dispute of the Faculties* (1798) 'is not content to enjoy a pleasant life.' 'Virtue', he made clear in *The Metaphysics of Morals*, 'is the strength of a man's maxims in following his duty. All strength is known by the hindrances which it can overcome; with virtue, these are the natural inclinations, which can come in conflict with the moral prescription; and since it is man himself who puts these hindrances in the way of his maxims, virtue is not only compulsion of oneself . . . but a compulsion according to a principle of inner freedom.' According to the new ethical ideal associated with the concept of inner liberty, then, a man's will becomes fully moral only to the extent that he submits it to perpetual torment and trials. Struggle and conflict become the hallmark of virtue, and morality acquires the character of a dynamic process in which men seek to realize themselves by confronting more and more severe challenges to their will.

The new concept of freedom, it will be evident, was thus more closely allied from the start to a spirit of fanaticism than to one of moderation. When Mussolini wrote, in *The Doctrine of Fascism*, that the centre of life must be placed inside man and not outside him; when he explained that the fascist ethic is captured in the mood and motto (*'me ne frego'*) of the *Squadrista*, who love risk and despise comfort, caution and prudence, he was of course adding a dose of romantic bravura which was quite alien to Kant himself. Mussolini's moral posture, however, would be unintelligible without the new doctrine of inner freedom which had entered European life at the time of the French Revolution.

Against this background, it is possible to sympathize with the difficulties which Mussolini found in converting Italians to the new activist morality. As early as 1939, one historian reminds us, 'Their reluctance to enter the war at all . . . had already driven him to fury. The cold winter of 1939–40 had pleased him. He watched the snow falling in December and said, "This snow and cold are very good. In this way our good-for-nothing Italians, this mediocre race, will be improved. One of the principal reasons I wanted the Apennines to be reforested was because it would make Italy colder and snowier." ' There were more moral delights in store for Mussolini, however. 'In January when there was a coal shortage he was gratified again, because it was good for the people to be put to tests which would make them shake off their "centuries old mental laziness". "We must keep them disciplined", he said, "and in uniform from morning to night. Beat them and beat them and beat them." '[35]

In Hitler's writings, as in those of other leading Nazis, the new ethic of struggle was to be clothed in the language in which it became particularly fashionable during the nineteenth century: the language, that is, of Social Darwinism, with its stress upon the survival of the fittest. The detail of Darwinian theory, however, may safely be ignored in the present context, since the minor writers (like Haeckel) who popularized it during the second half of the nineteenth century, and converted it into the pseudo-scientific key to life which Hitler claimed to find in it, were merely offering a vulgarized form of the new metaphysic of ethics which had appeared long before with Kant.

It may well be objected, however, that to move from Kant's ethical theory to Mussolini and Hitler is to postulate a purely fanciful intellectual connection. By way of reply, it will be useful to recall that the activist style had provided practical evidence of the destructive implications of the new concept of freedom as inner struggle quite independently of Kant's speculations.

For Robespierre, as for Kant, inner freedom was the supreme good for man. Like Kant, Robespierre also believed that this freedom could never be achieved without struggle, for the end of liberty is virtue, in which lies self-realization, and the road to virtue is not an easy one. From this, Robespierre rapidly concluded that liberty is not only compatible with terror, but actually requires it. 'The mainspring of popular government in time of revolution', he observed, 'is both *virtue and terror*: virtue, without which terror is evil; terror, without which virtue is helpless.'[36]

In the new activist style of politics, in short, fanaticism and terror were not only inseparably linked to the idea of liberty from the very beginning; they actually came to count as evidence of virtue, and to indicate a passionate commitment to liberty. 'There is nothing', exclaimed St Just, 'which so much resembles virtue as a great crime.' Virtue, indeed, might henceforth seem to be quite unattainable without great crimes: 'There is something terrible', St Just also said, 'in the sacred love of the fatherland; it is so exclusive as to sacrifice everything to the public interest, without pity, without fear, without respect for humanity . . . What produces the general good is always terrible.'[37]

Rousseau's dream of liberating the suffering masses by rallying them to the activist cause, then, had rapidly turned out to be a more bloody and ruthless business than its progenitor had foreseen. By the end of the nineteenth century, nevertheless, the pitiless violence which had been moralized by the philosophers and practised by the French revolutionaries had become sufficiently respectable for it to provide the basis of a new profession. This was the now familiar profession of terrorism; the profession, that is, of the dedicated revolutionary who will stop at nothing in order to seize power, under the pretext of 'liberating' the people. His credo, hinted at long before by St Just, was first clearly spelt out (in 1869) in Michael Bakunin's *Revolutionary Catechism*. From this work we learn that, 'All the tender feelings of family life, of friendship, love, gratitude and even honour must be stifled in the revolutionary by a single cold passion for the revolutionary cause.' Bakunin's stress on the cold, merciless and dispassionate spirit in which violence is to be perpetrated is particularly striking, for it is 'tirelessly and in cold blood' that the revolutionary 'must always be prepared to die and to kill with his own hands anyone who stands in the way of achieving [the revolution]'. Nothing is to be exempted from the holocaust of this destructive violence, for the only true revolution 'is one that destroys every established object root and branch, that annihilates all state-traditions, orders and classes'. Only in the midst of this devastation are the conditions for perfect freedom finally established.

Perverse as it may seem, then, the modern European activist style of politics had established an intimate connection between freedom, virtue, and terror long before fascism openly elevated violence to the central principle of political life. Once this is appreciated, it is not very difficult to understand such aspects of twentieth-century activism as the organized destruction of the Jews by Nazism. Destruction and fanaticism, after all, had become morally respectable parts of the western tradition as soon as the new activist style had won general acceptance. It is unnecessary, in consequence, to invoke elaborate intellectual constructions of the 'totalitarian' kind devised by Arendt in order to understand such features of twentieth-century life as mass murder by men like Eichmann; it is only necessary to recall the extremism towards which the new activist style has always been prone. The man who is really serious about bringing inner or spiritual freedom to his people will naturally pride himself, as Bakunin had insisted he should, on his cold, impersonal, merciless attitude towards the enemies of the freedom he seeks to realize. For Robespierre, the enemies of this freedom were priests and aristocrats; for Lenin, they were 'bourgeois' groups like the Kulaks; for the Nazis, they happened to be the Jews. In each case, 'freedom' was to be achieved only by the appropriate extermination campaign.

Within the context of this activist tradition, what could be more natural than the conduct of the notorious Commandant of Auschwitz, Rudolph Hoess, who voluntarily admitted having gassed two million persons at Auschwitz between 1941 and 1943? His only regret was that the extermination programme had made Germany unpopular throughout the world, and had therefore 'in no way served the cause of anti-semitism, but on the contrary brought the Jews far closer to their ultimate objective'.[38] And what could be more plausible – within the context of the activist style of politics, of course – than the final paragraph of Hoess' memoir? 'Let the public continue to regard me as the blood-thirsty beast, the cruel sadist and the mass murderer,' he wrote there, 'for the masses could never imagine the Commandant of Auschwitz in any other light. They could never understand that he, too, had a heart and that he was not evil.' Hoess' claim that he was not evil is worth pondering upon. True to the creed of Bakunin, he prided himself, indeed, on the very fact that he had to carry out actions which were frequently at odds with his natural inclination. 'Nothing is harder than to grit one's teeth and go through with such a thing, coldly, pitilessly, and without mercy,' he wrote of his extermination duties.[39] Here the idea of moral perfection through moral struggle is taken to its extreme, but the idea itself, as has been seen, had been perfectly respectable for a century and a half, in spite of the extremism which Robespierre, St Just, Bakunin and others had previously shown that it encouraged.

This same fanaticism, deriving from the pitiless idea of freedom as a will striving to release itself from natural and prudential considerations, was the source of the S.S. morality at large – a morality in which freedom, self-sacrifice, and loyalty to the leader and the nation became inseparable from terror. In this morality, the categorical imperative (as Kant had termed the unconditional moral law to which man is subject) is merely shifted from the noumenal sphere to the nation and the fascist leader. Consider, for example, the words with which Himmler appealed to S.S. leaders at Posen in October 1943, in connection with the extermination programme. 'To have stuck it out and at the same time remained decent fellows, that is what has made us tough . . . We had the moral right, we had the duty to our people, to destroy this people which wanted to destroy us. But we have not the right to enrich ourselves with so much as a watch, a mark, a cigarette, or anything else . . . All in all, we can say that we have fulfilled this most difficult duty for the love of our people. And our spirit, our soul, our character has not suffered injury from it . . .'[40]

Terrorism, however, was not the only form of extremism fostered by the new concept of freedom which inspired the activist style. Transferred to the international level, the idea of struggle could mean only one thing. It meant war. As fascism was eventually to demonstrate, however, the activist style of politics endows war with a significance entirely different from any associated with it in the past. War, as has often been remarked, is the normal condition of human societies, and peace the exception. Within the activist style of politics, however, war is not merely a normal condition of things, but an intrinsically desirable way of conducting international affairs. War alone, Mussolini explained in *The Doctrine of Fascism*, 'brings up to their highest tension all human energies and puts the stamp of nobility upon the peoples who have the courage to want it'. Indeed, within the activist style of politics war becomes of such paramount significance that it is no longer relevant whether a country wins or loses. Just as in private life the important thing is to engage in ceaseless moral struggle for its own sake, so, in political life, the important thing is to fight, regardless of the chance of victory or the prospect of defeat. As Mussolini explained to Ciano, 'It's humiliating to remain with folded arms, while others make history. It doesn't matter much who wins. To make a people great it is necessary to send them into battle, even if you have to kick them in the pants.'[41] After the near annihilation by the Russians of his personal S.S. division, the Leibenstandarte Adolf Hitler, Hitler interrupted General Reichenau's report on the fiasco in order to inform him that, 'Losses can never be too high,' since 'they sow the seeds of future greatness.'[42]

Within fascist ideology, then, the logic of the activist style was finally accepted, and war became the supreme test of a people's fitness for historical survival. War, as a result, becomes the sole raison d'être of the state, irrespective (as has just been seen) of the prospect of success. Now this militant outlook has frequently been regarded as a total departure from the enlightened and pacific morality which is generally ascribed to the previous two centuries of European cultural development. Fascist ideology itself, for example, was proud to proclaim that it had restored the martial and heroic spirit in an age of 'decadence'. On closer inspection, however, fascist militarism proves to be an unforeseen but intellible outcome of the idea upon which the West had most prided itself during those centuries, rather than a total departure from it. This is the idea of progress in which the concept of freedom was fused with the cult of moral striving and inner struggle.

In one perspective, the belief in progress was the natural concomitant of the new theory of evil as an evanescent feature of the human condition. In the present context, however, the most important aspect of the idea of progress is the necessity it created for finding some way of rationalizing the continuing part played by evil in human affairs until its final disappearance, with the advent of individual and social perfection. The solution adopted was ingenious. Instead of being treated as a purely negative phenomenon, as the traditional theological and philosophical systems of western thought had conceived of it, what was now suggested was that it might actually be a positive force for good in human affairs. According to the most widely favoured theory, evil could be justified when the struggle, conflict and violence which it entailed were regarded as the historical mechanism through which progress was promoted. It was this theory which, in its most ambitious form, provided the basis of Hegel's vision of history as a dialectical progress in which human consciousness rises to an ever higher awareness of its freedom. Marx adopted a modified version of the theory in order to defend a view of human history as the story of progress towards a communist utopia, in which freedom would finally be achieved by the triumph of the proletariat in the class struggle. Long before Hegel and Marx, however, Turgot had argued in a lecture *On the Successive Advances of the Human Mind* (1750), that, 'It is only through turmoil and destruction that nations expand and civilizations and governments are in the long run perfected.' Thereafter Kant, for example, had argued (in 1794) in his *Idea of a Universal History on a Cosmopolitan Plan*, that it is through war that nature mysteriously pursues its ultimately benign end of developing man's reason and moral freedom to the full.

The intention of thinkers like Turgot and Kant was not to idealize war; they were merely speculating about the possibility that human history conceals some higher moral purpose to which even misery and suffering may ultimately contribute.

71

The result, nevertheless, was that violence was endowed at a very early stage in modern European intellectual life with a positive moral significance, to the point where Kant could suggest, in his treatise on *Perpetual Peace* (1794), that even war was rationally preferable to the static, stagnant peace of despotism which a universal monarchy would establish.

The fascist cult of struggle, violence and war, then, did not mark a radical departure from a previous European tradition of pacific idealism. During the nineteenth century, it is true, the idea of progress had encouraged a complacent optimism about a future era of world peace, especially in liberal and socialist intellectual circles. The process of reasoning which had contributed to this optimism, however, had arbitrarily singled out the more attractive side of the idea of progress for exclusive attention. But the same process of reasoning, it will be evident, might equally well be used to defend a militant ethic of a very different kind. The fascist ethic, in this perspective, is just as much the child of modern optimism, as exemplified in the idea of progress beloved by the western democracies, as is the pacific liberal idealism which produced the ideal of perpetual peace.

Finally, yet another consequence may be derived from the ethical ideal which inspired the activist conception of liberty as endless striving and struggle. This is that within the new activist style, politics became primarily a sphere for youth; a desperate crusade, that is, for adolescents and for those still tied to the dreams of adolescence. In this style, the wisdom brought by age, and the sense of political limitations that age alone inculcates, can find no place. What alone matters is the vigour demanded by the endless struggle for perfect liberty. Old age weakens this vigour and fanaticism, thereby atrophying the activist impulse demanded by the new style of politics. Wisdom, in consequence, is now transferred from age to youth, since it is youth, and not age, which ignores the limitations of human existence and embarks gladly upon the restless quest for endlessly changing experiences.

Within the new activist style, then, politics becomes predominantly the province of the young. The nationalistic and democratic sentiment which inspired activism from the outset has often been interpreted in class terms, but stress on class conflict merely obscures the deeper discontinuity that has characterized western life during the past century and a half. This discontinuity consists in the conflict between generations produced by the rapid political and social change which marked the nineteenth and twentieth centuries, and was intensified by the war. The more acute of nineteenth-century activist politicians, however, were keenly aware of the implications of the new political style for the younger generation at a relatively early stage. Thus the Carbonari revolts of 1830, Mazzini believed, had been unsuccessful largely because they were led by middle-aged men who had inevitably failed, just because they were middle-aged, to establish contact with the masses. In 1831, therefore, he founded 'Young Italy', and explicitly excluded from membership (except in special cases) anyone over forty. The advice he offered to those who wished to maintain an activist momentum amongst the masses was simple: 'Place the young at the head of the insurgent masses,' he instructed, 'you will find in them a host of apostles for the new religion . . . youth lives on movements . . . spread through their ranks the word of fire, the word of inspiration; speak to them of country, of glory, of power, of great memories.'[43]

What is significant about the recruits to Young Italy is not so much the fact that they were mainly middle class, as the fact that they were young men – men, that is, who were prepared to sacrifice life and everything else in the ardour of a children's crusade. 'Here are we,' said one of Mazzini's recruits, Jacopo Ruffini, to his fellow conspirators at Genoa, 'five young, very young men, with but limited means, and we are called on to do nothing less than overthrow an established government.'[44] This might be considered an excellent beginning for one of Richmal Crompton's amusing *William* books, were it not for the fact that shortly afterwards – in 1848 – it was a student march on the Vienna Landhaus that overthrew Metternich and triggered the revolution in the Habsburg capital.

It was not in class terms, but in terms of a generational conflict between fathers and sons, that both Turgenev and Dostoevsky were to provide a compelling interpretation of the ideological conflicts of the modern age. Yet neither Marx nor Lenin, obsessed as they were by class, paid any attention to the conflict of generations which has characterized European life since 1789. The crucial importance of youth for the activist style, however, was seized upon by the fascist leaders from the outset. Those made desperate by poverty and distress, Hitler wrote in *Mein Kampf*, created an important foundation for Nazism, but, 'Above all we turn to the vast array of our German youth.'[45]

In practice, all activist movements have endeavoured to enlist the support of youth. A distinguishing mark of fascism, however, is that for this ideology youth is not merely one possible source of support amongst others but is the very pivot upon which its hopes are hinged. It may be contrasted, in this respect, with Marxism. For the Marxist revolutionary ideal, it was sufficient to overthrow the capitalist economic order and transfer the means of production to the proletariat. The fascist ideal, by contrast, involved nothing less than the creation of an entirely new kind of man. The character of this man would be martial and heroic, with a will which recognized no obstacles. For that reason Marxism, in fascist eyes, was no better than liberalism. It offered, that is, only one more materialist ideal, and by its stress upon the laws of history it deprived the will of its potential creative power. For the Nazis, racial theory implied that the new man was in fact already in existence, but lay buried by a mass of corrupt liberal, democratic and materialist values, which had therefore to be destroyed in order to reveal the Aryan prince hidden beneath them. For the Italian Fascists, on the other hand, the new man had still to be created. In both cases, however, the practical result was the same: it was that fascism stood more deeply and radically opposed to the existing order than was Marxism. This was why fascism, unlike Marxism, had to look totally outside the existing social order for the way to the fascist future. It had to turn, in consequence, to those whose will had not yet lost its purity and vigour – that is, to youth. Youth alone is in a position to uphold the fascist ideal of freedom and struggle uncompromised by the pedestrian and egotistical concerns of modern life; youth alone believes in the boundless potency of human will, and youth alone is ready to sacrifice everything, even life itself, in a spirit of uncritical devotion to the fascist leader. It was with this consideration in mind that Hitler appealed to the youth of Germany. 'Most of all', he said in his address to youth at Berlin on 1 May 1936, 'we ask of you, German youth, that you fashion the German people of the future, and in yourselves be for it a model.'[46]

Given the central place of youth within fascist ideology, both the great fascist movements were naturally concerned to institute compulsory educational methods for imparting and sustaining the activist impulse. The 1937 Handbook of Reich Youth Leadership illustrates one such method. The outline of a fortnight's camp suggests as the motto for one day: 'It is not necessary for me to live, but certainly necessary for me to do my duty!'; for another, 'Let struggle be the highest aim of youth!' This last motto was to be followed by an invigorating pep talk by the camp leader: 'The camp leader speaks about the fact that we all have to become fighters . . . He who fights has right on his side; he who does not fight has lost all rights!'[47]

With the institution of such wretched features as compulsory membership in youth movements, the activist style of politics had obviously moved a long way from the early years of the nineteenth century, when the new ethical idea of freedom as endless struggle had first been clearly formulated. In this, as in every other sphere, however, the novelty afforded by twentieth-century political life lay partly in the propaganda techniques and institutional methods devised to implement the requirements of the activist style, and partly in the sheer scale of the atrocities themselves. From a purely theoretical point of view, neither fascism, nor indeed any other activist movement, has added significantly to the pattern of political ideas with which the European world was already familiar by 1815.

4. The potency of human will   So far, three of the intellectual prerequisites of fascism inherent in the activist style of politics have been brought into focus. A closer scrutiny of the years between 1789 and 1815 indicates, however, that this portrait of the potential sources of extremism which the new activist style of politics made available for fascism to exploit is not yet complete. What remains to be considered is a fourth idea, implied in what has already been said but not so far explicitly considered. This is a belief in the boundless capacity of human will to control history and shape human destiny. 'In Hitler's presence,' Albert Speer reflected, 'we felt ourselves as lords of the world we had created; we truly believed in his mission.'[48] When the belief that man's will may make him the 'lord of creation' is combined with the previous three prerequisites of the new activist style, the result is the basic pattern of ideas from which the ideology of fascism was to be constructed. But when, it must be asked, did this fantastic belief originate? Once again, it is necessary to return to the beginning of the modern period, with the French Revolution and the Napoleonic era.

Whilst it was the scale and rapidity of the destruction carried out during the early years of the French Revolution that first suggested how powerful the impact of the human will might be, it was the subsequent career of Napoleon which fostered the idea that men might refashion the world in a way which brought it into conformity with their dreams. In the course of this career, Napoleon himself had deliberately done much to fan the flame of activist sentiment throughout the European world, whenever it had seemed to serve his purpose. Consider, for example, the part he played in fostering it in Hungary and Poland. In the course of quarrelling with the Habsburg Emperor in 1809, he issued a proclamation to the Hungarians declaring: 'You have national customs and a national language; you boast of a distinct and illustrious origin; take up then once again your existence as a nation. Have a king of your choice, who will rule only for you, who will live in the midst of you, whom only your citizens and soldiers will serve . . . Meet therefore in a National Diet, in the manner of your ancestors . . . and let me know your decisions.' Likewise, when Napoleon decided to invade Russia, he played upon Polish nationalist sentiment. 'Show yourselves worthy of your fore-fathers,' he told a Polish deputation, 'they ruled the House of Brandenburg, they were the masters of Moscow, they took the fortress of Widdin, they freed Christianity from the yoke of the Turks.'[49]

In a broader perspective, however, the significance of Napoleon's career extends far beyond the immediate impetus he gave to the activist vision of a 'general insurrection of the peoples' (in Danton's phrase). 'In a short career, of less than twenty years,' we are reminded, Napoleon 'laid low the fabric of international order in Europe. Things which had not been thought possible were now seen to be indeed possible and feasible. Revolutions could succeed, empires be overthrown, and frontiers changed. A man, a handful of men, by resolution, audacity, and ruthlessness could raise masses of other men to decide the fate of governments and the frontiers of states.'[50] The lesson taught by Napoleon has haunted the imagination of activist politicians down to the present day. The power of man's will to reshape the course of history was no longer in doubt. Whether this power could create as well as destroy, however, is a question which no activist ideologue has ever paused to consider carefully.

It was the new belief in the potency of human will that now rapidly produced the prototype of the demagogic figure who was finally to spearhead the transformation of states into movements in our own century. The make-up of this figure was clearly identified as early as 1818, in a satirical portrait of the activist mentality which has lost none of its contemporary relevance. The portrait is the one of Scythrop – based in reality upon Shelley – provided by Peacock in *Nightmare Abbey*. In it one may already discern the mixture of romantic fantasy, conspiratorial politics and apocalyptic yearning which was to become a familiar part of the activist style, not only in the West but throughout the whole world, over a century later. Hitler's Wagnerian dreams, for example, his obsessive belief in a secret Jewish conspiracy which was holding the world in thrall, and his vision of an elite which would rescue the masses by binding them into a coherent whole, are mere variations upon the pattern of political ideas to be found in this lucid sketch of the kind of man to whom the new activist demagogy now gave birth. 'In the congenial solitude of Nightmare Abbey', Peacock wrote,

the distempered ideas of metaphysical romance and romantic metaphysics had enough time and space to germinate into a fertile crop of chimeras, which rapidly shot up into vigorous and abundant vegetation.

[Scythrop] now became troubled with the *passion for*

77

reforming the world. He built many castles in the air, and peopled them with secret tribunals, and bands of illuminati, who were always the imaginary instruments of his projected regeneration of the human species. As he intended to institute a perfect republic, he invested himself with absolute sovereignty over these mystical dispensers of liberty. He slept with Horrid Mysteries under his pillow, and dreamed of venerable eleutherarchs and ghastly confederates holding midnight conventions in subterranean caves. He passed whole mornings in his study, immersed in gloomy reverie, stalking about the room in his nightcap, which he pulled over his eyes like a cowl, and holding his striped calico dressing-gown about him like the mantle of a conspirator.

'Action', thus he soliloquized, 'is the result of opinion, and to new-model opinion would be to new-model society. Knowledge is power; it is in the hands of a few, who employ it to mislead the many, for their own selfish purposes of aggrandizement and appropriation. What if it were in the hands of a few who should employ it to lead the many? What if it were universal, and the multitude were enlightened? No. The many must be always in leading-strings; but let them have wise and honest conductors. A few to think, and many to act; that is the only basis of perfect society . . .'

Scythrop proceeded to meditate on the practicality of reviving a confederation of regenerators. To get a clear view of his own ideas, and to feel the pulse and the wisdom and genious of the age, he wrote and published a treatise* . . . which he thought would set the whole nation in a ferment; and he awaited the result in awful expectation, as a miner who has fired a train awaits the explosion of a rock. However, he listened and heard nothing; for the explosion, if any ensued, was not

* Probably an allusion to a pamphlet on Ireland which Shelley published in 1812, intended to secure its moral and political regeneration (Penguin ed., note 7, pp.262–3).

sufficiently loud to shake a single leaf of the ivy of the towers of Nightmare Abbey; and some months afterwards he received a letter from his bookmaker, informing him that only seven copies had been sold, and concluding with a polite request for the balance.

Subsequent radical authors, of course, have fared much better at the hands of the media; had Scythrop published his book a century or so later, it is unlikely that his bookmaker would have had much to complain about. For the time being, however, the Scythrops of the world remained isolated figures on the European scene, living in an underground realm of small conspiracies and student politics which provoked Metternich's harsh Karlsbad Decrees (1819), but otherwise left the restored political order largely undisturbed. There was no question, at this stage, of activist fantasies being translated into the reality of mass movements. After the kings had been restored to their thrones in 1815 the European world waited silently – as de Musset wrote in 1836 – whilst its poets sang of despair, its young men denied everything, and its uneasy monarchs pretended not to notice that beneath their crowns, their hair was standing on end with fright.[51]

The monarchs had good reason to be frightened, as the new upsurge of revolutionary sentiment in 1848 demonstrated. It was in that year that Guizot commented caustically upon the inroads into political life now being made by the new band of activist politicians who were fast becoming a familiar spectacle in western life. These were men, he observed, who 'busy themselves with making and unmaking governments, nations, religions, society, Europe, the world . . . They are intoxicated with the greatness of their design, and blind', he added, in a phrase worthy of special note, 'to the chances of success.' They were, in a word, fanatics. The new type of politician created by the activist style, Guizot noted, impiously conferred upon the human will a potency which had hitherto been ascribed to God's will alone. To hear such men talk, 'One might think that they had the elements and ages at their command . . . and that these were the first days of creation.'[52]

At the extreme, fanaticism of the kind identified by Peacock and Guizot could have only one conclusion. This was a wholly destructive political nihilism. That extreme, however, was not to be reached until our own century, when nihilism became the ruling principle of the two great fascist leaders in their respective attitudes towards their unfortunate subjects. In Mussolini's case, it was displayed throughout the war in his tendency to blame every Italian setback or defeat on 'a soft and unworthy people', or on a people 'made flabby by art'.[53] In Hitler's case, it is sufficient to recall what happened on 18 March 1945, when Speer wrote to inform him that in military and economic terms, the war was lost, and appealed to him to save what remained of his country's resources for his people. Sending for Speer, Hitler replied that, 'The nation has proved itself weak, and the future belongs solely to the stronger Eastern nation. Besides,' he added, 'those who remain after battle are of little value; for the good have fallen.' The same day new orders were issued by Hitler and Bormann: the war was to be continued 'without consideration for the German people'.[54]

Nihilism of this kind is often dismissed as originating exclusively in temperamental peculiarities of Hitler and Mussolini. Thus, Hitler is commonly described as psychopathic, bloodthirsty or insane, whilst Mussolini is regarded as a colourful demagogue who eventually became so deeply caught up in the propaganda and mythology with which he surrounded his own existence that he could no longer distinguish fact from fiction. Whilst few would wish to dispute such views, the nihilistic idealism which culminated in fascism becomes both more intelligible and more disturbing when it is seen to be no more than the extreme implication of the essentially restless and egotistical cult of will, with its concomitant morality of self-realization, which the western world at large has increasingly favoured since the end of the eighteenth century. Ever since that time it has been apparent that the new cult of will tended to suggest that life only acquired meaning and significance in the face of extreme challenges and struggles; habitual, settled conduct, that is, has long since ceased to be considered, in the modern world, an adequate sphere for the satisfaction of human nature, since such conduct is considered fit only for unreflective and unimaginative robots. From this point of view,

Schleiermacher was entirely consistent when he concluded, at the time when the activist tradition first appeared, that freedom, once it is identified with a spiritual odyssey conducted through endless struggle, inevitably ends in a love of death. 'May it be the mission of my freedom', he wrote in his *Soliloquies* (1800), 'to bring me nearer to this necessity. May it be my highest goal to be able to wish to die!'

A long line of thinkers, from Max Stirner through Dostoevsky and contemporary existentialists, have since familiarized everyone with the posturing of tortured individuals confronted by extreme situations in which they seek to resolve the meaning of life by emulating lemmings. Transferred from the private to the political world, the disastrous implications of this manner of thinking and living might seem to be obvious. The fact that in the event they were not can perhaps best be explained by assuming that men had smiled for a century at the Jekyll which they beheld in their mirror, without noticing the lineaments of Hyde in his countenance. When Hyde finally escaped from under the skin of the idealistic Jekyll, however, it was natural that he should assume the guise of the nihilistic fascist leaders.

In the event, it was not until the First World War completed the dislocation of the traditional order of European political life begun by the French Revolution that the kings at length fled from their thrones, or else finally accepted that their crowns were held entirely on popular sufferance. Now at last, over a century after the rickety restoration of the old European order by the Congress of Vienna, the day of the activist had arrived. Amidst the debris of the old order and the uncertainties and fragility of the new, three great condottieri – Mussolini, Hitler and Lenin – saw their chance and seized it.

Of these three unsavoury stories, that of Lenin is the least relevant for an understanding of the dangers which confront the modern democratic state. Marxist ideology had little to do with his acquisition of power, in spite of his elaborate protestations to the contrary. The truth of the matter, we know, is that, 'Lenin seized power not in a land "ripe for socialism", but in a land ripe

81

for seizing power.'[55] As might be expected, it was only in quite untypical moments of candour that Lenin himself ever cared to recognize that fact. One such moment occurred, for example, in 1922, when Lenin became angry with Sukhanov, a Menshevik opponent who had the temerity to suggest that none of his actions conformed to Marxist orthodoxy. Stung by this outrageous idea, Lenin retorted: 'Napoleon, if I remember rightly, wrote, "On s'engage et puis . . . on voit." '[56]

The success of Mussolini and Hitler, by contrast with that of Lenin, is an altogether different matter, for (as George Mosse remarks), 'The most important fact about fascism's triumph in Germany and Italy was that it came to power legally.'[57] This triumph owed at least as much to the folly of its enemies as it did to the enthusiasm of its supporters; the idea that fascism was carried to power on the crest of an irresistible wave of nationalist sentiment was merely a creation of fascism's own activist mythology. By this time, however, the activist style had for long been so deeply entrenched in the European world, and so intimately connected with 'progressive' politics, that even many of the enemies of fascism, like the German Social Democrats, for example, subscribed to it in one or other of its meliorist forms.

In Italy, likewise, the socialist party, which by 1919 was easily the largest party in the country, indulged in vague activist fantasies which the socialists never contemplated implementing, in spite of their bombast. In practice, the socialists 'simply sat back under the cosy illusion that time was on their side and that universal suffrage inevitably signified the approaching end of liberalism and the coming of the dictatorship of the proletariat. There was no hurry to carry out reforms, no need to compromise or win allies, no obligation even to make their policy attractive or practicable.'[58] Other Italian parties (such as the Catholic *Popolari* and the liberals) preferred to fight against each other, and even to ally with fascism in the hope that they could use it for their own purposes, rather than to ally against it.

In this way, then, opposition to activist politics was weakened in both Italy and Germany. Conservative and liberal parties, on the one hand, tended to believe that they could ride the activist tiger as Napoleon, Cavour and Bismarck had ridden it before them; whilst socialist parties, on the other hand, entertained their own brand of activist fantasy, thereby blurring the dividing line between limited and activist politics. It was to this confusion, rather than to any intrinsic merit of its own, that fascism owed its success. What it offered was not the coherent 'third way' between capitalism and socialism which some of its more intelligent supporters liked to pretend, but a hotch-potch of vague (and frequently incompatible) ideas. It was the very vagueness of the brew which enabled it to unite lukewarm activists, half-hearted adherents of limited politics, opportunists and outright extremists amidst the quicksands of an ideal of unity and national regeneration which could mean all things to all men.

But what, it must now be asked, was the specific form which fascism gave to the new activist style of politics? In the present chapter, this question has only been touched upon obliquely, since the main concern has been to identify the general ideas and tendencies which brought about the transformation of states into movements. The ideas and tendencies behind this transformation – a transformation which was to find its most complete ideological expression in the fascist *Weltanschauung* – have been traced back to the era of the French Revolution and the Napoleonic period. Attention has been concentrated, in particular, upon the four ideas which were most crucial for the new style of politics.

It is out of these ideas that the fascist *Weltanschauung* was to be constructed; and yet, it will be clear, none of them was peculiar to fascism. In rival permutations they comprise the basis of every activist movement: whether we turn to the democratic idealism of the French revolutionaries, or to communism, or to fascism, politics is regarded by each of these ideologies as a crusade against evil, in which despotic governments, claiming to act in the name of the masses, purport to offer 'true liberty', whilst at the same time encouraging their followers to believe in the malleability of the social order and in their ability to reconstruct it in accordance with their preferred version of utopia.

But if the ideas upon which the fascist *Weltanschauung* were based are merely the ideas which have inspired the new activist style of politics as a whole, it becomes still more vital to ask once again what it is that distinguishes activism in its peculiarly fascist form. In outline at least, the answer to this question has in fact already been given: it is that fascism was the most extreme, ruthless and comprehensive expression of the new activist style of politics which the western world has yet experienced. Although the implications of this answer have still to be developed, it has two merits which may be noticed immediately. On the one hand, it relates fascism to the broader context of modern European intellectual and political history. On the other hand, it also establishes a perspective in which the otherwise disparate Italian and German movements may be treated as two members of a single political species – the species of activism, that is, known as 'fascism'. This answer is clearly insufficient, however, to illuminate fully either the fascist programme itself or the character of the *Weltanschauung* by which fascism sought to implement it. It is now necessary, therefore, to consider in more detail the nature of fascism.

3 Fascism as Theatrical Politics

In 1946 Friedrich Meinecke, a thoughtful German critic of Nazism, made a determined intellectual effort to disregard the ruin to which Hitler had reduced Germany, in order to try to understand how fascism had ever come to power. In the course of his book on *The German Catastrophe*,[1] Meinecke paused at one stage to confront an interesting question. Was there, he asked, a 'positive' dimension to Nazism, in spite of the devastation which Hitler's politics had brought about in practice? He concluded that there was. Hitler, he wrote, had found 'something which corresponded to the objective idea and needs of our time'.[2] This positive element Meinecke described as 'the big idea that was floating in the air – the idea of the amalgamation of the national and socialist movements'. In Hitler, he observed, we 'unquestionably find . . . the most ardent spokesman and the most ardent practitioner' of this great project. Even though Hitler perverted the project, Meinecke insisted, 'His share in the great objective idea must be fully recognized.'[3] The same judgment might be made about Mussolini, who could claim that he had tried to implement a similar ideal by uniting nationalism with syndicalism, which was the most influential form of socialism in Italy at the time. In this chapter an attempt will be made to determine whether fascism really does have a positive dimension, as Meinecke believed. Anticipating what follows, it will be suggested that this was not so, mainly because the means of creating unity adopted by fascism meant that politics would inevitably become indistinguishable from a highly destructive theatrical performance. Before explaining how the transition from politics to theatre occurred, however, it is important to acknowledge that Meinecke achieved something very unusual: unlike most of the intellectuals of our age, he managed to take the fascist project seriously, instead of dismissing it as something which only fools, madmen or villains would ever have supported. Following his example, it will be best to begin by looking more closely at how the fascists themselves conceived of their project.

By the end of the First World War the project of amalgamating nationalism and socialism could plausibly be regarded – as Meinecke still regarded it in 1946 – as the central problem of modern European politics. The war had not only completed the demolition work of the Napoleonic era by finally destroying whatever remained of the traditional European order; it had, in addition, brought the masses permanently into the political arena. 'The war', as Mussolini observed in March 1919, 'has not driven the masses back into the pre-historic darkness of their life before the war, but has called them with a loud voice to reassert themselves. It has broken their chains . . . A war of masses ended with the triumph of masses . . .'⁴ The immediate result of this triumph of the masses was the spectre of a 'red peril'. In both Italy and Germany the claim made by fascism was that it had rescued the homeland, and indeed the whole of the western world, from this danger. In reality, there was no red peril in either of these countries, since socialists were either too timid or else too divided to present the challenge which fascism attributed to them. The real danger came partly from fascism itself, partly from the indecision of its opponents, and partly from a widespread doubt about the ability of representative institutions to restore order in conditions which seemed constantly to tend towards civil war. There was, in addition, the incompetence and collusion of the ruling authorities, who proceeded (in both Italy and Germany) upon the unprincipled assumption that they could use the fascist squads for their own purposes.

Whilst the red peril was a figment of fascist propaganda, the social and political dislocation which marked the post-war years nevertheless lent the fascist diagnosis of the situation a certain persuasiveness. Hitler's description of the post-war plight of Germany may be regarded as typical of the view of many of those who were to respond throughout the western world to the fascist call for a radical reconstruction of society. 'Looked at from a purely political point of view,' he wrote at the end of the first volume of *Mein Kampf*, 'the situation in 1918 was as follows: A nation had been torn into two parts. One part, which was by far the smaller of the two, contained the intellectual classes of the nation . . . On the surface these intellectual classes appeared to be national-minded, but that word meant nothing else to them except a very vague and feeble concept of the duty to defend what they called the interests of the State, which in turn seemed identical with those of the dynastic regime.' Over against this impotent nationalist class stood a second class. To this, Hitler wrote, belonged 'the broad masses of manual labourers who were organized in movements with a more or less radically Marxist tendency. These organized masses . . . had no nationalist tendencies whatsoever and deliberately repudiated the idea of the nation as such . . . Numerically this class embraced the majority of the population and, what is more important, included all those elements of the nation without whose collaboration a national resurgence was not only a practical impossibility but was inconceivable.'[5]

From Hitler's simple portrait of Nazism as an endeavour to unify the two opposed camps of nationalism and socialism within Germany it is possible to derive an elementary classification of European fascist movements at large.[6] All of these sought to re-establish social unity by amalgamating nationalism with socialism. The nature of the balance they endeavoured to strike between the two ideologies, however, differed greatly. Using the character of the balance at which they aimed as the principle of classification, it may be said that Nazism, at one extreme, sacrificed socialism, in all but name, to racialist nationalism. At the opposite extreme may be placed the British fascists, who started off (under the leadership of Oswald Mosley, a former socialist minister) from a position much closer to socialism than to nationalism, with the shift towards nationalism as a subsequent development. In between these two positions, every possible form of balance was struck by the multiplicity of fascist leagues which sprang up in France during the inter-war years. So far as the Italian movement is concerned the position is far more ambiguous, at first sight anyway, since the balance seems constantly to have shifted. At the outset, and again at the very end, during the period of the Italian Social

Republic in northern Italy, the balance was tilted in a socialist direction. During the intervening period, by contrast, the movement was tilted overwhelmingly in a nationalist direction, in which Mussolini's imperial dream increasingly became the centre of fascist policy and ideology. Within the confines of the overall classification, however, the ambivalent nature of the synthesis of nationalism with socialism at which every fascist movement aimed is well illustrated by the 'Hungarist' programme devised by Ferencz Szalasi for his Hungarian movement, the Arrow Cross. 'Hungarism', Szalasi explained, 'means socialism', in the sense that it has as its goal 'not the happiness of particular privileged individuals or classes, but of the totality of individuals and classes. But', he added, 'Hungarism at the same time means national socialism, because it fights for the happiness of . . . the people, for the welfare of the nation, and through this of every working individual.'[7]

The schema is especially useful in so far as it is designed to take account of the fact that fascism could appeal just as readily to a monarchist or a socialist as to a nationalist. The appeal of fascism for unprincipled or panic-stricken conservatives needs little explanation – the fascist squads seemed, after all, to represent order in its most simple and direct form. The claim of fascism to be a genuinely socialist movement, on the other hand, is too often dismissed as a prime example of fascist hypocrisy and double-talk. In practice, it is true, the brand of socialism which fascism offered was merely state collectivism, consistent only in its professed rejection of any affinity to Marxist socialism. Since the meaning of socialism has always been controversial, however, with no agreed definition even amongst its disciples, only the outraged socialist believer will take the complacent and dangerous step of dismissing the fascist form of socialism with the vague assertion that it was not 'true socialism'. Unpalatable though it may be to socialists, Drieu la Rochelle, for example, spoke with perfect sincerity when he said, 'I place my only hope in the continuation of socialist progress through fascisms.'[8] Hitler always regarded himself as a socialist, and Mussolini claimed that he had never rejected the spirit of socialism, but only the Marxist form of it.

The speech which Mussolini made on 23 March 1919, the

day the Fascist movement was founded in Milan, is of especial interest in this connection. In it, he outlined the new movement's position on the economic, social and political issues of the time. The result was somewhat embarrassing, since his speech made it difficult to distinguish at all clearly between fascism and socialism. As Mussolini was compelled to acknowledge towards the end of the speech, 'upon examination our programme may be found to resemble others. Specifically, one may discern premises analogous to those of the official socialist party.'* How then was the new movement to be distinguished from socialism? Although the fascist position did not differ from it in substance, Mussolini hastened to explain, it nevertheless differed greatly 'in spirit'. It is different in spirit, 'because it is based on the war and the victory'.[9] This different spirit, Mussolini hoped, would dissociate fascists from the socialists who had advocated Italian neutrality in 1915, on the one hand, whilst also enabling them to take advantage of Italy's position amongst the victors by an appeal to nationalist sentiment, on the other.

To reject the fascists' claim to be a genuinely socialist movement is unnecessary. To do so is merely to pit self-righteous socialist dogmatism against the rival (and equally unsatisfactory) dogmatism of fascist ideology. As in the case of their claim to be the defenders of true liberty and true democracy, it is far better to acknowledge that the fascists were simply exploiting once again the ambiguity of the modern European political tradition.

Fascist movements, then, may initially be classified according to the nature of the balance which they struck between nationalism and socialism. A moment's reflection, however, indicates that this form of classification is too superficial to do justice to the complexity of the phenomenon. It is unsatisfactory, in particular, because it leaves three crucial aspects of fascism unaccounted for.

In the first place, it lays exclusive stress upon the 'positive'

---

* The resemblance to socialism is hardly surprising in view of the fact that the programme had been drawn up by Alceste Di Ambris, one of the founders of the syndicalist *Unione Italiana del Lavoro* in 1914.

dimension which Meinecke detected in the fascist project. It fails, in consequence, to cast any light on the reasons why this project went so badly astray. 'Strange paradox of dreams that turned into nightmares,' as Eugen Weber reflected recently, 'the Fascist phenomenon leaves us with the question, as yet unresolved – at what point and under just what pressure do high ideals turn into tales of dread?'[10] Taken by itself, then, the schema clearly does nothing to eliminate this paradox.

Secondly, the schema merely adopts the conventional left/right method of classifying fascist ideology whose limitations have already been considered. It therefore fails to explain why fascism transcends these categories and defies classification as either a 'reactionary' or a 'radical' movement, in the usual loose usage of those terms.

Finally, it will immediately be remarked that the amalgamation of nationalism and socialism was neither a novel nor a peculiarly fascist project. During the half-century or so before 1914, indeed, the European world had been littered with projects of this kind. They were not, it should be stressed, peculiar to conservative thinkers, but were entertained by ideologists of every complexion. In the middle of the nineteenth century, for example, the so-called 'father of German socialism', Ferdinand Lasalle, had based his thought upon the ideal of uniting nationalism with socialism to form an organic, authoritarian state in which universal suffrage could be used as a convenient device for burying the propertied classes beneath the proletarian vote. In Austria, Karl Lueger's German Workers' Party had attempted to fuse nationalism and socialism within a demagogic framework that profoundly impressed the young Hitler, who lamented the fact that Vienna, that 'incarnation of racial depravity', was unsuited to the establishment of the necessary racial foundation.[11] In France, Maurice Barrès had described himself as a National Socialist, committed to uniting extreme nationalists with extreme syndicalists in mutual opposition to capitalism. In Italy, Enrico Corridini had reported to the First Nationalist Congress in Florence that Italian nationalism must become what he called 'our national socialism'. This, he explained, 'is to say that just as socialism taught the proletarian the value of the class struggle, we must teach Italy the value of the international struggle. . .'[12]

Neither Hitler's National Socialist ideal, then, nor Mussolini's National Syndicalist one, marked a new programme for the western world. Indeed, as Meinecke remarked, to draw the masses into the state system, and thereby re-establish national unity in the aftermath of the French Revolution, had been the main problem of European politics ever since the Napoleonic era. In one perspective for example, it was precisely the creation of 'national socialism' which British statesmen and politicians had pursued from at least the time of Disraeli until the National Coalition in 1931 which effectively ended Oswald Mosley's bid to establish an independent political platform. British statecraft adhered firmly to the established constitutional framework, and the New Party formed by Mosley failed to dislodge the existing two-party system. Mosley's subsequent attempts to carry his cause out onto the streets were merely a desperate response to the reluctance of both politicians and electorate to follow his irregular modes of proceeding.

What then distinguished the specifically fascist programme for the amalgamation of nationalism and socialism? It was, of course, the dynamic, militant, total, completely anti-constitutional and ultimately nihilistic *Weltanschauung* which fascism adopted in order to implement this project. It was, that is, the *way* in which fascism sought to create social unity, rather than anything peculiar to the content of the fascist ideal. Even racialism, as has been said, was not peculiar to it.

The novel way of creating social unity envisaged by fascism was succinctly formulated by Hitler, none of whose predecessors in the long European tradition of previous 'national-socialist' speculation had found the key to creating an organic society where he found it. The masses, he wrote in *Mein Kampf*, must first be 'set in motion . . . by men of superior talents', and thereafter treated as 'a fly-wheel, in as much as they sustain the momentum and steady the balance of the offensive'.[13] For Mussolini, likewise, the objective was to launch the masses into perpetual motion, through which, under the guidance of a leader and a party elite, they would become the fly-wheel of history.

91

Again, if we ask how this perpetual activism is to be generated and sustained, both Hitler and Mussolini reply in a way very different from previous advocates of social unity. The basis of unity, they assert, cannot be reason, or parliamentary government, or regard for economic interests. What inspires men to action is never these things, but is always a faith, or myth. 'The driving force which has brought about the most tremendous revolutions on this earth has never been a body of scientific teaching which has gained power over the masses,' Hitler noted, 'but always a devotion which has inspired them, and often a kind of hysteria which has urged them to action.'[14] When Mussolini remarked that, 'I am not a statesman. I am more like a mad poet,' he captured the flavour of this novel way of synthesizing nationalism and socialism. 'Hitler and I', as he observed in a similar vein, 'have surrendered ourselves to our illusions like a couple of lunatics. We have only one hope left; to create a myth.'[15]

The final outcome of this transformation of politics into an affair of myth, lunacy and perpetual revolution was the nihilistic 'revolution of destruction' identified by Rauschning as the core of Nazism, and by Megaro as the core of Italian Fascism.[16] These thinkers, however, were exceptional in their intellectual penetration. Not only at the time, but even down to the present day, fascism has been widely regarded as a basically constructive movement. Meinecke, as has been seen, still entertained that opinion about Hitler's movement in 1946. Even twelve years after the collapse of the Hitler regime, a thoughtful ex-Nazi like Melita Maschmann records that she remained convinced that the Nazi movement was at bottom a creative one, in spite of its record of atrocities. With hindsight, of course, few would now wish to present Nazism in that light; but the nebulous and unsatisfactory character of hindsight as a basis for forming any clear judgment about the nature of fascism is dramatically illustrated by the continuing disagreement amongst contemporary scholars over the Italian case. For Megaro, writing during the 1930s, the Italian movement was every bit as destructive as the German one, even if the means and extent of the destruction fell far short of the Nazi holocaust. This impression is reinforced at the present day by the work of scholars such as Denis Mack Smith, who has exposed with meticulous care the sterile duplicity with which Fascism infected Italian life.[17] Yet by other scholars, such as A.J. Gregor, the Italian regime is now hailed instead as offering the pattern to which political development may be expected to conform during the remainder of the present century.[18]

Clearly, there is a difficulty here which is not resolved by retrospective contemplation of Nazi nihilism. Setting hindsight to one side, it is necessary to confront again the question posed a moment ago by Eugen Weber. The fascist phenomenon, as he observed, 'leaves us with the question – as yet unanswered – at what point and under just what pressures do high ideals turn into tales of dread?'[19] Why, in other words, should the synthesis of nationalism and socialism which Meinecke identified as the great need of our age turn out, in its fascist form, to be so destructive in practice?

In order to deal with this seeming paradox it will be useful to consider briefly what is still the most coherent exploration of the practical implications of the activist style. This is to be found in the writings of Jean-Jacques Rousseau. The enduring relevance of his thought lies, indeed, precisely in the fact that two centuries of subsequent experience and speculation have not superseded, but only modified, the portrait of activism which he provided. It would be foolish, of course, to conclude that Rousseau is about to be maligned once more as a direct forerunner of fascism, or as an advocate of some primitive version of the fascist state. Such a view would invite both anachronism and oversimplification. What remains true, nevertheless, is that Rousseau exposed, solely by an inspired flight of his imagination, the political pattern to which any activist movement will inevitably be driven to conform, in so far as it seeks to create social unity by appealing to the patriotic emotions of the populace at large.

Using Rousseau's early portrait of the implications of the activist style as a point of departure, it is possible to determine the distinctive manner in which fascism later reshaped the activist heritage. The result was a *Weltanschauung* wholly alien to Rousseau himself. At the same time, however, it is only within the context provided by the historical development of activism between Rousseau's *Social Contract* and Hitler's *Mein Kampf* that the gradual conversion of the activist ideal of social unity into the nihilistic frenzy of fascism becomes intelligible.

Rousseau's starting-point is particularly instructive, since it provided the first clear statement we possess of the grounds given by activists for rejecting the entire modern state tradition in favour of the new style of politics. This starting-point, it will be recalled, was his conviction that modern states fail dismally in the task of achieving true social unity. They lack true unity because they do not endeavour to create virtuous citizens imbued with a deep love of their country. That, indeed, was why Rousseau rejected a limited style of politics. The states which accept this style, he wrote, 'imagine they have done everything when they have raised money'. They are content in other words, to ensure peace and tranquillity in society, and to that end they seek nothing more than a routine, outward, passive compliance with the law. But in order to produce a true citizen, deeply imbued with a love of his country, governments must encourage men not merely to obey the state, but to love it actively.[20]

States which refuse to undertake this task, Rousseau asserts, court disaster in two respects. On the one hand, they fail to generate that intense sense of solidarity or spiritual unity which is the hallmark of a truly great and free people. On the other hand, they impoverish and corrupt their subjects by failing to inspire in them the desire for those heroic acts of self-sacrifice without which life lacks proper human dignity. A heroic self-sacrificing ideal of political life, Rousseau assumed, is possible only when men accept that, 'It is certain that the greatest miracles of virtue have been produced by patriotism . . . which [alone] gives to the force of self-love all the beauty of virtue, [and] lends it an energy which . . . makes it the most heroic of all passions. This it is that produces so many immortal actions, the glory of which dazzles our feeble eyes.' The aim of political activism, then, is to regenerate men by converting them from passive subjects into lovers of their state, thereby endowing the state itself with the maximum of spiritual unity whilst at the same time conferring meaning and dignity upon the life of individual subjects by endowing it with heroic stature.

Here, in outline, is a foreshadowing of the problem of national unity, as activist politicians were to interpret it in Italy after 1861, and in Germany after 1870. Like Rousseau, these politicians were to insist that neither external obedience nor domestic prosperity were sufficient for the creation of true national unity; and like him, they were to demand that unity should be given that moral or spiritual character which both Mussolini and Hitler were subsequently to make their central concern. It is appropriate, then, to consider by what methods Rousseau believed the creation of this unity might be achieved. How, we may ask, did he think a whole people was to be drawn into active participation in the life of the state?

In the first place, Rousseau makes clear that the activist concept of social unity requires that the division between public and private life should be completely abolished – politics, in other words, must be transformed from a limited into a total activity, since only a system of total politics can create the spirit of 'mutual emulation' from which will arise 'that patriotic intoxication which alone can raise men above themselves, and without which liberty is but an empty word, and laws but a chimera.'[21] What the new freedom would be like can be gleaned from Rousseau's observation that 'it is necessary to abolish . . . the ordinary amusements . . . of gambling, drama, comedy, opera; all that makes men effeminate; all that distracts them, isolates them, makes them forget their fatherland and their duty; all that makes it possible for them to be happy anywhere as long as they are entertained.'[22]

In the second place, Rousseau explains how the new activist style is to be imposed upon men's inner life by an elaborately organized and completely superintended system of public education. This politicized system of education must begin as soon as a child is born, since, 'Every true republican has drunk in love of country along with his mother's milk. This love is his whole existence; he sees nothing but the fatherland, he lives for it alone.'[23] The most important part of this education, Rousseau added, is also the most neglected one: it does not consist of 'boring studies', but of physical education. Accordingly, 'In every school a gymnasium, or place for physical exercise, should be established for the children.' In this way, it is possible to ensure that children are not allowed 'to play alone as their fancy dictates, but altogether and in public, so that there will always be a common goal towards which they can aspire, and which will excite competition and emulation'.[24] As a rather grudging concession to parents whose enthusiasm for the activist style may be only lukewarm, Rousseau allows that the formal education of their children may be domestic and private, but insists that they 'ought nevertheless to send their children to these exercises', since 'it is only public and common games which are capable of accustoming them at an early age to rules, to equality, to fraternity, to competition, to living under the eyes of their fellow-citizens and to desiring public approbation'.[25] The whole system of education must be placed firmly under state control, being supervised by a college of magistrates who can discharge or dismiss, entirely at their discretion, any teacher within the system.[26] By this method it will be possible to give men's souls 'a national physiognomy which will distinguish them from other peoples' and also 'prevent them from mixing, from feeling at ease with those peoples, from allying themselves with them'.[27] For present purposes, however, the most important thing about this system of education is that it inevitably requires the destruction of limited politics, since none of its aims can be achieved without total supervision of life by the state.

In the third place, the activist conception of social unity requires, as Rousseau was at pains to argue in the *Social Contract*, that all divisive social groups (such as interest groups and political parties) should be brought into line with the general will by being submerged in it. The constant mobilization of the population, in a word, is incompatible with permitting the existence of any form of organization outside the confines of the state structure.

Fourthly, Rousseau made clear that social unity, within the activist style of politics, is incompatible with representative institutions. The style points, indeed, entirely away from parliamentary government towards a wholly different form of democracy. A form of democracy which actively engages the people in politics requires, Rousseau maintains, a highly theatrical manner of conducting public life, since only a theatrical idiom can create amongst the masses a constant sense of identification within the community. What is especially noteworthy, in this connection, is Rousseau's insistence upon the need for public spectacles, as the device most likely to create a sense of national unity.

In the opening chapter of his essay on *The Government of Poland*, Rousseau emphasized this aspect of the new style above all others. How, he asked, can the hearts of the masses be reached? Neither coercion, nor material rewards, nor just administration, he concluded, will ever catch their imagination in a way which engages them in the cause of national unity. How then is the activist impulse to be created? 'Dare I say it?' Rousseau asked. His recommendation was simple: teach them children's games. Use, in other words, political techniques 'which seem idle and frivolous to superficial men, but which form . . . invincible attachments'. Games, ceremonies, festivals, spectacles – any mass ritualistic activity, that is, which reminds the people of its distinct national identity, increases its pride and self-esteem, and conjures up before it a vision of its own majesty and importance – such were to be the substitutes for constitutional forms employed by this new, popular style of politics.[28] In this way the people is continually encouraged, as it were, to worship itself, as it marvels at the symbols of its own corporate identity; through spectacles, games and rituals, in other words, the individual is to be pulled out of his isolation and submerged in the mass. By a series of colourful rites and rituals, then, the activist style must generate amongst the mass a spurious sense of warmth, unity and solidarity, in ways which are excluded by a limited style of politics.

For Rousseau himself, this theatrical style of politics always remained a dream which never left the pages in which he sketched its contours. Indeed, his thought as a whole is most properly seen, not as forward-looking or anticipatory, but as standing in line with that long tradition of utopian speculation to which belong such earlier thinkers as Campanella and Sir Thomas More.[29] If, however, we reflect for a moment on the subsequent course of European history, it is obvious that a style

97

of politics which was a mere paper project for Rousseau was subsequently to provide the inspiration for the fascist regimes of our own century. 'As early as 1919,' Hitler wrote in *Mein Kampf*, 'we were convinced that the nationalization of the masses would have to constitute the first and permanent aim of the [Nazi] movement.' It is this 'nationalization of the masses' – the gathering of the masses into the fold of activist politics – which also comprises the drift of Mussolini's exposition of fascist doctrine in his 1932 article in the *Enciclopedia Italiana*. Fascism, we read there, binds individuals and generations together in 'a mission, suppressing the instinct for a life enclosed within the brief round of pleasure in order to restore within duty a higher life free from the limits of time and space: a life in which the individual, through the denial of himself, through the sacrifice of his own private interests, through death itself, realizes that completely spiritual existence in which his value as a man lies'.

What was it, we may now ask, that paved the way for the translation of Rousseau's early activist dream into political reality? If we examine the problem more closely, it is not too difficult to discern the specific intellectual and political developments which mark the evolution of the new activist style into the form which we refer to as fascism. Of these developments, the first to emerge as a significant political tendency in the European world was one which took the form of the progressive elaboration of, and refinement upon, the theatrical techniques for arousing the people which Rousseau had invoked in the *Government of Poland*. Since it was these techniques that fascism was subsequently to adopt and modify so successfully for its own purposes, it is important to recall that the techniques themselves were originally fostered by democratic, nationalist, and even socialist crusades on behalf of the masses. In one perspective, indeed, the history of the nineteenth and twentieth centuries may even be seen as little more than the development of an extensive repertoire of emotional, dramatic, and quasi-religious rituals through which some semblance of unity might be given to 'the sovereign people' which had now become the sole source of legitimate power in western states.

Consider the way in which, for example, Mussolini announced the Abyssinian war. The announcement was not made in the form of a note addressed from one head of state to another, as tradition and diplomatic etiquette required, but in the form of a radio broadcast by the leader to his followers. 'On the evening of October 2nd,' we are reminded, 'the ringing of church bells at last proclaims the great event . . . In clipped, ringing words Mussolini announced his decision; twenty million people heard him, gathered in the squares of their towns, all over Italy; twenty million people thrilled (as it was claimed) to a sense of their spiritual oneness with this unique man.'[30] Obviously, to address twenty million people in this way remained as inconceivable during the nineteenth century as it was in Rousseau's own day; only the technological advances made in mass communications during the present century have made it possible. Yet technological advance did not bring with it any discontinuity in the fundamental idea upon which Rousseau himself had established the new activist style – the idea, that is, of lending popular appeal to the ideal of organic unity by translating the ideal itself into a highly theatrical manner of conducting politics. It will be useful to consider, from this point of view, the impact of democratic doctrine on Germany and Italy in the period between 1789 and the advent of fascism, in order to illustrate how strongly the democratic ideal itself pointed from the beginning towards a theatrical, extra-parliamentary form of 'movement' politics.

In Germany in particular, the organic ideal of social unity came to be associated from almost the beginning of the French revolutionary era with a variety of extra-constitutional methods for drawing the masses into a form of democracy which had no connection with parliamentary forms and procedures. The result was a 'liturgical' or 'ceremonial' form of mass democracy intended to promote nationalist sentiment, in the hope that this would give rise to a more spiritual, intimate and personal form of social unity than any which had hitherto existed. In Germany, the public cults advocated by Rousseau, and subsequently put into practice by the French revolutionaries, were rapidly assigned a central position in the campaign for national unity triggered off by the doctrine of popular sovereignty.

99

Initially, these public cults were small-scale affairs, like the patriotic festivals advocated by nationalists such as Jahn and Arndt. The Wartburg festival of German student organizations (1817) is an instance. As Treitschke remarked, however, it must be remembered that a seemingly inconsequential assembly of fifteen hundred German students from all parts, 'meeting solely on behalf of the fatherland, was to this generation a phenomenon so astounding as to seem almost more important than the world-shaking experiences of recent years'.[31] Even more significantly, there occurred in 1832 what has been described as 'the first mass meeting in modern German history', when 32,000 men and women gathered for a national festival at Hambach.[32] By the 1860s, national festivals of this kind had acquired a definite order and format: processions, unison singing, patriotic plays and speeches, specially erected halls, choral representations, and sporting events were all incorporated as standard parts of activist liturgy. In particular, the wearing of uniform was sometimes made compulsory.[33]

It was in Germany, above all, that the theatrical trappings which marked the subsequent development of all nationalist movements acquired a character that was eventually to find its purest expression in fascism. From the beginning, German thinkers responded to the success of the French armies by a wholesale and increasingly militant attack upon the original democratic ideology in whose name the French had carried out their European conquest. Rejecting what they dismissed as the excessively abstract and rationalistic conception of democracy offered by French ideology, German thinkers claimed to offer instead a more concrete democratic ideal than the French one.

This might be achieved, they maintained, by releasing the democratic ideal from the cold and insipid trappings of Enlightenment theory, with its abstract talk about reason and mankind, and re-establishing it upon the more tangible foundation provided by historical reality. Only if the democratic ideal were relocated in actual historical reality, rather than in abstract appeals to reason, the German thinkers believed, would it come to play a living part in the hearts of the populace at large. It was for this reason that an early German nationalist like Friedrich Jahn, for example, 'advocated the celebration of the great deeds of the people themselves and thought the battle of Merseberg in the Middle Ages a particularly suitable memorial occasion, for here the peasants had defeated kings and bishops'.[34] Similarly, Ernst Arndt, another early nationalist, advocated (in his book *German Society*, 1814) the celebration of 'holy festivals' of the people. These were to be partly pagan in inspiration, such as the summer solstice, and partly recent, like the victory over Napoleon at the battle of Leipzig.[35]

It was this attempt to weld the masses together by a variety of theatrical devices which finally culminated in the political style of the Third Reich. From this point of view, Franz Neumann's remark about Nazism holds good also of Italian Fascism. 'National Socialism', he wrote, 'has transformed the institutional democracy of the Weimar Republic into a ceremonial and a magic democracy.'[36] Of the many familiar illustrations of this transformation, one may suffice. This is the Christmas play performed before the employees of the German railroads, after Hitler came to power in 1933. 'The play', we are told, 'took place around a Christmas tree in the middle of the auditorium. The commentator drew a parallel with the Greek theatre. The struggle and victory of Christianity provided the theme: crusaders appeared, and mercenaries, the S.A. marched to the crib, with the Swastika flying. Final victory is achieved in the end: "God sent us a saviour at the moment of our deepest despair: our Führer and our wonderful S.A." '[37]

In every sphere of life, both in Italy and in Germany, fascism resorted to similar theatrical techniques, in order to replace institutional forms of integration with a purely emotional sense of unity. In this respect, however, it did not initiate but only completed the long quest for emotional unity which, during the century and a half after Rousseau, had increasingly chiselled away any remaining connection which the democratic ideal had retained with the preservation of limited politics. The appeal and power of the propaganda techniques used to fabricate this emotional sense of unity should not, however, be underestimated, since it was only in the face of wartime setbacks that the fascist regimes encountered significant internal opposition. The efficacy of these techniques during

101

peacetime – and even during the war itself – is testified to by, for example, Melita Maschmann, the B.D.M. leader. In spite of the regimentation which the new style of politics entailed, it succeeded to a considerable extent in generating a sense of participation which the institutions of limited government can never create. As Maschmann records, the feeling that social inequality and class differences, for example, had been successfully transcended in a warmer, more personal and truly organic social order was generated by the camp communities around which the youth movement centred. 'Our camp community', Maschmann writes, 'was a model in miniature of what I imagined the National Community to be. It was', she continues, 'a completely successful model. Never before or since have I known such a good community, even where the composition was more homogeneous, in every respect. Amongst us there were peasant girls, students, factory girls, hairdressers, schoolgirls, office workers and so on . . . [Through the camp] we each recognized one another's particular value, after coming to know one another's weak and strong points, and everyone strove to be willing and reliable. The knowledge that this model of a National Community had afforded me such intense happiness gave birth to an optimism to which I clung obstinately until 1945.'[38]

In Italy, the conversion of democracy into an affair of popular cults and rituals was slower to develop. The colourful, extra-constitutional style of politics favoured by Mazzini and Garibaldi had pointed in this direction, but the indifference of the masses to the ideal of national unity, the prevalence of regional loyalties, the sober Machiavellism of Cavour and his successors, and the cultural monopoly of the Church, all worked against the appearance of a theatrical political style. The situation changed, however, when the aftermath of the war brought disunity to a head, in an atmosphere of general discontent and disillusionment. It was at this time that there occurred an incident which would be too trivial to deserve attention, were it not for the miniature dress rehearsal which it provided for the later development of Italian Fascism.

This incident was the occupation of the town of Fiume by Gabriele D'Annunzio in 1920. Until the end of 1920, the newly formed Fascist movement lacked coherence of any kind: it had neither a distinctive programme, nor a strong organization, nor a clearly determined leadership. What was to hold this inchoate movement together? The inspiration came, not from Mussolini himself, but from the theatrical style with which D'Annunzio welded together at Fiume the same combination of miscellaneous elements upon which Mussolini was to rely – an alliance, that is, 'of nationalists, army veterans, dissident socialists, idealists, and adventurers who turned up at the first smell of blood'.[39]

Nationally renowned before the war as Italy's greatest poet and novelist, D'Annunzio's daring exploits during the war had added glory to his name. Now, with the war ended, and his life well into middle years, D'Annunzio confronted a serious problem – the prospect, that is, of dying of boredom. The three deities who had hitherto ruled his existence and saved him from this most dreadful of human fates threatened at length to desert him: the god Dionysus, who had inflamed his imagination in pursuit of a literary cult of romantic nihilism; the goddess Aphrodite, who had enabled his senses to run roughly in tandem with his imagination; and the god Mars, who had smiled kindly on the exploits of the black-shirted special legion (the *Arditi*) which D'Annunzio had created during the war. Now all this was behind. In desperation, D'Annunzio petitioned the Prime Minister, Nitti, for three million lire with which to visit the East, in order to rekindle his imagination and revive his artistic sensibilities.[40] When the petition failed, D'Annunzio sought the exotic nearer to home. He turned to politics.

At the end of the war Fiume had been claimed by the Italian delegation at the peace conference as an Italian-speaking town, in spite of the fact that the hinterland round the port was Slav-speaking. This brought Italy into conflict with Yugoslavia, which needed the port for access to the Adriatic, and also placed Italy at odds with America, Britain and France, who compromised between Italian and Yugoslav claims by declaring Fiume a free state. The claim to Fiume, nevertheless, became the focal point for a propaganda campaign, foolishly condoned by the Italian government, which crystallized Italian dissatisfaction with the peace negotiations. It was against this background that D'Annunzio took matters into his own hands. Inspired by the thought of Garibaldi's invasion of Sicily, he led a small pack of demobilized *Arditi* and other malcontents to Fiume and occupied the town, as the first step towards occupying the whole east coast of the Adriatic. Even liberals and socialists applauded this first open display of contempt for the new world-order projected at the Peace of Paris. The main matter of relevance, however, is the theatrical political style with which D'Annunzio conducted affairs in the tiny 'Regency of Carnaro' which he proclaimed at Fiume, where (styling himself *Comandante*) he now proceeded to rule for just over a year.

Fiume, D'Annunzio declared, was more than a new political order; it was the beginning of a new concept of life, freed from the insipid rationalism, materialism and general decadence of the old western civilization. 'Here', he asserted, 'is life bursting forth! Here is life on the rampage!'[41] The Peace of Versailles was accordingly described as 'decrepitude, infirmity, obtuseness, deceit, betrayal and cruelty, which look out on the world with eyes dilated with fear'. Fiume, by contrast, 'means youth, beauty, daring and cheerful sacrifice, broad aims, profound newness'.[42] So far as external affairs were concerned, the 'broad aims' to which the Comandante referred seem to have meant the conversion of politics into a world crusade, not only against the decrepit West, but also against what he called the 'flood of Balkan tribes, the flood of Slavic barbarians'.[43] In due course, as Michael Ledeen observes, this crusade became formalized in the institution of the League of Fiume, an anti-League of Nations that undertook to represent the interests of the young, emerging nations of the world, which were coming out from underneath the oppression of the colonial powers of an aging western civilization. D'Annunzio, Ledeen concludes, 'thus became one of the first leaders of what we call today the Third World revolution, although he did so in the name of his own peculiar brand of cultural imperialism, for he was entranced by the idea of a revolution' of the oppressed peoples of the world under his own leadership.[44]

So far as the fate of democratic government is concerned,

D'Annunzio's political style prefigures the fascist style even more directly. His aim, he said, was the creation of direct intercourse between the masses and their leader. This, he maintained, was the first instance of true democracy since Greek times.[45] Osbert Sitwell, who visited Fiume during D'Annunzio's period of rule there, talked to him about this. D'Annunzio 'proceeded to tell us of the strange conversations which he held with the people. A silent crowd would begin to gather, and then swell quickly outside the palace. He would go out and ask them what they wanted. A voice would answer, and there would gradually build up a system of direct intercourse between the people and their ruler.'[46] In the 'dialogue' between speaker and masses which followed, another writer tells us 'excitement mounted until it became a paroxysm, and to the question *A chi l' Italia?* a thousand echoed back like thunder *A noi*'.[47]

Oaths of loyalty to the leader, uniforms, flags and insignia were all greatly favoured by D'Annunzio, as ways of binding his followers to him. Demonstrations of a military or semi-military character served to instil a martial sense, whilst enhancing the feeling of popular unity. On one occasion, for example, D'Annunzio invited an eminent Italian conductor to bring his orchestra over from Trieste to give a series of concerts at Fiume. In keeping with the new 'life force' style of politics D'Annunzio arranged for a fight to be laid on for the conductor and his orchestra to watch during their visit. 'Four thousand troops', we learn, 'had taken part in the concert, and one hundred men had been seriously injured by bombs. The members of the orchestra, which had been playing during the quieter intervals, fired by a sudden access of enthusiasm, dropped their instruments, and charged and captured the trenches. Five of them were badly hurt in the struggle.'[48]

But attention to particular incidents like this, with which the short history of Fiume abounds, must not be allowed to obscure the wider political implications of D'Annunzio's theatrical flair. As Michael Ledeen remarks, the most important of these implications was the destruction of the traditional boundaries between the religious and political spheres of Italian life and their replacement by 'a kind of political passion play'[49] in which the aim was mass manipulation by myth and symbol – a style of politics, that is, which has now 'become the norm in the modern world'.[50] Ledeen concludes his study with a word of caution about the dangers of reading too much significance into the Fiume incident. Although D'Annunzio's style provided the model for the subsequent rituals developed by Fascism under Mussolini, Ledeen observes, 'the substantial differences between Mussolini and the Poet make it impossible for one to claim that there was an important ideological continuity between D'Annunzio's Fiume and Mussolini's Italy'.[51]

Whilst Ledeen's caution is to be respected, he nevertheless appears to overrate the extent of this ideological discontinuity. It is true that D'Annunzio's temperament was very different from Mussolini's, and that it is, as Ledeen insists, 'unthinkable that D'Annunzio would have presided over the creation of a regime as reactionary and oppressive as that of Fascist Italy',[52] if only because D'Annunzio would have wearied of the whole thing long before a totalitarian state could have been brought into existence. Whilst the Comandante and the Duce are firmly separated by their different personalities, however, it is by no means as evident as Ledeen claims that their divergences produced a fundamental ideological discontinuity between Fiume and Fascist Italy. What Ledeen inexplicably ignores in this connection is one of the most interesting documents of twentieth-century political history. This document is the Constitution of Fiume itself.

A glance at the Constitution indicates that Ledeen is wrong to believe that it is only the stylistic ingredients – viz. the leader cult, the ideal of direct democracy, and the love of theatricality – which Italian Fascism took over from Fiume. In addition to these, D'Annunzio also came up with a strange blend of ancient, medieval and modern ideas, of pagan and Christian principles, and of nationalist and socialist ideology, from which he claimed to extract a doctrine which would replace both capitalism and socialism. This was the doctrine embodied in the document just mentioned, the 'Outline of a New Constitution for the Free State of Fiume' which appeared on 26 August 1920.[53] Like Rousseau's *Government of Poland*, the

Constitution of Fiume never amounted to more than a paper project. The ideas it contains, nevertheless, deserve close attention, partly because they gave definite ideological content to D'Annunzio's political style, but also because Mussolini's own movement added nothing to the farrago of ideas to be found there.

How then did the Constitution of Fiume propose to replace both capitalism and socialism? The starting point was a rhetorical appeal to the sovereignty of the people of Fiume as the basis of the new state. The democratic doctrine of popular sovereignty was immediately modified, however, by fusing it with a doctrine emanating from syndicalist theory which was to exert a powerful influence on the Italian form of fascism. According to syndicalist doctrine, the democratic doctrine of the sovereignty of the people is a sham, a doctrine without substance, since the people is believed to be composed of individual citizens. The 'citizen', syndicalists maintained, is an abstraction; the reality is the producer. The citizen must therefore be replaced by the producer, and a man's contribution to the productive activities of his nation must be accepted as the true measure of his worth. In this vein, article III of the constitution declares that Fiume is 'a State chosen by the people which has for basis the power of productive labour'. Article IV further stressed the sovereignty of man as producer by declaring that 'above and beyond every other right [the constitution] maintains the right of the producer'.

Fascist doctrine, which took over this revolutionary emphasis on production as the basis of an individual's participation in the state, was anticipated in other respects by the flirtation with syndicalist socialism with which D'Annunzio now diverted himself. Since D'Annunzio was the most colourful of Italy's nationalists, in order to reconcile syndicalism with the nationalist cause it was obviously necessary to free it from its connection with the socialist doctrine of class conflict.

The constitution of Fiume sought to achieve this by adopting a form of 'national syndicalism', in which the central idea was corporatism. The basis of the new state, according to the corporatist ideal, was no longer to be the individual, either

107

as citizen or as producer, but the corporation. 'Whatever be the kind of work a man does,' article XVIII announced, 'he must be a member of one of . . . the Corporations.' These corporations 'receive from the commune a general direction as to the scope of their activities, but are free to develop them in their own way'. Within each corporation the members of each sphere of economic activity would be brought together. Thus one corporation, for example, was to comprise wage-earners of industry, agriculture and commerce, small artisans, and small landholders. A second was to include the technical and managerial staff in any private business, industrial or rural; a third was to comprise all public employees; a fourth, the intellectual sector of the people, such as teachers; a fifth, the liberal professions, and so on. A further corporation was to include all employers.

The corporatist arrangement was intended to eliminate class conflict partly by recognizing the 'productive' character of citizens (such as employers and salaried staff) who would otherwise be labelled as parasites by Marxist theory; partly by the provision of 'Labour judges' who would decide cases of controversy between employers and workers (article XXXIX); and partly by an extensive system of cultural and educational indoctrination which would infuse all citizens with an overriding sense of national unity. There would, in addition, be a second chamber based upon functional representation: sixty delegates (called *provvisori*) were to be elected by the corporations, in order to represent the people in its primary role as the body of producers.

The 'socialist' ingredient in this national syndicalist synthesis was further reinforced by the qualified hostility towards private ownership expressed in the constitution – a hostility which was to be characteristic of both Italian Fascism and German Nazism. 'The state', article IX declared, 'does not recognize the ownership of property as an absolute and personal right, but regards it as one of the most useful and responsible of social functions.' Property, in other words, is held by the individual in trust for the community, and can be withdrawn if he leaves it unused, uses it badly, or proves to be bone idle. What this might mean when translated into law may be partially gleaned from, for example, the Nazi Law concerning Hereditary Homesteads, 29 September 1933. The purpose of that law was to implement the *volkisch* utopia by turning Germany into a peasant-based society, and it was therefore vital to decide what qualifications were necessary in order to claim the title of peasant. What is relevant at present is the fact that not even pure German blood was sufficient for this: according to the law, a man could only continue to be a peasant so long as he behaved honourably; as soon as he did anything dishonourable, he would immediately cease to be a peasant, and would lose all his peasant property rights. The inevitable uncertainty of tenure created by the inherent difficulty of deciding what is 'honourable' might seem to an ordinary mortal to be no more than a formula for agricultural disaster and arbitrary government; but for men like Hitler and the *Comandante* of Fiume, such considerations were of no importance, believing as they did that they were creating a new form of ownership which would avoid the evils of both capitalism and communism.

In order to complete the portrait of the new form of ownership, one more supposed advantage must be noticed. This is the fascist conviction that it would not only end class conflict and personal feelings of alienation, but would at the same time create a more beautiful, graceful and dignified world than any at which liberal and communist ideology aim. In the case of the Constitution of Fiume, this was to be the work of the College of Aediles. The task of the college, whose members were to be 'wisely selected from men of taste, skill, and a liberal education', would be, amongst other things, to 'convince the workers that to add beauty, sure sign of joy in the building, to the humblest habitation is an act of piety, that a sense of religion, of human mystery, of the profundity of Nature may be passed on from generation to generation in the simplest symbol, carved or painted on the kneading trough or the cradle, on the loom or the distaff, on the linen chest or the cottage beam' (article LXIII).

This *volkisch* rhetoric, which Nazism was to take more seriously than Italian Fascism, was combined with the most theatrical of all the elements in the new style of politics heralded by D'Annunzio's Fiume experiment. 'Music', article LXIV of the constitution declared, 'has power to bring spiritual peace to the strained and anxious multitude.' Accordingly, the ideal of social unity must find its ultimate guarantee in the incorporation of music into the structure of the state as 'a social and religious institution'. Music binds the whole state together, because 'the instruments of labour, of profit, and of sport, and the noisy machines . . . fall into a poetical rhythm' from which music itself may henceforth be expected to 'find her motives and her harmonies'. Hence 'the teaching of choral singing based on the genuine poetry of the people (folk songs) will hold a first place', and in every commune of the state a choral society and an orchestra will be subsidized by the government.

The aesthetic side of fascism was intended to provide far more than mere edifying entertainment for the masses; as the Nazis in particular were quick to appreciate, a cult of beauty could be used to legitimate the regime's industrial policy. This was the task of the Bureau of Beauty of Labour (*Amt Schönheit der Arbeit*), for which Albert Speer was responsible. As Speer explained, Beauty of Labour's aim was to transform work by removing the 'joyless compulsion' with which capitalist wage-slavery had hitherto infected it.[54] In this respect, it provided Nazism's answer to the Marxist vision of a society in which work would be a pleasure instead of a curse. But it performed, in addition, a further ideological function which was no less valuable. On the one hand, the *volkisch* theme in Nazi ideology was anti-modernist; but on the other hand, a highly modernist programme of industrial efficiency was adopted after 1936, when the Four Year Plan and the ideal of a 'war economy in peacetime' became the *ultima ratio* of the regime. In Beauty of Labour the regime found a means of partially reconciling the conflict between its traditionalist and modernist objectives. Through an ambiguous aesthetics of technology and rationalization Beauty of Labour could pose as a vaguely traditionalist institution which pointed to a return to the organic relationship supposed to have existed between workers and employers in the Middle Ages; but through a quasi-religious cult of productivity it could at the same time secure the regime's practical needs by legitimating the cult of productivity and technology required by an efficient modern

110

war economy. Implicit in this cult was the intriguing idea that modern industrial production has nothing to do with economics; as Anatol Von Hubbenet's *Das Taschenbuch der Schönheit der Arbeit* succinctly put it, 'we do not consider the factory as an association for economic purposes'.[55] In practice, as Anson Rabinbach observes, this endeavour to raise industry above economics was mainly a cosmetic device for masking the destruction of the legal trade unions, suppression of working-class organizations, and the freezing of wages at depression levels throughout the Nazi period. Despite Beauty of Labour's assertion that joy in work and genuine satisfaction could only be created when work is removed from the sphere of purely material considerations and given a higher, ethical meaning, Rabinbach continues, reports of the factory inspectors' office indicated the reluctant response of workers to the campaign. He concludes, nevertheless, that the bureau eventually succeeded in overcoming much of the initial scepticism about the effect of its measures and achieved considerable ideological success.[56]

Returning now to the Constitution of Fiume, it has already been said that this was to remain a paper project. At the end of 1920 the Italian government finally pulled itself together and sent a gun-boat to Fiume to bring D'Annunzio – who had been contemplating a march on Rome in order to end the government's vacillation – to heel. After the first shot, D'Annunzio withdrew and went into retirement. His departing words, however, foreshadow the attitude of both Mussolini and Hitler in face of the defeat they encountered, and may be regarded as integral to the mentality of political leaders inspired by activist mythology. 'Mindful of his oaths for "Fiume or death" he continued to bewail that death had not taken from him the shame of being an Italian, but then he concluded that Italy was not worthy of such a loss.'[57] Within the format of this mythology, in a word, the leader is always right. Even military defeat, in consequence, never indicates the unsoundness of his own political judgment, but only establishes the cowardice of his followers and their consequent unfitness for historical survival.

In both Italy and Germany, it is clear, fascism represents, in

111

the first instance, an intensified development of the highly theatrical style of politics which Rousseau, long before, had shown to be an inevitable concomitant of any attempt to mobilize the masses in the cause of establishing social unity within the framework of direct, participatory democracy. Such novelty as fascism brought to this idea consisted, in the first instance, in stripping the activist style of the remaining constitutional restraints which it still possessed in Rousseau's thought, and then transferring its theatrical ingredients – with the aid of techniques and devices only made possible by technological advances – to the context of mass society.

Fascism, however, did more than convert activism into an entirely theatrical style of politics, deprived of even those vestigial constitutional connections to which apologists for the activist style had previously paid at least lip-service. It also completed a radical revision of the new activist style which may best be described in terms of a shift from 'spontaneous' to 'directed' activism. Since it is its explicit and open commitment to 'directed' activism which distinguishes fascism most clearly from the activist forms of democratic, nationalist and socialist ideology encountered during the last century, the meaning of these terms, and in particular the nature of 'directed' activism, must now be explained with some care.

4 The Fascist Revision of the New Activist Style

'Spontaneous' activism is a convenient phrase for describing the basic belief which had inspired activist idealism during the century after 1789. This belief was that it was only necessary to call or beckon to the masses, as it were, in order to draw them into the political arena. It was this hope which had inspired Rousseau, for example, to advise the peoples of both Poland and Corsica on the form of government which they should adopt in order to terminate their slavery. It was the same hope which soon afterwards inspired the crusade of liberation undertaken by the French revolutionaries. It was the same faith in the capacity of the people to undertake enlightened action on its own behalf that inspired the radicals of 1848, over half a century later. And it is the ideology of spontaneous activism which is still preserved by Marxism (in its more liberal, non-Leninist forms at least), although even the best-intentioned Marxists find it impossible to avoid an authoritarian tone when dealing with the failure of the masses to show any sign of the evolutionary tendencies expected of them. To this first or 'spontaneous' phase of the activist style fascism, as was seen in the last chapter, was heavily indebted. It was from the spontaneous phase of activism that it derived, in particular, the emotional and theatrical political format upon which activists had relied in order to infuse the masses with a sense of participating in the control of their own destiny.

Fascism was to be no less deeply indebted, however, to a second phase through which the activist style has passed. This phase, which is the one in which we still live at the present day, commenced towards the end of the nineteenth century. It was in the last decade of that century, in particular, that the idea arose that a successful activist movement could never rely upon the spontaneous political enthusiasm of the masses. It must concentrate, instead, upon activating the masses entirely from

113

above, even in face of their open indifference, or outright hostility, to whatever crusade the activist politician might wish to undertake at their expense. The activist style of politics, in a word, now began to acquire the 'directed' character which was later to find its supreme expression in the fascist ideal of perfect and unquestioning submission to the will of a leader. More generally, just as fascism stripped the highly theatrical element in the spontaneous phase of the activist style of all connection with a limited style of politics, so it finally stripped directed activism of any similar connection, thereby reducing directed activism to its three stark essentials, viz. a leader, a movement, and a 'myth' or *Weltanschauung*.

The idea that a successful activist movement must be a directed rather than a spontaneous one was not, it is true, an altogether novel departure within the activist style. Even in Rousseau's own early portrait of activism, a deep-rooted underlying pessimism about the people had led him to suggest that only the intervention of a god-like leader, in the form of a Legislator modelled on the great figures (like Solon) of antiquity, would ever make the idea of organic social unity a living reality in the hearts of subjects. During the course of the nineteenth century, moreover, the dramatic career of Louis Napoleon had lent concrete support to a possibility which Rousseau's discussion of the Legislator had previously opened up. This was the possibility that the democratic ideal of popular sovereignty might point, not towards popular participation in politics, but towards rule by a national leader who claimed to embody the general will in his own person. In the course of 1852, in particular, Louis Napoleon had indicated how easily the appearance of spontaneous support 'from below' might be created. It was in that year that he organized a massive plebiscite, in order to ratify retrospectively his unconstitutional seizure of power during 1851. As one historian remarks, 'his system has left its own unhealthy legend, a jackal-ghost which prowls in the wake of the "Red spectre". Napoleon III and Boulanger were to be the plagiarists . . . of Napoleon I; and Mussolini and Hitler were to be unconscious reproducers of the methods of Napoleon III. For these are inherent in plebiscitary [dictatorship] . . . with its direct appeal to the masses:

demagogical slogans; disregard of legality in spite of a professed guardianship of law and order; contempt of political parties and the parliamentary system, of the educated classes and their values; blandishments and vague, contradictory promises for all and sundry; militarism; gigantic, blatant displays and shady corruption. *Panem et circenses* once more – and at the end of the road, disaster.'[1]

What is distinctive about the period from 1890 to the present, however, is the increasingly explicit intellectual recognition which was given within the activist style itself to a possibility which had previously only been dimly discernible, at both the theoretical and the practical level. This was the possibility that the masses would have to be totally directed, in order to rally them behind the activist crusade. In order to understand how this possibility gradually acquired theoretical recognition, it is necessary to recall the mood of disillusionment with the masses which triggered off the final revision of the activist style.

That mood is not hard to understand. In both Italy and Germany, national unity had been achieved, not by the masses, but entirely over their heads, by the traditional diplomacy of Cavour and Bismarck. In France, the Third Republic was a rickety structure, which entirely failed to display any of the activist zeal that had burst forth in 1870, at the time of the Paris Commune. It was natural, in view of the continuing failure of the masses to convert the external formality of unity into the inward reality of active participation in a common national life, that men should now emerge who eyed the masses with a contempt far more profound than that which had permeated Rousseau's own activist idealism. Amongst the ranks of these men there were, for example, elite theorists like Pareto, Mosca and Michels, who all dismissed the idea that the masses could ever play any independent role in history. It is this mood of contempt* which, in an accentuated form deprived of its

---

* This contempt was to find its most extreme expression in the writings of Nietzsche. It would be a mistake, nonetheless, to look in his direction for anything which remotely resembled a directed form of activism. Loathing the

original paternalist overtones, was to be perpetuated by the fascist condottieri; as when Mussolini, for example, declared that a dictator might well be loved by the masses, provided that he treated the crowd like a woman.[2]

Elite theory, however, was not the only child of the contempt for the masses which now began to supplant the fond hopes about them which had been entertained by men like Mazzini. In the face of continuing mass inertia, the appearance of elite theory was accompanied by a cynical concern with the techniques of crowd manipulation. In 1885 the English thinker, Sir Henry Maine, had published his study of *Popular Government*, in which he had already forecast this development, at a time when John Stuart Mill's qualified optimism was still the ruling orthodoxy of the age. Modern mass democracy, Maine had argued, would inevitably reduce politics to an affair of 'wire-pullers'. In the United States Henry Adams published, at roughly the same time, his novel *Democracy*, which was a study of wire-pulling in action. It was from the France of the Third Republic, however, that there emerged, a decade later, the first detailed treatise on how the wire-pulling was to be conducted. This was Gustave le Bon's study, *The Crowd*.

Setting all the other literature of the period to one side, we may allow Le Bon's short and elegant study to serve as a convenient dividing line between the previous era of spontaneous activism and our own century of directed activism. Le Bon himself, one must hasten to add, had no sympathy at all with activism. In spite of his elitism and political pessimism, he remained committed to a limited style of politics, concluding his book with the view that 'parliamentary assemblies are the best form of government mankind has discovered as yet'.[3]

masses, Nietzsche loathed activism, in all its forms. His own ideal was the Greek 'tragic vision' of life, which he made the basis of an ethic so intensely individualistic that it culminated in his worship of the super-man. In spite of his later popularity amongst fascist writers, the essence of Nietzsche's position was so wildly unpolitical, and even anti-political, that it is impossible to view his brand of elitism as contributing anything at all to the revision of the activist style.

116

Nevertheless, Le Bon's incisive exploration of crowd psychology constitutes a turning-point in modern political theory, since in it the centre of political gravity is no longer a more or less vague set of hopes about the political capacity of the people, but moves, instead, to the figure of a leader who can manipulate the masses from above. A short review of the ideas advanced by this most succinct of the new Machiavellian writers will provide a background against which it will then be possible to view the three manuals later contributed by our century to the fully revised (or 'directed') version of the activist style. The advice contained in these three manuals, which merely refined upon Le Bon's work, was finally given its most perfect synthesis in the last of them. This was Hitler's *Mein Kampf*. Before that work appeared, however, two other manuals had contributed significantly to the revision of activism. One was Lenin's pamphlet, *What Is to Be Done?* The other was Georges Sorel's *Reflections on Violence*. But first let us briefly consider Le Bon's study.

Writing in the last decade of the nineteenth century, Le Bon began his book by prophesying that, 'The age we are about to enter will in truth be the ERA OF CROWDS.'[4] In this new era, the destinies of nations will be elaborated 'in the hearts of the masses, and no longer in the councils of princes'.[5] This does not mean, however, that the masses will be the moving force in history, as the theorists of spontaneous activism have fondly believed. It means, rather, that the character of politics will inevitably be transformed, since henceforth 'to know the art of impressing the imagination of crowds is to know at the same time the art of governing them'.[6]

What then is the secret of this new art of governing the masses? The most interesting part of Le Bon's study, from this point of view, is the long chapter which he devoted to the figure of the new Prince, whose emergence he foresaw as the natural concomitant to the 'era of crowds'. This Prince, whom Le Bon described simply as 'the leader', must be able to use the irrational psychological laws which rule the mentality of crowds in order to mould them to his purpose. The great leader is one who appreciates intuitively that 'crowds do not reason, that they accept or reject ideas as a whole, that they tolerate neither

117

discussion nor contradiction . . . [and] that crowds suitably influenced are ready to sacrifice themselves for the ideal with which they have been inspired'.[7] He is the man, above all, who can organize the crowd politically by calling up in its soul, not the voice of reason or material interest, but 'that formidable force known as faith, which renders a man the absolute slave of his dream'.[8] In order to impart this faith to the masses, however, Le Bon stresses that the great leader must himself be possessed by it, as were 'the Luthers, the Savonarolas, the men of the French Revolution', for example.[9] He must also possess what Le Bon called personal 'prestige' – the quality, that is, which has subsequently come to be extensively discussed by political scientists under the name later given to it by Max Weber, viz. 'charisma'. Assuming that he possesses these qualifications, then the question arises of the actual techniques by which the leader will convey his creed to the crowd. How was this to be done, in the coming era of crowds?

The leader, we learn, will rely upon three main 'means of action', to which Le Bon devotes a separate section of his study. These he calls affirmation, repetition, and contagion. It is by these means that the leader will 'imbue the mind of a crowd with ideas and beliefs'.[10] In the case of affirmation, the principle involved is an elementary one: 'The conciser an affirmation is, the more destitute of every appearance of proof and demonstration, the more weight it carries.'[11] Repetition, however, is equally important, since, 'The thing affirmed comes by repetition to fix itself in the mind [of the masses] in such a way that it is accepted in the end as a demonstrated truth.'[12] Finally, affirmation and repetition generate between them 'contagion'. Of contagion, Le Bon notes that 'a panic that has seized on a few sheep will soon extend to the whole flock'. The operation of contagion is 'so powerful a force that even the sentiment of personal interest disappears under its action'. He adds the significant observation that amongst men, physical proximity is not essential for the operation of contagion: 'An example is the revolutionary movement of 1848, which, after breaking out in Paris, spread rapidly over a greater part of Europe and shook a number of thrones.' What is also to be remarked is that contagion does not operate in a one-way direction, from the upper classes down to the masses. On the contrary, 'every opinion adopted by the populace always ends in implanting itself with great vigour in the highest social strata, however obvious be the absurdity of the triumphant opinion'.[13]

With Le Bon's study in mind, it is now possible to examine more closely the currents of thought united by fascism in the course of its synthesis of the revised or directed form of activism towards which his work had pointed. It is especially necessary to disengage these currents of thought from one another in order to understand, in particular, the marked similarities between fascism and rival versions of directed activism, of which communism and syndicalism are the most important – irrespective of what their original protagonists may have had in mind. For this reason it is necessary to consider in turn what each of the three manuals produced by Lenin, Sorel and Hitler added to Le Bon's sketch of the means by which a leader may hope to unite the masses in an activist crusade in the new 'era of crowds'.

Anticipating what follows, it may be said that Lenin pointed to the need for an elite corps of dedicated revolutionaries as an indispensable ingredient in shaping the leader's success; that Sorel extended the 'faith' in which Le Bon had found the principal moving force in mass behaviour into a full-blown and systematic theory of activism as a style of politics based entirely upon what he described as a 'myth'; and that Hitler, along with Mussolini, finally crystallized the distinctively fascist form of activism in two ways. On the one hand, both Hitler and Mussolini were far more shrewd than Sorel had been in identifying the precise character of the myth which would eventually serve the interests of an activist leader who aimed at the overthrow of established forms of government; and on the other hand, they both found in the war the key to the form of organization best suited to the movement regime by which they sought to overthrow the state tradition. It will be convenient, for purposes of examining these contributions to the revision of activism more carefully, to consider the three manuals which contain them in the chronological order in which they appeared, taking Lenin's first.

The disillusionment with the masses which appeared in the

119

late nineteenth century and found theoretical expression in Le Bon's work was especially marked amongst the socialists, whose situation had become increasingly embarrassing. After half a century, the revolution forecast by Marx in 1848 had still not occurred. What was worse, capitalist development had brought about the spread of prosperity, instead of the impoverishment upon which Marxism had relied as the agency for generating revolutionary discontent. The result was that the prospect of the spontaneous proletarian uprising upon which socialist activists had pinned their hopes could no longer be seriously entertained by a determined socialist ideologue. What then was to be done? This was the problem faced by Lenin, in a pamphlet he issued in 1902. His reply was simple: the activist must no longer wait for the spontaneous uprising of the masses, but must accept that the revolution is to be imposed upon the masses from above, regardless of whether or not they want it, by a small, dedicated elite of professional revolutionaries. Here, then, is a significant addition to Le Bon's study of the techniques by which the leader would acquire power and control the masses: he would need, above all, a disciplined and totally dedicated party of his own.

In the revised form of activism, then, the revolution is to be imposed from above by the leader and his elite corps, whilst the masses are to be downgraded to passive recipients of the revolutionary idea. What is still not clear, however, is the nature of the ideological appeal best calculated to win over the masses. In Lenin's case, the assumption was that this appeal would ultimately be a rational and scientific one, grounded in the laws of dialectical materialism. Le Bon, however, had already made clear that if history had any lesson at all to teach, it was not the power of reason and materialism to move the masses, but the power of faith. This lesson was not to be fully incorporated into the revision of activist ideology, however, until some years later, when the task was carried out by the least orthodox but most profound of all the thinkers who have been influenced by Marx. He was the French writer, Georges Sorel, whose *Reflections on Violence* constitutes the second great manual upon which the revision of the activist style had been based.

Reviewing the century of activist enthusiasm after 1789,

Sorel immediately grasped the secret which fascism was later to utilize. The masses, he saw, would never rally either to the rationalism which had inspired the liberal-democratic dream of liberty and equality, or to the materialism which had inspired the socialist dream of a proletarian paradise. The only thing that would rally them, Sorel insisted, was the purely emotional appeal of a myth.

For Sorel, the nineteenth-century activist tradition as a whole had gone astray precisely because it had neglected the need for a spiritual foundation of the kind which myth alone could provide. This had meant that activism had tended constantly towards ineffective theories of utopia, rather than towards a true theory of revolution. Utopia, he explained, 'is the work of theorists who, after having observed and discussed the facts, try to establish a model against which existing societies can be compared in order to measure the good or evil they contain'.[14] The misfortune of Marxism is that it persistently tended to degenerate into a theory of utopia. The most that can issue from this utopian tradition is a series of revolts; but revolt is a very different thing from revolution.[15] It is here that the vital historical role of myths becomes apparent, for it is only myth that can convert revolts into revolution, since 'revolts can be spoken of indefinitely without ever provoking revolutionary action as long as there are no myths accepted by the masses'.[16]

The importance of myth, in the first instance, is that it raises the masses above their desire for pleasure and for a consumer's utopia by imbuing them with a desire for glory and a willingness to undertake the endless heroic struggle which glory demands. From this point of view, 'remarkable examples of myth [are] those which were constructed by early Christianity, the Reformation, the French Revolution and by Mazzini's followers'.[17] All these myths illustrate the true moving force in history, which is the fact that 'men who participate in great social movements represent their immediate action in the form of images of battles assuring the triumph of their cause'.[18] It is these 'images' which Sorel calls myths. Myths have three characteristics.

In the first place, they cannot be rationally questioned or regulated, since they express, not abstract thought, but the

121

fundamental convictions of a group.[19] This does not mean, it must be stressed, that they blind men to practical realities, since 'we know that these social myths do not prevent any man from learning to profit from all the observations he makes in the course of his life and that they are no obstacle to the fulfilment of his normal business'.[20] Secondly, myths are not empirical forecasts of the future. On the contrary, myths are to be judged entirely 'as means of acting on the present; any discussion of applying them materially to the course of history is devoid of sense'.[21] What is more, in order to perform its function of inspiring action, the myth must be taken as a whole, and not broken up into parts by rational inquiry. And it is necessary, above all, to ignore the outcome of actions inspired by myths, and to attend only to their ability to inspire action.[22] Finally, the myth is essentially a dynamic entity, which expresses the boundless freedom of the human spirit. The myth, in other words, shatters all stable historical frameworks and puts in their place an ideal of life as pure movement.[23] Myths point, in other words, towards 'absolute' or permanent revolution.[24] As might be expected, Sorel's belief in the energizing power of a dynamic myth was accompanied by a profound hatred for constitutional politics which led him, at a later date, to express admiration for both Lenin and Mussolini.

Whether Sorel's critique of Marxism and the concomitant revision of the activist style directly influenced Mussolini and Hitler is not important for present purposes. Certainly Sorel was praised by fascists, as Talmon (amongst others) notes,[25] and in particular by Mussolini. In Hitler's case, there is no evidence that he had ever read Sorel. What really matters is the fact that fascist ideology, unlike communism, found the key to political success in revising the activist style along lines similar to those originally proposed by Sorel. Only the fascist form of activism, in other words, has openly accepted and proclaimed that myth is the sole basis of true social unity and historical greatness. Although Sorel is not on that account to be held responsible for fascism, fascist ideology itself never added anything of significance to the theory of myth with which Sorel had proposed to underpin the activist style, in place of the rationalist and materialist foundations previously offered by democratic and socialist radicals.

If we now turn to the third manual, in which the fascist version of directed activism finally received its most notorious formulation, Hitler's *Mein Kampf*, then it is evident that the main divergence of fascism from Sorel arises from the different content which fascism gave to the myth, rather than from any dispute about the necessity for openly re-establishing activism upon the new basis. The new content is most readily apparent in the case of the Nazi elaboration of a racialist version of Sorel's myth. Long before Hitler's name became so intimately associated with that development, however, the racialist version had already been mapped out in the writings of men like H.S. Chamberlain, Julius Langbehn and Paul Lafargue. Even the Nazi obsession with 'decadence' added nothing of intellectual substance to what might be found, at the beginning of the nineteenth century, in the writings of men like Max Nordau, whose book *Degeneration* had appeared in 1895.

Where Hitler went beyond Sorel in putting the finishing touches to the directed phase of activism was solely in tactical and organizational finesse. He merely carried the myth, that is to say, out of literary speculation and onto the streets. Any attempt to bring a myth or *Weltanschauung* to victory, Hitler wrote, must fail unless the myth is translated into 'a great, homogeneous fighting association'.[26] The secret by which this militant association is to be formed and sustained is simple: the successful movement must be modelled on an army. 'The principle which made the former Prussian Army an admirable instrument of the German nation', Hitler wrote in *Mein Kampf*, 'will have to become the basis of our statal constitution.'[27] The army, then, suggested the instrument by which nationalism and socialism were to be fused within the fascist version of the activist style. All training and all education in the new Reich would in fact be regarded as preparation for subsequent service in the army, which is 'the final and supreme school of patriotic education'.[28]

It was from the army, indeed, that nearly all fascists were to take the central organizational principle of the new organic state which they aimed to create; the principle, that is, of 'authority downwards and responsibility upwards'. In the case of Italian

123

Fascism, the military origin of the organizational principle of the regime is as evident as it is in the Nazi case. The preamble to the Statuto of 20 December 1929, for example, had this to say about the nature of fascism: 'The National Fascist Party is a civil militia for the service of the nation. Its objective: to realize the greatness of the Italian people. From its very beginnings, which are indistinguishable from the renaissance of the Italian conscience and the will to victory, until now, the party has always thought of itself as in a state of war, at first in order to combat those who were stifling the will of the nation, today and from henceforth to defend and increase the power of the Italian people. Fascism', the Statuto stressed, 'is not merely an Italian organization connected with a programme partly realized and partly still to be realized; it is above all a faith . . . under the impulse of which the new Italians work as soldiers, pledged to achieve victory in the struggle between the nation and its enemies.' Not only the ethos but also the structure of the Fascist Party, and indeed of the state at large, were determined by the military character of the fascist enterprise. 'In the hour of vigil', the Statuto continues, the organization of the Party 'was fixed according to the necessities of battle, and the people recognized the Duce by the marks of his will, his strength and his achievements. In the heat of the struggle, action took precedence of law. Every stage was marked by conquest, and the assemblies were only gatherings of officers and men dominated by memories of the dead.'[29]

By itself, however, the army principle of organization is insufficient; as the embodiment of an unchanging myth or *Weltanschauung*, directed activism finds an additional model in the dogmatic practices of the Catholic Church. Like the Church, Hitler wrote, the Nazi movement 'holds fast to its fixed and established dogmas which alone can give to the whole system the character of a faith'.[30] The programme of the twenty-five points of the N.S.D.A.P. was accordingly never altered, after its adoption in 1926. After reading Lenin, this frank admiration for the army and the Catholic Church may seem very refreshing. Neither Mussolini nor Hitler ever troubled themselves, at any rate, with the empty rhetoric about 'democratic centralism' with which Lenin endeavoured to conceal the transition from spontaneous to directed activism.

The quality which entitles *Mein Kampf* to pride of place amongst the three works which have contributed most to the conceptual revision of the activist style during the present century, however, still remains to be noticed. It consists of Hitler's instinctive grasp of the master-key to successful demagogy – a key which may be described in one word: simplification. In the third chapter of *Mein Kampf*, Hitler described the art of simplification with admirable clarity. 'The art of leadership, as displayed by really great popular leaders in all ages', he observed, 'consists in consolidating the attention of the people against a single adversary and taking care that nothing will split up that attention into sections . . . The leader of genius', he continued, 'must have the ability to make different opponents appear as if they belong to the one category . . . As soon as the vacillating masses find themselves facing an opposition that is made up of different groups of enemies their sense of objectivity will be aroused and they will ask how is it that all the others can be in the wrong and they themselves, and their movement, alone in the right.' Mussolini, with a successful career in journalism behind him, had no difficulty in rivalling Hitler's capacity for simplification.

It was in this way, then, that the activist style was finally made to yield the highly destructive and entirely extra-constitutional ideal of spiritual unity contained in the fascist *Weltanschauung*. Whilst the Italian and the Nazi versions of the ideal society differed as regards specific details, of which the racial issue is the most obvious, these differences reflected variations in demagogic rhetoric rather than a fundamental divergence in the structure of the fascist style itself. Mussolini derived his own pattern of demagogy partly from the syndicalist tradition and partly from the colourful rabble-rousing in which his fellow-countryman, D'Annunzio, excelled; Hitler, emerging from a different tradition and adapting himself to different circumstances, drew instead upon the racial and anti-semitic ideas which had flourished in the world of pre-1914 Vienna. The basic achievement of the two great fascist leaders, however, was that they both succeeded in simplifying the directed phase of activism into an unprincipled regard for

125

whatever moved the masses, coupled with a boundless contempt for the hapless dupes who embraced the myth offered to them.

The transition from spontaneous to directed activism, however, might well have remained a mere affair of radical scribblers had it not been for the Great War. Just as the French Revolution had given substance to the original spontaneous phase of activism to be found in Rousseau's writings, so now the war gave practical relevance to the ideas and dreams of those who abandoned spontaneous for directed activism. In the case of fascism, neither its theory, nor its practice, nor its success would be intelligible, were they to be considered apart from the profound impact of the war on European intellectual and political life. Since the last contribution to the revision of activism – Hitler's *Mein Kampf* – was conceived and written in the shadow cast by the war, it is only within the new political context created by the war that its full significance can be appreciated. The same is true of the course taken by Mussolini's life and thought.

Once the revised version of the activist style had been placed upon the new foundation of myth, an unscrupulous politician was henceforth faced with only one problem. This was that of determining which faith or illusion was best calculated to mobilize the masses. From this point of view, Sorel's proposed revision of the activist style was unsatisfactory, for an obvious reason. This was that he failed to appreciate the precise nature of the myth which would appeal to the masses. The myth upon which Sorel himself had pinned his hopes was that of the General Strike. The advent of the First World War, however, revealed that the myth most likely to influence the masses had nothing at all to do with the socialism of Marx and Lenin, let alone with the syndicalism of Sorel. It pointed, instead, to nationalism as the one force capable of uniting the different members and classes of a nation behind their government.

In every European country, the intense wartime experience of national unity and social cohesion seemed to many thinkers to make the war a blessing in disguise, rather than an unmitigated evil. The enthusiastic reflections of W. Trotter, in his *Instincts of the Herd in Peace and War* (1919), are illuminating in this respect. Prior to the war, he wrote, 'the individual led a life emotionally thin and tame because the social feelings were localized and faint. With the outbreak of war the national unit became the source of moral power, social feeling became wide in its basis and strong in its intensity. To the individual life became more intense and more significant, and in essence, in spite of horror and pain, better worth living; the social fabric, moreover, displayed a new stability and capacity for resisting disturbances that would have effectively upset its equilibrium in time of peace . . . With the cessation of war', Trotter concluded, 'this great stream of moral power began rapidly to dry up at its source.'[31] In Germany, the impact given by the war to nationalist sentiment was still more powerful, as the reflections of those who experienced the life of the trenches frequently testify. 'The war, for all its destructiveness,' Ernst Jünger wrote, 'was an incomparable schooling of the heart.'[32] The effect of this schooling, he said, was to make the idea of the nation a living reality for the first time. 'The nation', he observed, 'was no longer for men an empty thought veiled in symbols.'[33]

It was the response of European nations to the war, then, that indicated the precise character of the myth which was most likely to serve the activist cause. The war, however, had a further consequence for the activist style which the fascists, above all, were quick to appreciate. Not only did it reveal the power of nationalist mythology and provide a concrete model (the army) for the type of organization in which the new activist style of politics might find the structure appropriate for a 'movement regime'. It also revealed that the collectivist requirements of a war economy might 'socialize' the political life of states far more effectively than any amount of socialist ideology ever could. It was in this 'war socialism' that fascists immediately recognized the means by which their project of synthesizing nationalism with socialism might eventually be carried out.

In England, Oswald Mosley was amongst the first to appreciate this 'positive' aspect of the war, long before he adopted a specifically fascist programme as the means of

127

pursuing its implications. In Germany, however, a thoughtful book on the likely impact of the war upon the future structure of the European world had already appeared before the war was over. In his work *Mitteleuropa* (1915), Friedrich Naumann drew attention to the fact that it was not only the old political order of western Europe which had been brought to an end by the war; the old social and economic order of capitalism, he maintained, had also been radically transformed. Naumann's observations are interesting, not only for the light they throw on the socio-economic conditions which provided the background to the rise of fascism in Germany, but also because they anticipated at many points the contemporary discussion of post-capitalist or 'post-industrial' society. In spite of the typically German admixture of *volkisch* ideology which they contain, it is therefore worth pausing to consider them briefly.

The war, Naumann explained, meant that Germany had far outpaced the rest of the western world in terms of socio-economic development. As a direct result of the war, Germany was now well into 'the second capitalistic period, which can be described as the transition from private capitalism to socialism, provided only that the word socialism is not taken to mean the phenomenon of purely proletarian big-business but is broadly understood as folk-ordering with the object of increasing the common profit of all for all'.[34] The war and technological change, he announced, meant that capitalism was dead; or rather, it meant that the old-style capitalist entrepreneur had been quietly led, without being aware of it, into the kind of collectivized, state-interventionist economic order to which he had originally been thoroughly opposed. The upshot was that 'what appeared forty years ago to be the ideology of socialist and state-socialistic dreamers, remote from reality, now appears with incredible certainty as a form of reality which has become an accomplished fact in the meantime'.[35] In this way, then, Naumann was able to reconcile himself to the failure of his own earlier attempt to found a National-Socialist party, since what his party had failed to achieve, the war had done for him.

Where then did the future lie? It lay, Naumann believed, in the final union of nationalism with socialism in a new organic state. In order to complete the German conversion to national socialism, all that was necessary was that Germany should now convert the unforeseen changes brought about by war into a deliberate, conscious principle of social and political organization. The lesson of the war, in a word, was that economic and political individualism must be rejected in favour of national-socialist policy: 'When we emerge from the war we shall no longer be the same economic beings as before. Past, then, is the period of fundamental individualism, that period of imitation of the English economic system, which was clearly in decline; but at the same time, past also is the period of an internationalism which boldly vaulted beyond the present-day state. Upon the basis of wartime experiences we demand a regulated economy.'

This demand, Naumann added prophetically, was one which would not be confined to Germany: 'Such movements will also manifest themselves elsewhere in the world among other peoples, even among the English, but with us, in our cut-off state, they are riper than anywhere else.' His conclusion was ominous: 'On all sides state-socialism or national socialism grows up; "regulated economy" grows up . . . after the war for the first time the German becomes an economic state-citizen body and soul; his ideal is and remains the organism, not free-will.' The creation of this organism inevitably involved, he added, a programme of territorial expansion, since the work of Bismarck was to be completed by extending the frontiers of Germany to include Austria and Hungary. The national-socialist state, more generally, necessarily entailed a militant policy of autarky.

Naumann himself optimistically relied upon a rational appreciation of the natural course of history and an understanding of the consequences of the war to bring about the ideal of organic unity of which he dreamed. In the event, the 'sane reconciliation' between nationalism and socialism for which he hoped was to be affected by methods far different from any he had in mind.

These methods were those which both Mussolini and Hitler were to adopt. It was they who gave tactical and organizational reality to the fascist ideal of unity, by continuing the war into

129

peacetime. 'An old world is gone forever', Alfred Rosenberg jubilantly announced at the end of the war, and 'a romanticism of *steel* has taken the place of one of dreams. This longing is alive and groping for form in millions of people.'[36] Society, that is, was to be unified by converting it into a military encampment, with a leader and party elite presiding over the highly collectivized economy which war requires, and spiritually regimenting the encampment along the authoritarian lines of the Catholic Church, by the imposition of an all-embracing myth or *Weltanschauung*. It is to a more detailed consideration of this myth, along with the organizational means by which it was imposed, and the results it entailed, that we must now turn.

5 The Fascist Weltanschauung

It has been argued that, far from being a monstrous deviation from the western political tradition, the fascist *Weltanschauung* stands in a direct line of continuity with it. To stress this continuity would be misleading, however, if it meant minimizing the importance of ideas which may properly be regarded as distinctively fascist, in the sense that they figure more prominently within the fascist *Weltanschauung* than in any other form of activist ideology. It is for this reason that five ideas in particular must now be given more detailed consideration than they have so far received, even though they are not peculiar to fascist ideology but are part and parcel of the activist style of politics at large.

The first idea, which remains controversial down to the present day, is the fascist concept of the corporate state as a 'third way' between capitalism and socialism. The second is the fascist rejection of reason and stability in favour of a stress upon myth and dynamism which culminates in the ideal of permanent revolution. The third is the so-called leader principle. Although this principle is now a familiar ingredient in activist movements throughout the world, it was fascism which originally proclaimed it to be the key to the organizational structure of the movement regime with which the activist style of politics seeks to supersede the traditional western state ideal. The fourth idea is the messianic concept of a redemptive mission. The fifth, and last, idea is that of creating an autarkic (i.e. self-sufficient) state through a programme of world conquest. Blended into one great intellectual mish-mash, these five ideas provide the structure of the fascist *Weltanschauung*.

1. Corporatism The most important claim made by fascism was that it alone could offer the creative prospect of a 'third way' between capitalism and socialism. Hitler, in *Mein Kampf*, spoke

131

enthusiastically about the 'National Socialist corporative idea' as one which would eventually 'take the place of ruinous class warfare';[1] whilst Mussolini, in typically extravagant fashion, declared that 'the Corporative System is destined to become the civilization of the twentieth century'.[2] To decide what corporatism really means, however, is a difficult matter. Today, the concept has become highly topical once again, but even now there is still widespread uncertainty about what corporatism actually is. In the interest of clarity, it will therefore be best to begin by attempting to indicate briefly how the current concept differs from the fascist one.

Contemporary writers on corporatism use the concept only in a restricted sense, to refer to a shift of the centre of political gravity away from the parliamentary system to decision-making by representatives of the three great groups which dominate modern industrial society, viz. labour, capital and government. Corporatism in the fascist sense, by contrast, is a concept which is ultimately intelligible only within the all-embracing vision of an organic, spiritually unified and morally regenerated society. Within this context corporatism refers, more especially, to the various economic policies and institutions by which the union of employers and workers is to be brought about. What mainly characterizes these policies and institutions is an attempt to unite both groups by means which will imbue them with a desire for mutual self-sacrifice in the national interest. Fascists claim, more generally, that only the organic society created by these measures would offer true freedom, by which they mean a release from the petty, egoistic concerns of everyday life and an opportunity for total devotion to the nation and its leader.

This, at least, is true of Italian Fascism; the Nazi corporatist ideal was different, mainly because Nazi doctrine required that economic considerations should be completely subordinate to racial ones. As Werner Sombart made clear in his book *German Socialism* (1934), the ultimate aim was 'a total ordering of the German Volk', which must 'above all be uniform, born from a single spirit and extended from a single central point systematically over the entire social life'. In other words, the Nazi aim was to submerge all groups – peasant, workers and employers alike – in one racially pure organic society

(*Volksgemeinschaft*). It was corporatism in this romantic, *volkisch* sense, rather than corporatism in the more economically rational sense in which Italian thinkers tend to present it, which accounts (for example) for such measures as the abolition of independent trade unions and their replacement by the Labour Front in the Law for the Organization of National Labour of 20 January 1934. The primary function of this reform, as of all other Nazi economic reforms, was the purely ideological one of fabricating a sense of emotional participation in the mythical Nazi racial community. Those who persisted in emphasizing the economic aspects of corporatism were either repudiated by the regime or – as in Gregor Strasser's case – murdered.

It was during the early 1920s, when Hitler and various radical Nazi intellectuals still looked to Fascist Italy for inspiration, that the Nazis came closest to taking corporatist theory seriously. Subsequently, as they gained confidence and began to stress the exclusively German character of all their ideas, they naturally endeavoured to avoid any words which appeared to echo Italian propaganda. Even when the policies they advocated or adopted seemed to have a corporatist character, they therefore avoided the word 'corporatism' and preferred to speak instead of 'German socialism' or 'national socialism', in order to emphasize the wholly indigenous and exclusive character of a policy which was never thought of (unlike Italian corporatism) as being available for export: from the Nazi standpoint, any third way would be valid for Germany alone.

By the time the regime came to power, the result of Nazi ambivalence about corporatism was that the concept had become so vague that even Nazis themselves no longer knew what it meant. This is well illustrated by Dr Robert Ley's account of his dilemma in 1933, when Hitler made him directly responsible for implementing the corporatist ideal. 'I can tell you', he told the Fifth Annual Congress of the German Labour Front in 1937, 'that I did not sleep for several nights on account of the corporate system because I could not make head or tail of it.'[3] In practice, as Ley explained, he ended his confusion merely by implementing the principle which inspired all Nazi

133

institutions. This was the ubiquitous leader principle, which will be considered more closely in a moment. For the present, it is important to add that even though Nazi corporatist doctrine was never taken very seriously by Nazi theorists, the rhetoric nevertheless appears to have been partially successful in generating the ersatz sense of solidarity which Nazis themselves liked to describe as a 'socialism of sentiment'. This success, however, owed more to the tangible benefits of full employment than to active support for the *volkisch* ideal amongst the bulk of the populace. (What should be recalled in this connection is the fact that, whilst the level of employment rose, the level of wages declined. In this situation, *volkisch* rhetoric did more to console men for what they were losing than to inspire active enthusiasm for what Nazism offered.)

Italian corporatism, by contrast with the Nazi version, was generally confined to the economic sphere. For that reason, it has often been regarded as an altogether more constructive attempt to create a 'third way' between capitalism and socialism. Its non-*volkisch* emphasis on economic re-construction and state planning meant, in particular, that Italian propaganda could present Fascist corporatism as a universally applicable solution to the socio-economic cleavages inherent in all modern mass-industrial societies. On closer inspection, however, even Italian theorizing about corporatism completely fails to bear out any of the ambitious claims which Fascists were fond of making for it. Mussolini's own speeches and writings, for instance, are a complete muddle, containing at least three different and incompatible interpretations of the idea.

According to one of his interpretations, corporatism was intended to offer an entirely new conception of the function of the state. On this view, not only the traditional cleavage between state and individual but also the more modern division of industrial society into contending classes, were to be overcome by reconciling both within the framework of the corporation. The corporation, as Mussolini explained to the Senate on 14 November 1933, was to act as a cramp (*un vincolo*) that bound all members of society together in a single common faith. According to Fascist cant, the new corporate basis of social and political life would facilitate creative individual self-expression, on the one hand, whilst also facilitating the elimination of the wasteful laissez-faire system by a new, more positive ideal of state intervention directed towards securing communal goals, on the other. In practice, of course, the Fascist vision of a corporatist society based upon the self-regulation of producers under the aegis of the state was merely a veil for despotism. Mussolini himself acknowledged this when he explained that corporatism in this sense was only relevant to a totalitarian state like the Italian one, since the reforms it would require were so all-pervasive that the corporatist system could not possibly work within the context of limited politics.[4]

According to a second interpretation, however, the corporatist system was not tied to one particular political system but could be exported to any industrialized country in which individuals and groups wished to use the state as a non-coercive device for maintaining voluntary self-discipline (*autodisciplina*). This view, which was originally put before the Senate in a speech on 13 January 1934,[5] was subsequently embroidered by Mussolini in a way which identified corporatism with domestic socialism, on the one hand, and with a militant programme of national expansion, on the other.[6] Corporatism in this sense was obviously just a formula for warmongering, and Fascist 'socialism' was merely another name for the collectivism required by a war economy.

Finally, Mussolini made a third claim, according to which corporatism meant not so much a new function for the state, or a new kind of social order, as an entirely new conception of the form and structure of the state. Corporatism, according to this view, was the only form of democracy appropriate to the twentieth century. The corporatist system alone, it was held, would make the state structure truly representative by ending a fundamentally divisive parliamentary system based upon geographical particularism and upon divisive political parties. In place of this unsatisfactory system there would be an organic one, in which a corporatist parliament represented 'natural' (i.e. economic) social groups instead of abstract geographical and political ones.[7] In line with this manner of thinking, the remnants of the Italian Parliament were abolished in 1938 and replaced by a corporatist parliament. The result of this supposedly new 'organic' conception of the state, as might be expected, was merely a further enhancement of Mussolini's dictatorship, rather than the creation of an alternative to parliamentary democracy. The kind of politics which characterized the new organic state (or, as it was sometimes called, 'functional democracy'), may be gleaned from the Proceedings of the Chamber of Fasces and Corporations, 27 April 1940. From these we learn that, 'The Chamber and public galleries broke out with an enthusiastic ovation. The cry of *"Duce"*, *"Duce"* resounded through the hall again and again. The Duce responded with the Roman salute. The assembly then sang *"Giovinezza"*. The President ordered that the Duce should be saluted, and the Chamber answered with a powerful *"A Noi"*. When the Duce left his seat, the National Councillors crowded around him with enthusiastic and continual acclamations.'

It is obvious that no coherent theory of corporatism emerges from these conflicting views. It might be argued, nevertheless, that Fascist practice offers a more reliable guide to the nature of corporatism than does Fascist theory. Fascist practice, however, merely confirms the conclusion that Mussolini's corporatism was never a 'third way' but only a technique for extending state control over society. The growth of the state was so massive that corporatism might best be described as bureaucracy run riot: 'Party members and officials constituted a huge new vested interest, since the party, the militia, and the corporations provided what was admitted to be as many as a hundred thousand jobs for secretaries and organizers . . . The census returns of 1931 and 1936 reveal strikingly how the greatest increase in occupation statistics was made by administrators and professional categories.'[8] A correspondent of the London *Economist* observed pointedly in 1935 that, far from offering anything novel, the corporatist system 'has turned out to be nothing more than the most ordinary protectionism'.[9] Inevitably, the growth of state and party personnel brought about a corresponding growth of corruption, for which Mussolini's regime remains notorious.

The main conclusion to emerge from this analysis of fascist

ideas about corporatism is that there is nothing which is of continuing relevance for the structure of contemporary liberal-democratic society. In the case of Nazi theory, as has just been seen, corporatism simply meant the extension of racial ideas into the economic sphere. Even in the Italian case, the attempt to present corporatism as a coherent socio-economic ideal cannot withstand close scrutiny. In reality, Italian corporatism was largely an affair of empty rhetoric, inspired mainly by the need to create the impression that Mussolini's rule rested upon something more than force. Originally, Mussolini had not required any doctrine at all, since his success in 1919–22 was due less to any ideas of his own than to the shortcomings of his rivals. In such a situation, the absence of any doctrine was actually an advantage, since it even led an enemy of fascism like Croce, for example, to conclude that because fascism was devoid of doctrine, it was therefore innocuous.[10] From the time of the Matteotti murder[11] in 1925, however, Mussolini was under increasing pressure to defend himself from the charge that violence and bloodshed were his only title to office. The rhetoric about corporatism was the nearest he ever came to dealing with this problem. The fact that it was mere rhetoric should not, however, create the impression that it therefore served no useful purpose. In corporatist rhetoric, the regime stumbled upon a successful technique for rallying domestic support and winning international approval. On the domestic front, corporatism provided an ideological device for uniting four different and potentially incompatible groups; nationalist, syndicalist, and Catholic intellectuals were able to join with technocratically minded Fascists like Alfredo Rocco, under the impression that all were supporting the same cause. The existence in their midst of the technocratic group seems at first sight to give Italian Fascism a pro-modernist dimension which distinguishes it from the anti-modernist ideology of Nazism, but the apparent divergence is deceptive. Any 'modernizing' which the Italian regime conducted was largely inspired by Mussolini's personal delusions of national grandeur, rather than by the rational requirements of economic prosperity. On the international plane, the 'universalist' rhetoric which was a feature of Italian corporatist doctrine was

137

successful in lending the regime a veneer of intellectual respectability which was especially useful for purposes of overseas propaganda. Perhaps the best evidence for this success is the fact that, even at the present day, scholars are still sometimes hoodwinked into believing that in corporatism Mussolini had perhaps discovered a recipe for creating social harmony.

2. Permanent revolution Whilst corporatism lent a veneer of respectability to the Italian regime, the most remarkable feature of the fascist *Weltanschauung* is to be found elsewhere. It consists in the essentially fluid and dynamic conception of life and the world which fascism sought to oppose to both liberal and socialist political theory, as well as to the traditional forms of conservative ideology.*

A dramatic illustration of the initial incomprehension encountered by the new view of life even amongst fascists themselves may be found in a conversation which took place between Hitler and Herman Rauschning in 1934. The core of National Socialism, Hitler explained to Rauschning, 'is a revolutionary creative will that needs no ideological crutches'. This, he added, is what primarily distinguishes the Nazi revolutionary ideal from the Marxist one. Rauschning, however, was not at all clear about what the Nazi 'revolutionary creative will' actually was, and he was therefore compelled to ask Hitler to explain. Hitler tersely observed that, 'It has no fixed aim.' To Rauschning, whose views were of a traditional conservative kind, this aimless dynamism was so novel that

---

* Fascists always denied that there could ever be an official fascist text, of the kind provided for Marxism by *The Communist Manifesto*, or for liberalism by Mill's essay *On Liberty*, or for conservatism by Burke's *Reflections on the French Revolution*. It is true that, in 1932, Mussolini's article on the *Doctrine of Fascism* appeared to give the Italian regime an official doctrine, but Gentile, the regime's principal ideologist, was quick to explain that even an official doctrine could not permanently bind the will of the leader. Mussolini did not act inconsistently, therefore, when he recalled and destroyed all available copies of the *Doctrine of Fascism* in April 1940, after he had had second thoughts about certain phrases in it. (Mack Smith, *Mussolini's Roman Empire*, Penguin ed., 1979; first published 1976, p. 247).

Hitler was obliged to elaborate a bit further upon the nature of the Nazi revolution. 'We are a movement,' he informed Rauschning, adding that, 'Nothing could express our nature better. [Unlike the Marxists] we know that there is never a final stage, there is no permanency, only eternal change . . . the future is an inexhaustible fount of possibilities of further development.'[12]

In practice, very few thinkers subscribed to Hitler's doctrine of permanent revolution, and Hitler himself was always careful to pose in public as the defender of order and stability. Paradoxically, however, it was often non-Nazi intellectuals, who either despised the ideal of permanent revolution, or else rejected it out of hand, who played most effectively into Hitler's hands. They did so mainly because they tended to succumb to a corrosive, all-embracing sense of cultural alienation which made political moderation appear meaningless, or even treasonable. In order to account for the appeal of the Nazi *Weltanschauung*, it is necessary to step outside the relatively narrow circle of Nazi intellectuals themselves and consider the cultural and political vacuum unwittingly created by these profoundly alienated intellectuals, even though they were often either critics or avowed opponents of Nazism.[13]

The starting-point for most of these critics was Oswald Spengler's vision of the decline of the West. In one form or another, this vision may be traced back through a long line of earlier thinkers, including H.S. Chamberlain, Max Nordau and Nietzsche, to the wholesale revolt against modern rationalism and materialism begun by the German Romantic school at the end of the eighteenth century. The mere timing of Spengler's work, however, gave him an influence which far exceeded that of his predecessors. Unlike them, he spoke to a nation which had just been defeated in war and was therefore reassured to be told that Germany, far from being alone in her misery, was really experiencing a fate which would inevitably overtake her conquerors. Using a distinction which has been popular with German thinkers for the past two centuries, Spengler related the situation of Germany to the gradual triumph of a sterile and ossified world of 'civilization' over the living and creative reality of 'culture'. In Spengler's view, only a return to 'Prussian Socialism', by which he meant a return to the tradition of enlightened despotism begun by Frederick the Great, could prevent the desiccated spirit of modern civilization from degenerating into complete anarchy. With considerable misgivings, Spengler turned to Hitler as the man most likely to provide Germany with the new Caesar it required. Spengler, however, was entirely mistaken in identifying Hitler as a dictator in the tradition of Frederick; unlike Rauschning, he completely failed to recognize the nihilistic dynamism which separated Nazism from all previous forms of dictatorship.

Spengler's traditional kind of conservatism, however, might be brought closer to the Nazi brand of iconoclasm by superimposing upon it a conception of culture which was even more spiritual, romantic and vague – and hence even more hostile to modern industrial and democratic society – than Spengler's own. When that happened, the result was to radicalize conservatism by converting it into an ideology which entailed the total rejection of the modern urban and technical age. It is this total alienation from modernity which marks, above all, the disciples of the poet Stefan George. To the cold, impersonal and culturally barren world of modern *Gesellschaft* society they opposed the warmth and community of a lost world of *Gemeinschaft*. In a technical and academic form, this was the distinction popularized by romantic sociologists like Ferdinand Tonniës, in his book *Gemeinschaft und Gesellschaft*, which became an academic best-seller in the rootless intellectual world of Weimar Germany. For the George circle, however, hostility to the modern world at large, and to Weimar Germany in particular, crystallized in the form of a dramatic distinction between two Germanys. One was the spiritually arid Germany in which they felt they lived; the other, which became the idealized object of all their thought and work, was the 'secret Germany' which they wished to resuscitate – a Germany, that is, of warriors, aesthetes and beautiful youths, symbolized above all by Barbarossa, by Hölderlin, and by the Youth Movement.

It is this mood of total alienation from the cultural, moral and political world of Weimar which links the exotic George circle with artists and intellectuals like Gottfried Benn and

Heidegger. Benn's case is interesting mainly because his thought illustrates the kind of addled theorizing used by many artists in the inter-war era to defend their hostility to modern society and their predilection for political extremism. Such theorizing points in no particular political direction, and might therefore lead as readily to communism (as with André Breton and his surrealist followers, for example) as to Nazism. In Benn's case the path happened to lead to Nazism. His point of departure was the familiar belief that what our age is now witnessing is 'the disintegration of scientific reality, which [has] been the source of what [is] "real" for the last four hundred years'.[14] The consequent problem, according to Benn, was that of creating a new, more satisfactory reality; but where was this to be found? Benn's answer was that it lies in Expressionism. Expressionism abandons the futile search for a stable, external reality in order to discover a new reality by 'that difficult inward path to the creative state, to the primal images, the myths'.[15] Unfortunately, this intensely inward conception of reality, inspired as it was by a vision of twentieth-century European life as a 'ghastly chaos of crumbling reality and inversion of values', merely completed the very process of nihilistic disintegration which it was intended to arrest. In Benn's case, the rejection of the external world was accompanied by a naive identification of Nazism as the only movement which was capable of creating 'new realities, putting new concentrations, new layers of substance . . . on a foundation on which a new art can arise'.[16]

Heidegger, like Benn, was led to support Nazism for a brief period (1933–4) by an equally naive conviction that it was the only political movement that would make a clean sweep of everything which inclined the modern age towards nihilism. According to Heidegger's vision of the contemporary world, modern man is in danger, rather like the Lady of Shallot, of living confined to a world of shadows. It was this condition which Heidegger described, in great metaphysical detail, in *Sein und Zeit* (1926), where he characterized it as the condition of being totally cut off from Being. It will be recalled that the Lady of Shallot, who felt just like that, was finally ruined by the belief that Lancelot would end her *Angst* by leading her out of her world of shadows. With no less naivety, Heidegger

141

substituted Hitler for Lancelot as Germany's spiritual saviour. He hoped, in particular, that Nazi institutions such as the Labour Service would reintegrate the physical and spiritual sides of human nature, in a way which would produce the 'new man'. It was with this in mind that he announced to the students of Freiburg University, in 1933, that in the Labour Camps 'there is a new reality. The fact that our high school should be open to the new educational powers of the Labour Service symbolizes the new reality. Camps and schools intend to gather . . . the educational powers of our people in order to obtain that new unity in which the nation will drive towards its destiny under the State.'[17] After the war had ended, Heidegger developed a theory of 'historical errancy' to explain this error of political judgment.[18] The theory saved him from reflecting too closely on the extremism to which his own thought had left him exposed, but only at the expense of perpetuating his political naivety.

Almost invariably, the intellectuals who had initially given their more or less guarded support to Hitler soon realized that they had deceived themselves about the character of the Nazi revolution. Some stayed in Germany, others left. Amongst those who stayed, the Austrian writer Gerhardt Hauptmann deserves especial sympathy for the candour he displayed in 1937, when he was asked why he had not followed the example of Mann, Zweig and others and emigrated after withdrawing his support from the regime, 'What are you saying?' said Hauptmann, 'Why don't I leave Germany? Because I'm a coward, do you understand? I'm a coward, do you understand? I'm a coward.'[19]

It is perhaps worth repeating that the ideas and writings of the intellectuals just mentioned had no direct connection with the aimless dynamism of the Nazi *Weltanschauung*; they supported it only in an oblique fashion, by fostering an intense sense of alienation from modernity. It is just here, one must now add, that the most striking difference between German and Italian cultural life in the inter-war period is to be found. In Italy there was indeed cultural dissatisfaction, especially after 1870, but what is noteworthy about the thinkers who feared that Italian culture had become decadent is the relative mildness of the remedies they proposed; in Italy there was little of that desire for root and branch spiritual solutions which impelled German thinkers along the path towards nihilism. The Futurists, led by Marinetti, were the main exception to this generalization, but even Marinetti's colourful iconoclasm never envisaged the wholesale Wagnerian bonfire for which disaffected German intellectuals yearned. An incident which occurred in 1930 may serve to illustrate the vast gulf which yawned between German and Italian forms of 'cultural despair'.

In 1930 (so we learn from an excellent cookery book), Marinetti launched a national campaign against spaghetti, in the belief that it was a dish unworthy of the heroic inhabitants of the new Italy which Fascism sought to create. 'Spaghetti is no food for fighters', he declared, adding that it is also anti-virile, since 'a weighty and encumbered stomach cannot be favourable to physical enthusiasm towards women'. More generally, pasta 'is an obsolete food; it is heavy, brutalizing, and gross; its nutritive qualities are deceptive; it induces scepticism, sloth, and pessimism'. There was immediate opposition to this new Fascist culinary crusade. The Mayor of Naples, for example, declared to a reporter that, 'The angels in Paradise eat nothing but vermicelli al pomidoro.' Marinetti replied that this confirmed his suspicions with regard to the monotony of Paradise and the life led by the angels. What is characteristically Italian about Marinetti's attack upon the 'decadent', non-virile Italian diet, however, is the alternative diet he proposed. A good Nazi would have proposed some spartan replacement designed to steel the will and purge the bowels; but Marinetti resorted instead to exotic ingredients, such as an aphrodisiac drink composed of pineapple juice, eggs, cocoa, caviar, almond paste, red pepper, nutmeg, cloves and Strego. The cookery book in which this information is contained does not, alas, give the precise recipe; it does note, however, that the new meals were to be eaten to the accompaniment of perfumes, to be sprayed over the diners, who should hold the fork in the right hand whilst meanwhile stroking with the left some suitably erotic substance such as velvet, silk, or emery paper.[20]

The concept of decadence which worried Italian intellectuals, it is clear, was altogether more modest than the kind of cultural despair which fuelled Nazi nihilism. The main point, however, is that in both Italy and Germany discontent with the existing social order served as a bridge by which non-fascist intellectuals might unwittingly pass from traditional kinds of conservatism to the type of dynamism upon which the fascist *Weltanschauung* rested. Often, as has been seen, this discontent was expressed only in spiritual, aesthetic, or philosophic forms, but occasionally it took the form of highly developed, ultra-radical conservative political theorizing. This was especially so in Germany, where two thinkers in particular – Moeller van den Bruck and Ernst Jünger – broke completely with the tradition of reactionary conservatism represented by Spengler and blazed a radical conservative trail which stopped just short of Nazism but left those who followed it teetering on the brink.

It was in 1923 that Moeller van den Bruck published the work from whose title, *The Third Reich*, the Nazi movement was to take its name. Hitler himself had met Moeller a year earlier, in 1922, and had responded enthusiastically to the encounter. 'You have everything I lack,' he told Moeller. 'You create the spiritual framework for Germany's reconstruction. I am but a drummer and an assembler. Let us work together.'[21] Like other intellectuals, however, Moeller responded to Hitler with contempt: in his view Hitler could neither understand nor carry out the task which faced conservatism in the twentieth century. What was this task?

Moeller's starting-point, like that of other radical conservatives, was the belief that the only relevant form of conservative doctrine in the modern world is one which begins by accepting and embracing revolution, instead of by rejecting or suppressing it. 'Conservatism and revolution co-exist in the world today', Moeller wrote, with the result that the task now is to evolve 'a conservative revolutionary thought as the only one which in a time of upheaval guarantees the continuity of history and preserves it alike from reaction and from chaos.'[22] In the same context, he explained that 'conservatism and revolution would destroy each other, if the conservative had not . . . the political wisdom to recognize that conservative goals may be attained even with revolutionary postulates and by revolutionary means'.[23] The essence of the new, radicalized conservatism, then, is that it 'seizes directly on the revolution, and by it, through it and beyond it saves the life of Europe and of Germany'.[24]

Four features of Moeller's thought are especially relevant at present, since all four illustrate the basic structural similarities which exist between radical conservatism, on the one hand, and Nazi demagogy, on the other. In the first place, Moeller stressed that radical conservatism is much more than the ideology of a party. It is, he explained, an all-embracing *credo* or *Weltanschauung*, intended to inspire a threatened nation to fanatical, life-or-death effort at self-defence in the face of mortal danger.[25] Secondly, Moeller stressed that this new *Weltanschauung* cannot be reduced to a doctrine. A doctrine, indeed, is irrelevant to radical conservative thought, since the essence of the new political position is that it is 'a war for very life, for the nation's freedom'. It is this very absence of doctrine, Moeller insisted, which makes radical conservatism 'a natural cause, the cause of all whose elementary instinct is to turn and rise against the oppressor – without seeking justification in any doctrine'.[26]

Thirdly, the structure of Moeller's radical conservatism actively encouraged demagogy by reducing intellectual opposition to the Weimar system to a simple conspiracy theory which claimed to provide a comprehensive explanation for all Germany's misfortunes. It was the very nature of radical conservatism, indeed, to demand such a conspiracy theory, since only the spectre of a readily identifiable enemy could rally the masses behind the fanatical ideal of national unity upon which radical conservative activism relied. For Moeller, this enemy was not the Jew, but was rather the spirit of rationalism which (he maintained) had been eating away the core of western life for the past three centuries. As Moeller realized, however, the notion of rationalism was too abstract to mobilize mass political sentiment, and he therefore concentrated his attack upon what he took to be the more tangible expressions of it in the Germany of his day. Of these, parliamentary democracy, the capitalist economic system and the danger of Bolshevik socialism were the most important. The multiple facets which

145

rationalism reveals, however, should not obscure the fact that from the radical conservative viewpoint, all Germany's major problems were to be accounted for in terms of a single-factor conspiracy theory. All that was required in order to recast this wholesale attack upon Weimar in Nazi terms was to substitute anti-semitism for 'rationalism' as the basis of the conspiracy theory which was to be used to mobilize the masses.

Fourthly, the means by which the radical conservative programme sought to end the supposed anti-German conspiracy provides a further illuminating parallel with the structure of Nazi thought. The attack upon the conspiracy had to be total, as has already been seen; but what is no less instructive is the fact that, according to Moeller, a completely successful attack would have to take the form of a 'national socialist' programme. The principal object of this policy was to defeat Bolshevik socialism – an alien, perverse form of socialism, that is – by imbuing the masses with an 'organic' socialism of native German invention. This native German socialism had been transmitted (according to Moeller) from the essentially corporate, anti-individualist German past by a long tradition of guilds and professional bodies. Only the fusion of nationalism with Germany's own traditional brand of organic socialism, Moeller believed, could make modern conservatism relevant to the contemporary situation of the nation, in which the dynastic order had been destroyed for ever and the masses had been launched upon the irreversible path to full political consciousness.

When these four characteristics of the new conservatism are drawn together, then, they illustrate how easily radical conservative thought could pass over into sympathy for the kind of aimless, purely destructive revolution undertaken by Hitler. Moeller himself, needless to say, had never intended that the conservative revolution should be nothing more than a 'revolution of destruction'. To him, activist dynamism seemed, on the contrary, to be the only truly constructive way of realizing the greatest political ideal of the modern world, which is 'the state for the sake of the nation'. This ideal, he explained, is to be contrasted with the older ideal of 'the state for the sake of the state' upon which the unsatisfactory second Reich of

Bismarck and the Kaiser had rested.[27] The older ideal was to be rejected out of hand because it represented a static, purely reactionary form of conservatism which could never generate activist fervour amongst the masses and was therefore entirely irrelevant to modern social and political conditions. According to Moeller, it was this failure to win the active support of the masses which had been the main weakness of the second Reich inaugurated by the unification of Germany in 1870. To overcome the continuing political apathy of the masses, Moeller maintained, would be the principal task of the Third Reich. In this respect, the affinity between the Nazi ideal, on the one hand, and Moeller's vision of a 'conservative revolution' which would create a Third Reich, on the other, needs no comment: both envisaged a Third Reich built upon the activist fervour of the masses.

In the writings of Ernst Jünger, the connection between cultural alienation and political activism which was central to Moeller's radical conservatism was pressed even further, with the paradoxical result that from Jünger's standpoint Nazism itself seemed to be an excessively conservative affair. Whilst Jünger himself never became a party member, or even a fellow-traveller, his whole doctrine was nonetheless taken over by the Nazi regime for its own purposes after 1933.[28] The doctrine is of particular interest because it provided a mixture of heroism, nihilism and existentialism which was sufficiently vague and suggestive for it to attract individuals as diverse as Heidegger, at one extreme, and Freikorps adventurers like Ernst von Salomon, at the other.

The central concept in Jünger's doctrine was the idea of 'total mobilization' as the supreme end of the state. This idea was intended to preserve the supra-individual, highly collectivist ethos of a nation at war, on the one hand, whilst also inculcating a heroic and tragic view of life on the other. The result was Jünger's vision of a semi-military society in which work was to become indistinguishable from continual preparation for war. Such a society, Jünger hoped, would be sufficiently radical to win the workers away from socialism, whilst also deepening the spirit of nationalism throughout the country as a whole. The dominant figure in the new society was

147

to be the figure of 'the Worker', but Jünger's worker bore little resemblance to the type of worker around whom socialism had erected its scaffolding. For him, the whole purpose of the ideal society was to extract the worker from Marxist theory and remodel him instead in the totally different image of the Freikorps adventurer. Upon this image, drawn as it was from Jünger's own personal experience, were superimposed an impersonal cult of the machine age, on the one hand, and an extreme cult of suffering and *Angst*, on the other. The final outcome was a sustained hymn to political violence which easily shaded over into the completely extra-constitutional tendencies of Nazi politics. The result was so extreme, indeed, that it led Jünger himself to despise Hitler for his willingness to work within the framework of Weimar institutions.[29] In fairness to Jünger, it must be added that he always denied that the policies of the Nazi regime, when once Hitler came to power, corresponded with his ideal of total mobilization. All Hitler had offered, he subsequently explained, was 'the metaphysical solution, the purely technical execution of Total Mobilization'.[30] Jünger was of course entitled to reject the Nazi interpretation of his theory, but what is beyond doubt is the fact that his doctrine of total mobilization readily lent itself to an extremist interpretation of the Nazi type, since Jünger himself had openly proclaimed his indifference to truth or falsity on moral and political matters; the important thing, he had said, is 'to sacrifice oneself for a faith, regardless of whether that faith embraces truth or error'.[31] To that extent, he was ultimately at one with Hitler himself.

The various writers mentioned, then, illustrate the most important ways in which a profound sense of cultural alienation might produce an intellectual climate conducive to the ideal of permanent revolution. As has just been seen, the result of this alienation was that thinkers who were either not fascist at all, or else supported fascism only in a lukewarm or qualified manner, nevertheless prepared the way for fascism by advocating doctrines which released the will from all remaining moral and political restraints. In this respect, nothing they said was very novel. Their ideas were important, however, because they gave the most extreme expression yet seen to the philosophy of will which has inspired the activist style of politics ever since 1789.

What must now be considered is the critique of limited politics, and especially of parliamentary democracy, to which cultural alienation gave rise. This critique is most easily explored in connection with the leader principle, which is the third concept that distinguishes the fascist *Weltanschauung*. Since the leader principle holds the key to the type of society and system of government which fascism seeks to put in the place of parliamentary government, it must obviously be looked at in some detail.

3. *The leader principle*   The leader principle is now a familiar part of all contemporary activist regimes. Fascism, however, is the only modern ideology to place the explicit cult of a leader at the very centre of its teaching. The central significance of the principle in the fascist *Weltanschauung* can best be brought out by considering the three different functions which it performs.

For fascism, the first and most crucial of the leader's functions is to serve as a symbolic embodiment of the myth which shapes the historical destiny of his people. A single example will illustrate how radically this conception of leadership differs from that to be found within other modern ideologies. The example in question relates to the significance of a political speech. In liberal and socialist ideology, the purpose of a speech is primarily the rational one of instructing the listeners. Within fascist ideology, by contrast, the purpose of a speech (as Hitler himself put it) was to open the gates to the heart of the *Volk*, as with the blows from a hammer.[32] For fascism, in other words, the leader's task is no longer to instruct his listeners but to arouse their emotions, in a way which encourages them to 'live out' the fascist myth, rather than to examine it critically.[33]

In order to perform this first function the fascist leader must ensure that his movement is free from the disputes over the relationship between theory and practice which bedevil other ideologies. To achieve this internal harmony he must claim to be infallible in all matters of fascist faith, morality and politics. Consider, for example, the blunt terms in which Hitler felt obliged to spell out the doctrine of infallibility to Otto Strasser, in the course of a head-on clash over the scope of the leader principle which occurred in 1930. According to Strasser, the leader was ultimately subordinate to the Party, which was the true organ of Nazi infallibility. 'The Idea [i.e. the ideology]', Strasser asserted, 'is divine in origin, whilst men are only its vehicles, the body in which the Word is made flesh. The Leader is made to serve the Idea, and it is to the Idea alone that we owe absolute allegiance.' By contrast with the Idea, he maintained, 'The leader is human, and it is human to err.' Hitler's reply to this impertinent critique of his personal infallibility was brief and unequivocal. 'You are talking monumental idiocy,' he snarled. 'You wish to give Party members the right to decide whether or not the Führer has remained faithful to the so-called Idea. It's the lowest kind of democracy, and we want nothing to do with it! For us the Idea is the Führer, and each Party member has only to obey the Führer.'[34] In Italian Fascism, the same point was asserted still more directly; in the words of the Fascist Decalogue, 'Mussolini is always right.'

Both in theory and in practice, then, the fascist myth or *Weltanschauung* inevitably becomes inseparable from the will of the leader. The function of the leader principle, however, is not confined to giving symbolic embodiment to the fascist myth. It performs, in addition, a second function, which is that of providing the organizational basis of the movement regime with which fascism seeks to replace the state order. As an early study of Nazi ideology correctly noted, 'The factor of leadership is so prominent that it may almost be called the core not only of the constitution of the party, but also of its doctrine.'[35] Even before Hitler came to power, the supremacy of the leader principle had already been clearly established within his party. As early as 1927, for example, Gregor Strasser could exclaim enthusiastically: 'Duke and vassal! In this ancient German relationship of leader and follower, fully comprehensible only to the German mentality and spirit, lies the crown of the structure of the N.S.D.A.P.'[36] Once Hitler came to power, the leader principle became the foundation for all the institutions of the Third Reich. Under the Law for the Ordering of National Labour of January 1934, for example, the whole Nazi economic order was organized upon this principle.

The real problem, however, is to determine how effective the leader principle was in creating the kind of dynamic, spiritually unified community at which fascism aimed. At one level, it was undoubtedly successful. This was at the level of elite corps like the S.S., where the leader principle generated an intense spirit of camaraderie, equality and participation. In this respect, the testimony of an enthusiastic young French fascist, Christian de La Mazière, is of especial interest. It was in 1944, when Paris was on the point of being liberated, that de La Mazière's ideal of a rejuvenated Europe led him to join the Charlemagne Brigade of the Waffen S.S.* Reflecting on the first time he was called upon to give the raised arm salute to the leader, de La Mazière records approvingly that 'it struck me as signifying a new start . . . through it I felt I was entering an order where nothing was easy but where all was more pure and honest'.[37] In this 'more pure and honest' social order which fascism was to create, equality would be entirely compatible with the hierarchy and discipline required by the leader principle. These apparently incompatible ideals could be fused through the sense of emotional solidarity which de La Mazière experienced in the Waffen S.S. training camp. One detail recorded by de La Mazière indicates how effectively the organization of the Waffen S.S. managed to achieve a quasi-religious mixture of elitism, egalitarianism and socialism. 'In the Waffen S.S.', he observes, 'nobody ever said thank you. A soldier never thanked an officer; nor did an officer thank a soldier . . . The principle was that . . . everyone received what he had a right to and nothing more. There were no privileges such as those in the French military tradition. . . In the Waffen S.S., for instance, everyone ate together and the food was the same for all . . . If there was any schnapps, it was first distributed to the ordinary soldiers. The officers got what was left and, generally speaking, received less than the troops. One of the fundamental precepts

---

* More than half the Charlemagne Brigade came from outside Germany, and its members had no connection (or so La Mazière and others believed) with the Death's Head division of the S.S. that ran the extermination camps (*The Captive Dreamer*, U.S.A., 1974, p. 31).

was the higher the rank, the more numerous the duties and the fewer the advantages.'[38]

Combined with an elite atmosphere of camaraderie and harsh discipline, then, the leader principle was an effective means of creating and maintaining a fanatical spirit of loyalty and self-sacrifice amongst the Nazi elite. Considered as a general principle of social organization, however, it proved both administratively inefficient and ideologically counterproductive. It was administratively inefficient because the very concept of the leader principle was intended from the outset to destroy 'rational' (i.e. bureaucratic and legal) forms of state organization and replace them by *volkisch* ones based on direct contact between the leader and his movement. In addition, it was ideologically counterproductive, since in practice the leader principle did nothing at all to establish the *volkisch* society of Nazi propaganda. Indeed, far from creating the anti-modernist utopia of racialist fantasy, Nazi policies actually intensified the spread of an atomized, urban, industrial civilization. There were two reasons for this paradoxical outcome. One was that the attempt to replace the multiplicity of traditional social and family ties by the single tie of personal subordination to the Führer helped in practice to demolish the very values it claimed to uphold. The other was that Hitler's principal objective, which was territorial expansion, meant the creation of a war economy, which in turn inevitably intensified the growth of the very kind of urban industrial social order against which the Nazi *volkisch* ideal was aimed. In sum, the worst enemy of Nazi anti-modernization was Nazism itself, largely because the means adopted by the regime contradicted its ideological ends. The final irony, as one notable study observes, is that the Nazis, who came to power as the champions of the socially and economically most backward elements in the community, ended by taking Germany further and more rapidly forward on the path towards modernization than any of their predecessors.[39]

In Italy, by contrast with Germany, an early study already mentioned noted that 'the principle of leadership is less formally inscribed as the central and permeating principle of the whole community than it is in Germany'.[40] In the Italian situation, unlike the German one, the leader principle always had to compete with the independent political existence of a king whose legitimacy owed nothing to fascism. Unlike Nazism, moreover, Italian Fascism never sought to extend the leader principle to the economic order, where corporatism rather than leadership was the principal theme of Fascist propaganda.[41] For these reasons, the leader principle remained more of a mass cult of personality under the Italian regime than under the Nazi one. Nevertheless, the arbitrary word of the *Duce* remained the basis of the regime, and the principle that 'Mussolini is always right' was inserted in the Fascist Decalogue.

Finally, the leader principle performs a third function. This third function was clearly intimated by Camillo Pellizzi in 1922, when he explained that fascism 'fought for a principle of authority'.[42] The third function of the leader principle, in other words, was to create a new theory of legitimacy. According to this theory, the leader principle alone provides the means of creating a truly 'natural' political relationship. This natural relationship is marked by two things. In the first place, it eliminates the artificial and impersonal relationship created by law and puts in its place an entirely personal relationship between the leader and his follower. In the second place, it is one in which authority is exercised only by individuals whose personal qualities have enabled them to triumph in the struggle for existence. The leader's authority, in other words, reflects his mission and power to command, instead of being an artificial creation of the ballot box. In order to understand the broader implications of these ideas it is to Nazi rather than to Italian thinkers that one must once more turn. Foremost amongst these thinkers is Carl Schmitt, who has been aptly described as the 'crown jurist of the Third Reich', and who may claim to have offered the most impressive intellectual defence of Nazism ever devised.

In Nazi circles Schmitt is almost unique in that his thought did not rest upon a racialist foundation. What principally distinguishes him from other thinkers, whether Italian or German, however, is his attempt to free the fascist case for dictatorship, not only from dependence upon racialist ideology, but from ideological considerations of any kind at all. Having extracted fascism from ideology, Schmitt's primary aim was to present it instead in a completely naturalistic, non-ideological, or purely 'existential' light. In the later years of the Weimar Republic this made his thought especially influential, since what he offered to opponents of the Republic was an apparently scientific and value-free way of defending their cause. It was in this way that he created one of the principal bridges by which disaffected contemporaries could cross over into the Nazi camp. Ironically, however, it was precisely this non-ideological, quasi-scientific approach which caused Schmitt to fall into disfavour with the Nazi regime not long after Hitler acquired power; for whilst Schmitt's existential version of Nazism was by far the most impressive product of Nazi theorizing, his ideological detachment was at odds with the *volkisch* rhetoric of Nazi propaganda at large. It was therefore to less able but more conventional thinkers like Alfred Rosenberg that the party mainly turned for inspiration.

Before Schmitt fell from favour, however, he had equipped the Nazi regime with the most ambitious theory of dictatorship that the western political tradition has yet produced. This became evident in 1934, when Schmitt invoked the Führer principle in order to justify a regime which would henceforth be based upon murder. It was in that year that Hitler carried out the bloody elimination of those S.A. members who demanded a second, social revolution. In an essay entitled 'The Führer Protects Justice', Schmitt defended this action by arguing that it was the sole right of the Führer to take all necessary steps for the creation of a new German Reich. In the name of founding the new state, every action of the leader automatically becomes just. As a result, both an independent judiciary and an independent legislative body are superfluous. The Führer, as Schmitt puts it, 'creates justice directly as the supreme authority by virtue of his leader's office . . . the office of judge emanates from that of Führer. Anyone . . . wishing to separate the two is seeking to put the State out of joint with the aid of justice.' Should any doubts remain about the practical implications of his theory, Schmitt dispels them when he writes, 'The Führer himself determines the content and scope of a transgression against the laws.'[43] Here, in a word, is the perfect formula for total despotism – a formula which ensured that neither Hitler nor his subordinates would ever be called upon to answer for incidents like the Röhm purge. What were the theoretical considerations, one must now ask, which led Schmitt to confer such unlimited authority upon the leader?

The answer is that, for Schmitt, the unlimited power of the leader follows logically from the very nature of the political relationship itself. In order to understand the political relationship, Schmitt explained, we must first recall that every vital sphere of human life is ruled by two opposing categories. In aesthetics, for example, beauty and ugliness are the main categories. In economics, the main categories are those of utility and wastefulness. In morality, they are those of good and evil. What, then, are the opposed categories which provide the basis of the distinctively political relationship? They are, Schmitt replied, those of Friend and Foe. The political Foe, however, is not merely a competitor, or adversary; nor is he a private enemy whom we hate. What then is he? A Foe, in the relevant sense, has three characteristics. Firstly, his existence threatens the complete negation of one's whole way of life. The Foe must therefore be destroyed in order to protect one's own distinct existence. The relationship between Friend and Foe, in other words, is neither moral nor even personal; it is instead described by Schmitt as an ontological or 'existential' one, by which he means that the mere existence of the Foe is perceived as a threat to one's own life. Secondly, Schmitt makes clear that the terms Friend and Foe refer, in their political sense, not to individuals but to collectivities. In Schmitt's own words, 'A Foe exists only when one at least potentially fighting collectivity of people confronts another collectivity of the same kind.' Finally, because the existence of the Foe presents an absolute threat, the conflict between Friend and Foe must itself inevitably be a total one which only ends when the Foe is annihilated.

At this point, the connection becomes apparent between Schmitt's Friend and Foe concept of the political relationship, on the one hand, and the leader principle, on the other. According to Schmitt, the existential Foe can only be eliminated if the Friends have a leader round whom they can

155

rally. The task of the leader, however, is not merely to help them eliminate the Foe; his task, more generally, is to identify and define the Foe whose existence unites the Friends (i.e. his followers). It is in this way, then, that Schmitt legitimates the leader principle, by rooting it in his 'Friend and Foe' analysis of the political relationship. It will be useful, however, to flesh out the analysis by considering in slightly more detail its precise theoretical implications for the status of the leader and his relationship to his movement.

In the first place, Schmitt's analysis implies that the fascist leader cannot be regarded as a dictator, in the traditional sense of that term. In traditional dictatorships, the dictator makes no claim to be the representative of the people over whom he rules; in fascist theory, however, the leader claims to be the only truly representative ruler that a state can possess. According to Schmitt, the leader can make this claim because he is the embodiment of the people, who possess no independent existence (and hence no will) apart from their leader. It is no accident, one may note, that the fascist theory of 'embodiment' is worked out in quasi-religious terms distinctly reminiscent of those in which Christian theory explains the relationship of Christ to the Church; as Schmitt himself expressed the theory, 'our conception of leadership neither needs nor admits to any mediating image: it is a conception of immediate or real presence'.[44]

In effect, what this direct or 'unmediated' relationship means is that leader and people cease to be separate entities, as they are in traditional western liberal-democratic theory, and become instead synonymous terms. In this sense, the Nazi theorist Larenz reformulated the orthodox fascist conception of the leader when he explained (in 1933) that 'the statesman who wills the universal – that is to say, the State – is not only the organ or instrument of the State; *he is the State*'. On the other hand, Larenz stressed, 'since the State is also, at the same time, indubitably something more than any of its temporary representatives, it is true that even the active statesman is never, in himself alone, the State: he needs the complement, the other factor, that is to say the community of the *Volk* which acknowledges and recognizes itself in him'.[45] Setting these more or less technical formulations of the leader's status to one side, however, Hitler's own formulation of the fascist position is commendably succinct. 'What I am, I am through you; what you are, you are through me,' he once told his audience.[46] Similarly, the Nuremburg rally oath was: 'Adolf Hitler *is* Germany, Germany *is* Adolf Hitler.' Putting the same thing in a slightly different way, it may be said that the fascist theory of legitimacy is arrived at by taking the democratic theory of popular sovereignty, according to which the people is the sole legitimate possessor of absolute power, and then transferring this absolute power from the people to the leader. In this perspective, the fascist leader principle is the twentieth-century heir to the democratic doctrine of 1789: just as the democratic slogan was *vox populi, vox dei*, so the Fascist Decalogue, in like fashion, declared that, 'Mussolini is always right.'

In the second place, the leader rules neither by laws, nor by commands, nor even by personal charisma. In fascist theory, his claim to power is based on the belief that he intuitively understands and articulates the real will of the people, even if the people themselves are too confused or too stupid to be able to recognize their 'real' will in the decrees in which the leader formulates it. From this it follows that the fascist leader cannot be elected by the people, after the fashion familiar in liberal-democratic societies: what happens is that he emerges from amidst the people by virtue of his heroic personal qualities, and is then duly recognized and acclaimed by the people, who acknowledge his mission, admire the strength of his will and accept him as the embodiment of their own destiny. It is to Destiny, in the end, and not to the people, that the leader is responsible. It was on the basis of this theory that Carl Schmitt explained, for example, the constitutional basis of the Third Reich. Since the Weimar Constitution was never formally abolished, and since Hitler himself had been elected in 1933 in accordance with its provisions, it appeared to some non-Nazis that the Third Reich derived whatever legitimacy it possessed from the Weimar Constitution, and could therefore be challenged by appealing to that constitution. Schmitt, however, quickly got rid of this potential threat to the Nazi claim to a totally autonomous form of legitimacy. The election

157

of 1933, he explained, was not really an election in the old liberal-democratic sense at all, in spite of the fact that it was held in accordance with the provisions of the Weimar Constitution. It was, rather, an occasion which had given the German people the chance to recognize its destiny by acclaiming its leader. The election, that is to say, was a *de facto* affair and not a *de jure* one. What constitutes the consent of the people, in other words, becomes a matter which the leader himself is left free to define and determine. It is because the leader is not elected by the people, then, that he is not accountable to it.

Thirdly, the direct relationship which the leader requires with his movement in order to externalize the true will of the people means that fascism rejects institutional forms of any kind, in principle at least. In practice, as Hitler himself acknowledged, direct communication with the masses becomes increasingly difficult, and eventually impossible, as a movement grows in size; but the organization which then becomes imperative 'is only a necessary evil', since the 'natural and most ideal' way of promulgating an idea is always personal.[47] The most important consequence of this hatred of the impersonal element created by all organizations is that Nazism rejects any idea of the state as an independently valid form of political organization. The leader may hold state office, but his legitimacy never derives from this; it derives, instead, from the fact that he embodies the historic destiny of the *Volk*. The state, resting as it does on fixed, impersonal rules, would only fetter the dynamic progress of the *Volk* through history, and hinder the leader's ability to give intuitive expression to its needs and requirements. In Italy, Mussolini's need to compromise with the independent position of the monarchy and the Church gave the Italian regime an appearance of moderation, in contrast with Nazism, but this should not obscure the underlying iconoclasm which links the two regimes. In Italy, as in Germany, the fascist demand was for a direct, wholly personal relationship between the leader and the masses; not only in Italy, but in Germany as well, the regime had to compromise with entrenched opposition forces; yet there is nothing in Mussolini's career to contradict the radical hostility towards institutions revealed in his speech of August

1920. 'Down with the state in all its forms', he declared, adding that, 'To us, who are the dying symbols of individualism, there remains, during the present gloom and the dark tomorrow, only the religion, at present absurd, but always consoling, of Anarchy!'[48]

Finally, the leader principle brings with it an entirely new structure of organization for the political movements of the present century. Here, the writings of Schmitt on the typical form of modern despotism are once again amongst the most illuminating products of fascist literature. According to Schmitt, the history of modern western political experience is the disastrous history of the destruction of the state by a series of divisive dualisms. In Schmitt's eyes, the principal curse of the liberal-democratic tradition is that it has converted these ruinous dualisms into the very foundations of political life. Of the various dualisms in practice, the most notorious are those between 'the State and the Individual' or (what is the same thing) between 'State and Society'; the dualism of legislative and executive, expressed in the theory and practice of a division of powers; and the dualism of law and politics, which tries to stifle the dynamic movement of political life by imposing upon it the straitjacket of a fixed and static body of legal rules. According to liberal-democratic theory, the result of these dualisms is to secure freedom and protect individuality. In reality, however, what the various dualisms have meant is the complete paralysis of the state and the transfer of power into the hands of political parties which use it, not in the interest of the community, but solely to pursue their own sectional interest. Liberal-democracy, in a word, does not mean the creation of liberty, but of a plurality of irresponsible tyrannies which usurp the power of the state and destroy the rights of the individual. It is in this way, in short, that liberal-democracy brings about the complete destruction of the political realm.

The conclusion which Schmitt drew from this critique of liberal-democracy is that the modern world inevitably tends towards a condition of crisis from which there is only one sure form of escape. This is through a system of dictatorship which will create national unity by replacing the traditional liberal-democratic 'dualistic' structure of state and society by a new 'trialistic' structure. In the trialistic system, the cleavage between state and society will henceforth be healed by the introduction of a third element. This third element is a single party that reaches out to draw state and society into a single fully politicized political system.

It is this trialistic structure of party-state-society, according to Schmitt, which constitutes the typical political community of the twentieth century – not only in National Socialist Germany, but also (if in a different way) in Fascist Italy and Soviet Russia, where 'a trialistic system of State, party and labour has been attempted as the total expression of political and social reality'.[49] The great merit of the trialistic system is that it alone provides the perfect expression of the organic unity at which the activist style of politics aims: 'Distinct but not divided, connected but not coagulated, the three great fly-wheels run side by side, each according to its own internal law, but all in the unison of the political whole which is carried by the movement of the party.'[50] It was this trialistic vision of the future of twentieth-century political life that led Schmitt, even before Hitler's seizure of power, to hail Italian Fascism as a 'heroic attempt to preserve and assert the dignity of the State and national unity against the pluralism of economic interests'.[51]

What emerges from this elaborate piece of political analysis? The main conclusion to which Schmitt's work points is that fascist 'trialism' makes politics indistinguishable from a perpetual condition of total war. Although this is true of all forms of activism, it is only in fascist ideology that the militant implications of the activist style are made explicit. Fascism also makes clear that the activist style must, of course, mean unlimited despotism, since the 'Friend and Foe' analysis demands unquestioning submission to whoever leads the 'friends'. Finally, Schmitt's analysis may serve to highlight an unpalatable truth which has already been emphasized but will bear repeating once more. This is that the activist ideals of endless warfare and unlimited despotism cannot be seen as 'perversions' of modern democratic thought but are, on the contrary, perfectly logical ways of interpreting the ambiguous idea of 'the people' upon which the modern democratic tradition rests.

4. The messianic mission Schmitt's 'Friend and Foe' analysis of politics established beyond all doubt that the fascist claim to offer the only constructive ideal of social unity appropriate to the modern world really amounts to no more than a demand for ceaseless warfare. The full implications of the fascist *Weltanschauung* only become apparent, however, when an idea which has so far only been briefly touched upon is considered in more detail. This is the fanatical sense of mission, culminating in a programme of world conquest, which inspires the leader and his followers.

Messianic fanaticism, it will immediately be objected, is not peculiar to the modern world, let alone to fascism; on the contrary, it will be said, it may be traced back to antiquity. Thus the Jews regarded their God, Jehovah, not merely as the God of Israel, but as the God of all nations and all history. What distinguishes messianic fanaticism of this kind from the fascist type, however, is the fact that the Jews never claimed that their messianic status derived from any intrinsic excellence or merit on their part; they claimed only that God, by a free act of grace, had chosen Israel for his people, regardless of any peculiar merit of their own. Until the advent of modern nationalist doctrine, all messianic movements conformed to this pattern; they derived their mission, that is, from a source outside the chosen people rather than from a claim to intrinsic superiority over other peoples. Since it was the claim to intrinsic superiority which was to be exploited by fascism, it is necessary to consider how this idea entered the western political tradition.

The idea that one people might be intrinsically superior to another is in fact a relatively recent one, which appeared in Europe only towards the end of the eighteenth century. Until that time, the primary conception of order was of an international civilization to which all particular states and individuals were subject. In practice, this civilization was identified with the supra-national order of 'Christendom', whose cosmopolitan status was embodied in theories of natural law which can be traced back as far as classical antiquity. At the end of the eighteenth century, however, there appeared a new conception of international order which revealed an increasingly marked tendency to reject the ideal of an

161

overriding, universal order of civilization in favour of a stress upon the intrinsic value of particular national cultures. From that time down to the present day, the western world has been confronted by two potentially incompatible conceptions of order, one of which is universal, whilst the other is more or less nationalistic.

Not surprisingly, it was in Germany, where national hostility to the French victories was especially bitter, that the new stress upon the importance of preserving the diverse cultures and customs of the different nations of the world received its original theoretical formulation. The preservation of cultural diversity, indeed, was rapidly elevated to the status of a divinely ordained mission. As one of the proponents of the new nationalist doctrine, Schleiermacher, expressed the matter: 'Every nationality is destined through its peculiar organization and its place in the world to represent a certain side of the divine image . . . For it is God who directly assigns to each nationality its definite task on earth and inspires it with a definite spirit in order to glorify Himself through each one in a peculiar manner.'[52] The same sentiments are evident in the works of Herder, the thinker whose name is most closely associated with the early formulation of modern nationalist doctrine. 'All the works of God', Herder wrote, 'have this property, that although they belong to a whole, which no eyes can see, each is in itself a whole, and bears the divine character of its destination.'[53] Applying this to politics, Herder could confidently assert that 'every human perfection is national', and then move on to draw the conclusion that, 'He who has lost his patriotic spirit has lost himself and the whole world about him.'[54]

Herder himself was a man of pacific intent, but the nationalist doctrine which he advanced would obviously have devastating political implications if any attempt were made to apply it to the international order. These disastrous implications, it may be noticed, would inevitably be most apparent in the area of eastern and central Europe – the area, that is, which was to witness the rise of fascism and dictatorship after the First World War. In that part of the world diverse national groups, distinguished by differences of race, language and religion, were held together by traditional dynastic regimes. It was these regimes, above all, which were threatened by the new diversitarian creed, with its stress upon the desirability of securing self-determination for the different cultural units out of which they were formed. And it was the final collapse of these regimes during the First World War which destroyed the balance of power in Europe and opened the way to fascist dreams of world conquest in both Italy and Germany.

In retrospect it is clear that the two different visions of order which characterized the European political world at the end of the eighteenth century were in principle totally incompatible with one another right from the beginning. Not until well over a century later, however, was the advent of fascism to make the potential conflict between the old universalist ideal and the new 'diversitarian' one fully apparent. Why, one must ask, did this tension remain concealed from sight for so long? The explanation is simple: it is that the new nationalist doctrine was initially assumed to be a fundamentally pacific and progressive development of the democratic ideal of popular self-government. What made this belief a plausible one was the fact that most nineteenth-century nationalist thinkers disclaimed any intention of rejecting the old vision of a universal order; they claimed, on the contrary, that the new philosophy of diversity merely offered a way of re-establishing the old universal vision of civilization upon a far better – because more truly popular and democratic – foundation.

The idea by which they eliminated any potential conflict between the ideal of international unity, on the one hand, and respect for cultural diversity, on the other, is not difficult to detect. In the course of defending the diversity of the international order, thinkers like Herder always assumed that all the distinct cultures of the world possessed an equal value, since each was a manifestation of God's creation. For that reason these cultures constituted what Herder called 'shades of the same great picture, extending through all ages, and over all parts of the Earth'.[55] The diversity inherent in the cultural nationalism favoured by Herder, in other words, still remained firmly situated within a vision of international harmony and universal peace.

But was it realistic, one may properly ask, to assume that nationalist doctrine would be able to maintain this pacific attitude? Was it not far more likely that enthusiasm for a particular culture would instead breed contempt for other nations, with the result that the original belief in the equality of all cultures would increasingly be replaced by a tendency on the part of nationalist thinkers to stress the intrinsic superiority of their own? By the middle of the nineteenth century, at the latest, belief in the equality of all cultures had already worn very thin. By then, almost every country in the western world had learned to think of itself as morally and culturally superior to all other countries, and as entrusted with the divinely appointed mission of redeeming its 'decadent' neighbours. In France, for example, Michelet announced (in 1846) that the history of every nation was 'mutilated', with the sole exception, of course, of the history of France itself: 'avec elle, vous sauvez le monde'. Poland's greatest poet, Mickiewicz, had previously addressed the Poles in similar terms, informing them that Poland was 'the Christ among the Nations', and that all other nations worshipped false gods. Russia, likewise, was presented by nearly all her greatest writers, from Khomiakov to Dostoevsky, as the 'God-loving nation', entitled to look with contempt upon the decadent and decaying West.[56] It was in Italy, however, that the most colourful of this confused but well-intentioned generation of nationalist ideologues appeared. This was Mazzini.

Mazzini was typical of his age in his reluctance to abandon the idea that in some mysterious way a belief in the intrinsic superiority of the mission he assigned to the Italian nation was perfectly compatible with acknowledging the right of other nations to claim an equally valid mission of their own. With this reassuring thought in mind, he felt able to ignore problematic details, such as the fact that the lines upon which he wished to reconstruct the European world in accordance with the Italian mission would automatically have meant, for example, the destruction of Italy's neighbour, Austria. Nothing, in his view, must be allowed to obscure the fact that twice before the world had been united by Rome, Imperial and Papal, and that the greatest need of the age was for a new Roman hegemony, to be exercised by a regenerated Italy over a European world whose peoples no longer possessed any independent initiative of their own. 'Why', he asked, 'should not a new Rome, the Rome of the Italian people . . . arise to create a third and still vaster unity; to link together and harmonize earth and heaven, right and duty; and utter, not to individuals but to peoples, the great word Association – to make known to free men and equals their mission here below?'[57] The fact that Mazzini's rhetoric about the third Rome could eventually be taken over by Mussolini suggests how unpacific the universal aspect of nationalist ideology might prove to be.

It was not only the 'third Rome' ideal which was formulated long before Mussolini appeared upon the European scene, however. By the middle of the nineteenth century the foreign policy programme which Hitler was to implement in 1938–9 had also been clearly mapped out. Ironically, this programme of conquest was not the work of men who were considered reactionaries, or even extremists; it was the work, on the contrary, of the members of the Frankfurt Parliament – men, that is, who were generally considered to hold the most liberal and enlightened opinions of their time.

It was in 1848 that a group of German radicals formed the Frankfurt Parliament in order to create a unified, liberal German state within frontiers determined entirely by an appeal to 'natural', cultural and linguistic considerations. They believed that their enterprise was an inherently peaceful one. A very different impression, however, emerges when the methods by which they prepared to combine the different peoples of central Europe into a united Germany are considered.

Since the criterion of nationhood adopted by the Parliament was the linguistic one, it followed that the proposed Reich should include all German-speaking people. But this would have meant that the new Reich should definitely not include, for example, the whole population of Austria, since many subjects of the Habsburg Monarchy were not of the German race. Yet to reduce the size of the Reich in this way was not, of course, the purpose of the patriotic Frankfurt liberals. They therefore tried to have the best of every world. On the one hand, they appealed to the 'natural' linguistic frontiers, whilst also

165

appealing, on the other, to the 'artificial' historical frontiers of the Reich. Since these historical frontiers had of course varied at different times, this latter approach only provided a further source of ambiguity. In order to round things off, they appealed in addition to the German need for 'living-space'. Thus Trieste, for example, was part of the Habsburg Monarchy. The inhabitants of Trieste, however, spoke Italian: should they not therefore belong to a united Italy, rather than to a united Germany? Schuselka, a leading radical at the Frankfurt Parliament, easily settled the matter in Germany's favour in a fashion which makes clear that later Nazi rhetoric about living space added nothing to the rhetoric already found in nineteenth-century activist crusades. 'A great nation', he declared, 'requires space (*Raum*) to fulfil its world destiny, and I would rather die a thousand times than, for instance, renounce Trieste because they speak Italian.'[58]

In view of the policies by which Nazism subsequently undertook to unify Germany within its supposed natural frontiers, the attitude of the Frankfurt liberals towards the Poles is no less instructive. As liberals, the members of the Parliament proclaimed that they stood for the emancipation of all peoples. Inspired by this spirit, they expressed especial concern for the restoration of Polish sovereignty. But what then was to happen to the Polish-speaking districts of Prussia, in view of the fact that Poland was partitioned at the time between Prussia, Russia and Austria? Were these Polish districts to be given some measure of autonomy of their own, as consistency seemed to require, or would the Frankfurt liberals sacrifice their concern for national emancipation to their desire for German unity?

The Polish-speaking part of Prussia is of especial interest in this connection, since in that part Germans were in a minority; but the idea that this Polish-speaking region should enjoy autonomy merely because the Poles were in a vast majority was soon disposed of by the German radicals. A Prussian delegate, known for his liberal views, quickly solved the problem. 'Are half a million Germans to live under a German government and administration and form part of the great German Fatherland', he asked, 'or are they to be relegated to the inferior position of naturalized foreigners subject to another nation of lesser cultural content than themselves?' Here, the postulate of universal cultural equality originally made by early nationalists like Herder has obviously been rejected, to be replaced – by what? The same Prussian delegate provided the answer when he dismissed, not only the Polish claim to national independence, but any further claims to independence which might come from other directions, in so far as they seemed likely to prove detrimental to the ambitions of a powerful neighbour state. 'Mere existence', he observed, 'does not entitle a people to political independence: only the force to assert itself as a state among the others [gives that entitlement].'[59] The new cultural nationalism, then, revealed at an early stage how fanatical idealism might combine with naked power politics in a way which could easily inspire the kind of expansionist crusade fascism was to elevate into its ruling conception of international policy. Ironically, the sole interest of that later development lies in the fact already noticed, which is that it was supposedly liberal and progressive thought which had originally paved the way for fascist militancy.

Long before the appearance of Mussolini and Hitler, in short, the European world had become familiar with extravagant claims to a messianic mission advanced by activist politicians within every European nationalist movement. To this tradition of messianic nationalism, fascist ideology added no new intellectual ingredient. Even Nazi racialism involved no novel departure from the tradition, since claims to racial superiority had frequently jostled alongside the more usual nineteenth-century nationalist claims to cultural superiority. Whilst fascism added nothing of substance to the earlier messianic tradition, however, it nevertheless modified that tradition in one vital respect: it destroyed the complacent assumption that nationalism was a basically progressive doctrine which was inseparably connected with the twin ideals of individual liberty and international harmony.

5. *Autarky* The belief that a world composed of democratic, self-determining nation-states would inevitably be a peaceful and harmonious one derived a considerable part of its

167

intellectual appeal from an important but dubious assumption about the likely impact of modern economic development upon the international order. It is this assumption that must now be briefly considered.

The assumption, whose implausibility was not exposed until the advent of fascism, was that the world-wide growth of industry and commerce would gradually soften national rivalries and in that way intensify the overall trend towards world peace. It was this delusion which inspired, for example, the influential nineteenth-century Saint-Simonian school, whose doctrine provides a good illustration of the aspect of modern progressive orthodoxy in question. According to Saint-Simonian doctrine, once the industrialization process is properly organized it will necessarily create 'a state in which the different nations scattered over the face of the earth appear only as parts of a vast workshop, labouring under a common impulse to achieve a common goal'.[60] Unfortunately, what progressive sentiment of this kind failed to appreciate was that the concept of national self-determination was susceptible to two conflicting interpretations, which carried with them entirely different practical implications for economic policy.

On the one hand, self-determination might be taken to imply peaceful economic policies which aimed at preventing excessive dependence upon foreign countries for crucial raw materials. This, for example, was how the American statesman, Alexander Hamilton, interpreted the principle of national self-determination in 1791, when he submitted a report to the House of Representatives in which he urged the American government to adopt a policy of economic autarky. 'Not only the wealth, but the independence and security of a country', Hamilton stated, 'appear to be materially connected with the prosperity of manufactures.' Therefore, he concluded, 'Every nation, with a view to these great objects, ought to endeavour to possess within itself all the essentials of natural supply.' From this it followed, he observed, that the policy of the American Government should be the promotion of such manufactures 'as will tend to render the United States independent of foreign nations for military and other essential supplies'.[61]

On the other hand, this moderate and flexible approach

might be rejected in favour of an entirely opposite interpretation of the economic implications of national self-determination. Instead of being confined to securing peacefully what Hamilton called 'the essentials of natural supply', self-determination might instead be interpreted to mean the achievement of total economic self-sufficiency. A state which adopted the latter interpretation would then have to choose between two different ways of implementing it. One way was by minimizing its needs, in order to permit it to withdraw from the international order; the other was by a programme of world domination aimed at securing complete control over all the resources of the earth. It was this latter interpretation of the principle of national self-determination to which fascist ideology was openly committed, as both Hitler and Mussolini made clear.

In a conversation with Otto Strasser on 22 May 1930, Hitler vehemently rejected Strasser's demand for the creation of economic autarky by policies which would insulate Germany from the rest of the world. Replying to Strasser, Hitler insisted that Germany must acknowledge its dependence upon the world economic order, since, 'We are bound to import all important raw materials, and we are not less bound to export the goods manufactured by us . . . we cannot stop this nor do we wish to.' The proper task of the Nazi party, he continued, is therefore 'to organize on a large scale the whole world so that each country produces what it can best produce while the white race, the Nordic race, undertakes the organization of this gigantic plan. Believe me, National Socialism as a whole would be worth nothing if it were restricted merely to Germany and did not seek the supremacy of the superior race over the entire world for at least a thousand to two thousand years.' This then was what the Nazi programme of economic autarky implied. In Hitler's eyes, of course, it did not amount to a programme of domination or exploitation, since 'the lower race is destined for tasks different from those of the higher race'. The lower race would accordingly be grateful, if it were sufficiently intelligent, for the rational reorganization of the world which Hitler proposed to bring about.[62]

Like Hitler, Mussolini also adopted the militant,

expansionist version of the autarkic ideal. In the course of outlining his policy and ideas for the future in 1936, for example, Mussolini explained that, 'Italy can and must attain the maximum of economic independence for peace and war. The whole of the Italian economic system must be directed towards this supreme necessity, on which depends the future of the Italian people . . . This plan is determined by one single consideration: that our nation will be called to war.'[63] Mussolini's demand that Italy should be given a 'place in the sun' through the creation of a new Roman Empire, however, was at once more vague and less brutal than Hitler's expansionist programme. The Italian regime, indeed, was notable for the sheer ineptitude of its efforts to convert the Fascist economy into a self-sufficient military unit. In practice, what happened was that a regime which had always depended more upon ideological propaganda than upon deeds finally fell foul of its own mythology. This propaganda, whose purpose had been to vaunt Italy's superiority over other nations, succeeded in the end only in convincing Mussolini himself that victory would be almost effortless. Accordingly, he made no order for general mobilization, and even left Italian munitions production in a half-hearted condition, in order that the factories should be ready for the production of civilian goods which would be necessary to compete with Germany in the post-war economic boom which he expected to follow upon victory. To treat all this (in S.J. Woolf's phrase) as no more than 'cheerful pragmatism'[64] or, worse still, as a positive contribution to the 'modernization' of Italy, is wide of the mark. The fact is that Mussolini's autarkic policies kept the overall rate of Italian economic growth at almost the same level for two decades, and made sense only as a device for maintaining the economy and the masses in the barrack-room state of unity which Hitler, in a more successful way, imposed upon Germany.

The fascist policy of economic autarky is nevertheless instructive. Throughout the nineteenth century, as was just observed, the principle of national self-determination had generally been regarded as a natural extension of the democratic ideal of popular sovereignty, and hence as an important stage in the creation of a world without war. In 1919, the principle had been made the foundation of the peace settlement and the basis of the new democratic world order which it was intended to bring into existence. What fascism revealed was that the principle of national self-determination could never provide the foundation for a stable world order. Far from being a pacific principle, national self-determination might well be used to justify messianic claims to cultural superiority, on the one hand, and unlimited claims to world domination in the interest of achieving economic autarky, on the other. Once again, however, the sole novelty of fascist ideology in this respect lies in the fact that the fascists alone openly professed militant policies which other activists – most notably communist regimes – pursue without explicitly acknowledging it.

The implications of economic autarky for the internal structure of the state had in fact been made clear long before fascism appeared. They were spelt out right at the beginning of the nineteenth century by the German philosopher Fichte, one of the most influential early proponents of the activist style of politics. In his *Addresses to the German Nation*, Fichte demanded that Germany should free itself from dependence upon foreign countries by a policy of 'inner self-sufficiency and commercial independence'.[65] Almost a decade before his *Addresses*, Fichte reminded his listeners, he had explained how this was to be done: it was by the creation of what he termed a 'closed commercial state'. In a short work with that title, he had indicated what complete autarky involved. In the interest of brevity, we may accept the summary of the measures proposed by Fichte given by an acute but very indignant intellectual historian. Fichte, he observes, argued in favour of 'a planned economy, quota systems, concealed inflation, a blocked currency, state barter agreements, artificial production of substitute materials, intensive armament, living-space, forcible unresisted occupation of territory, complete economic co-ordination of such territory, transfer of population, and cultivated nationalism. The words', the same scholar continues, 'are different: *Lebensraum* and *Gleichschaltung* do not appear; it is as yet not *ersatz* but *stellvertretend*, not *Einmaschierung* but *Occupationszung*. But the ideas are the same [viz. as in Hitler's National Socialism].'[66]

171

In face of this fierce indictment, it is hardly surprising to find that other scholars have hastened to defend Fichte from the charge of embryonic Nazism.[67] The result, needless to say, has been an acrimonious but unprofitable debate which may be disregarded for present purposes because of the manifest anachronism which lies at the heart of it. Far from being an embryonic Nazi (whatever that may mean), Fichte was a latter-day disciple of the eighteenth-century Cameralist school, whose main concern was to make enlightened despotism even more enlightened and despotic than it had been under the Prussia of Frederick the Great. Nevertheless, Fichte's early delineation of *The Closed Commercial State* exhibits with relentless clarity the inner logic of the activist style of politics, which always points towards the total regimentation of society. His ideal of economic autarky, however, was to remain an intellectual's pipedream until well over a century later, when fascism finally brought it out of the world of political theory and into the political arena itself.

So far, attention has been concentrated upon the common framework of ideas which links Mussolini's movement with Hitler's. By way of concluding the present chapter, however, it must be acknowledged that the fascist *Weltanschauung* has, as it were, very ragged edges which severely restrict the extent to which it can be treated as a monolithic intellectual construction. In particular, three vital aspects of the two movements defy incorporation into a single framework.

The first of these aspects relates to a major point of doctrinal divergence between the two ideologies. Whereas Nazism rested on the doctrine of race, Italian ideologues always stressed the non-biological, voluntarist basis of their movement. The second aspect relates to an overall divergence in tone between the two ideologies, rather than to any specific point of doctrinal difference between them. Although the Italian Fascist movement prided itself on the brutality of the squads, the policies of the regime were mild by comparison with those associated with Nazism. Finally, a third divergence between the movements relates to the different degree of success each had in penetrating the national life of the two countries in which they occurred. In broad terms, Italian Fascism 'was too casual, and perhaps too self-consciously on the defensive, to be as insidious and deep-rooted an evil as Nazism'.[68] Since these differences between the two movements are intelligible only when they are related to the different cultural and political traditions of the two nations concerned, the relevant aspects of the traditions in question must now be indicated.

The first major difference between the two movements, which concerns their attitude to race, involves a major divergence over the status to be assigned to politics. For Nazism, Hitler wrote, 'The State is only the vessel and the race is what it contains. The vessel can have meaning', he continued, 'only if it preserves and safeguards the contents. Otherwise it is worthless.' From this, he said, it follows that 'it is not the task of the State to create human capabilities, but only to assure free scope for the exercise of capabilities that already exist'.[69] For Mussolini, by contrast, 'It is not the nation that guarantees the State, as according to the old nationalistic concept which served as the basis of the political theories of the national State of the nineteenth century. Rather the nation is created by the State, which gives to the people, unconscious of its own moral unity, a will and therefore an effective existence.'[70]

Why, it must be asked, did Hitler and Mussolini differ so greatly in their attitude towards politics in general and racism in particular? The answer becomes clear as soon as one notices the different historical situations created in Italy and Germany by unification. Whereas German nationalists could take for granted the cultural and linguistic unity of their country, Italian nationalists could not. As a leading nationalist ideologue, Corradini, remarked in 1911, 'Italy has never ever had and still does not have a national language, except in literature.'[71] In this situation, the idea that Italian nationalists might pose as the defenders of an Italian *Volk* was clearly a non-starter, since the Italian *Volk* was nowhere in evidence. Although frequent references to race may indeed be found in Italian nationalist literature both before and after the advent of fascism, the word was largely a rhetorical one without any of the biological connotations which were vital to it in Nazi usage. A leading

173

fascist writer like Gentile, for example, emphatically rejected any sort of naturalism, biological or otherwise, as a basis for nationalism – especially if its adherents were given to making assertions of collective superiority and inferiority.[72] In 1938, however, the position appears at first sight to have changed, with the declaration by the regime of an official racialist policy in the *Manifesto of Fascist Racism*.[73]

But although the Manifesto was undoubtedly influenced by Nazi ideas, it also reveals clearly the ways in which the biological concept of race was always qualified, in Italy, by totally non-biological ideas which were intended to reconcile racialism with the Italian stress on the voluntarist and therefore non-biological doctrine of fascism. Section 3 of the *Manifesto*, for example, explained that Italian racist doctrine was mainly intended 'to provide for the Italians a physical and psychological *normative model* of the human race . . . and to instil in Italians an ideal of superior consciousness of themselves . . .' (italics added). Not only was Italian racism given a 'normative' and 'psychic' character quite alien to Nazism, however; racial unity was held, in addition, to be based upon historical 'continuity of blood' rather than upon genetic purity (section 6). Italian racialist theory, in other words, opposed an historical, political and dynamic interpretation of race to the antihistorical, biological and entirely static race theory of National Socialism.[74] In Italian theory, furthermore, race has nothing to do with messianic claims to superiority, since, 'To say that human races exist is not to say *a priori* that there exist superior or inferior races, but only to say that there exist different human races' (section 1). Finally, unlike the Nazi concept of race, the Italian one did not identify racial unity with biological purity. Thus sections 2 and 3 of the *Manifesto* recognized that every European race was composed of diverse minor races; in accordance with the political and historical emphasis in Italian racist doctrine, national unity was thus explained by treating each nation as an historic breeding ground whose members would in due course acquire common physical and psychological characteristics.

Although the ideas of cultural, linguistic and racial unity used by Nazism were not suited to the ideology of Italian

174

Fascism, either because they did not seem to fit Italian history or else because they did not fit in with the regime's requirements, there was one obvious source of Italian unity from which Mussolini was able to derive some tactical advantage, in spite of its ideological limitations. This was religion. From the 1840s onwards, nationalists like Gioberti had already attempted to exploit this fact for political purposes by identifying Italy with Catholicism. The Pope, however, was naturally opposed to the politicization of religion, not only because Catholicism was essentially a supra-national creed, but also because secular nationalism threatened the territorial position of the Papacy in Rome. The Catholic religion, then, was hardly an adequate basis for Italian Fascism; but there was a strong Machiavellian touch, nevertheless, in the Lateran Pact (1929), by which Mussolini smoothed the ruffled feathers of the Papacy and won its qualified support for his movement.

It still remains, however, to notice the most radical of the techniques to which Italian Fascism resorted in order to provide an ideological basis for national unity. This was by the creation of an entirely New Man, *homo fascista*. Nazism, by contrast, never set out to create a New Man, since in Germany the ideal man was already supposed to be in existence: the Nazi problem was therefore not that of creating him, but of excavating him from the decadent overlay of modern civilization beneath which he was buried.

This fundamental divergence of the two movements becomes intelligible as soon as it is related to the entirely different situations faced by nationalists in each country after the achievement of unification. In Germany, as has just been noticed, linguistic and cultural unity could be taken for granted after political unification, but in Italy the situation was entirely different. Massimo D'Azeglio succinctly formulated the central problem of Italian nationalism when he observed (in 1870) that although Italy had been unified, there were still no Italians. It was this task – the task, that is, of creating new Italians to live in the new Italy – that Fascism was to claim as its unique contribution to Italian history. From this point of view, Fascism was merely a radical continuation (as the Fascists themselves insisted) of the *Risorgimento* ideal of national unity.

175

Unfortunately, the contrast between Nazi and Italian Fascist attitudes to the New Man has recently been seriously misinterpreted by eminent scholars like Renzo de Felice and Michael Ledeen.[75] In their view, Mussolini's concern with the New Man indicates that Italian Fascism was a fundamentally constructive movement, by contrast with the destructive anti-modernism of Nazism. Mussolini, however, was inspired far less by any constructive or modernizing intention than by a fanatical desire to convert the Italians into the kind of *dramatis personae* whom he needed in order to live out his dreams of heroism and national destiny. In this respect, the Fascist New Man and the Nazi buried one are not so very different; both, that is, belong to a style of politics which is ruled primarily by myth, and only incidentally by reality.

The various considerations just mentioned help to explain why the ideology of Italian Fascism could not afford to down-grade politics in the way in which Nazism did. There is, however, a second major difference between the two movements which still remains to be accounted for – that which relates to their overall tone rather than to any specific doctrinal divergence between them. Whilst it would be far too complacent to dismiss Italian Fascism as a mere piece of *opera bouffe*, the Italian movement certainly lacked the frenzied nihilism of the Nazi one. In order to understand why there was so much hot air in the ideology of the Italian movement by contrast with the German one, it is much more relevant to recall the entirely different international situation of the two regimes.

From the capture of Rome in 1870 down to the death of Mussolini in 1946, much of modern Italian politics had rested upon an illusion. This illusion was the belief that Italian unification provided a conclusive demonstration of Italian great power status and was merely the prelude to a period of Italian international expansion. According to the logic of the illusion, any politician who did not base Italian foreign policy upon a belief in Italy's great power status and historic destiny had perpetrated a shameful betrayal of the heroic *Risorgimento* heritage. Crispi, during the 1870s and 1880s, was the first to make a career out of peddling this gross misrepresentation of how Italian unity had been achieved; Mussolini's Fascist rhetoric merely followed in his footsteps, just as, in Germany, Nazi rhetoric followed in the footsteps of the 1848 Frankfurt pan-Germans.

The reality behind the grand illusion upon which Italian Fascism rested is worth recalling. The unification of Italy had been achieved, not from a position of international power, but from one of weakness. Cavour's diplomacy, above all, had skilfully exploited French, Prussian and British rivalry in order to achieve what Italian power alone would never have sufficed to achieve. To those who were not blinded by dreams about an Italian messianic mission, the weakness of the Italian position had for long been perfectly obvious: they saw clearly that Italy could succeed only by restricting herself to the modest and realistic policy by which Piedmont had skilfully managed to derive advantage from an intrinsically weak position. The art of Piedmontese diplomacy was to tilt the European balance of power in the Italian favour by exploiting conflict between the great powers. For Italy to desert this policy and seek instead an independent great power status in her own right would not only overburden her relatively primitive domestic economy; it would also inevitably reduce her foreign ambitions to a matter of mere pretence and posturing. The truth of the matter, as one scholar remarks of Italy, was that, 'Her most successful foreign ministers were those who recognized her essential limitations and were not lured by ambition to attempt more than preserving the balance or righting it when upset.'[76]

The divergent international realities which help to explain the occasionally comic posturing of Italian Fascism, on the one hand, and the destructive virulence of Nazism, on the other, should now be clear. From 1860 onwards grandiose dreams of Italian expansion rested on an illusory basis, whereas in Germany the expansionist policies of the Second and Third Reichs were built upon the reality of power. In this perspective, the aggressive international posturing which Mussolini began at the time of the Corfu incident[77] and maintained until his downfall was merely a desperate attempt to perpetuate the delusions of grandeur fostered by unification, long before the advent of fascism.

Even the cult of war for its own sake, it may be noticed, had been anticipated by extreme nationalist thinkers before Italian Fascism adopted the cult for its own ends. When Austria finally withdrew from Italy in 1870, there was naturally a danger that nationalist sentiment would lose the momentum it had previously been given by the presence of a foreign enemy. The simplest and surest way of maintaining that momentum was by substituting a new enemy for the old one. In practice, however, this was not so easy, since there was no enemy in sight. The only thing to do, therefore, was to invent one. That was the technique pioneered by Crispi, who was later to be hailed by Fascist intellectuals like Volpe as the precursor of Mussolini and the true heir of the heroic *Risorgimento* vision of Italian destiny. An example of Crispi's policies is provided by the anti-French war scare which he manufactured in 1889. Crispi informed England that the French Navy was moving on Spezia. Subsequent British information revealed that Crispi had acted entirely on the basis of an unsubstantiated rumour from a secret agent in the Vatican.[78] It was not until a little later, however, with the appearance of extreme nationalists like Papini and D'Annunzio, that Crispi's war scare policies were converted into a systematic war cult, accompanied by all the predictable verbiage about its moral, spiritual and political benefits. 'Life is really lived', Papini declared, 'only when opposing others and the struggle of nations has till now been forged in the mighty blaze and blood of war.'[79] The Fascists merely perpetuated this already well-established cult when they hailed Italian entry into the war (in 1915) as the initial step towards that condition of national spiritual unity which Cavour, Garibaldi, and their successors had failed to bring about. The aim of the Fascist revolution, in this perspective, was to consolidate the wartime experience of national unity by giving it an external and material political embodiment. In the phrase used by Gentile and Mussolini, the spiritual unity experienced during the war was to be consolidated by creating the Fascist 'ethical State'.

The third major contrast between Italian Fascism and Nazism is that relating neither to doctrine nor to tone, but to the different degree of penetration into the life of the two countries which each achieved. By comparison with Nazism, the degree of penetration which the ideology of Italian Fascism achieved in

Italian life was relatively shallow. For this there were a number of reasons. One was the restriction upon Mussolini's totalitarian aspirations created by the need to compromise with the rival authority of the monarchy and the Church. Another was the power of the provincial leaders (*ras*) and traditional local clientèles, for which there was no equivalent in Germany, where Hitler was able to establish a centralized party organization from the start. A third was the existence of the South, which created the problem of the 'two Italies' which has lain at the heart of Italian political life from unification down to the present day. In the South, the highly personal, non-ideological pattern of political life reduced Fascism to little more than a cult of 'Mussolinism'. In Germany, no comparable division in national life existed. In Italy, an early recognition of the extent of the problem presented by the South had come shortly after unification, in Villari's *Letters from the South*, which condemned the folly of all those who used delusions of international grandeur in order to distract attention from Italy's internal problems. 'It is high time', Villari proclaimed, 'that Italy began to realize that she has inside herself an enemy which is stronger than Austria. Somehow,' Villari continued, 'we must face up to our multitude of illiterates, the ineptitude of our bureaucratic machines, the ignorance of our professors, the existence of people who in politics are mere children, the incapacity of our diplomats and generals, the lack of skills in our workers, our patriarchal system of agriculture, and on top of all, the rhetoric which gnaws our bones. It is not the quadrilateral of fortresses at Mantua and Verona which has arrested our path,' Villari concluded, 'but the quadrilateral of seventeen million illiterates.'[80]

Over half a century later, during the 1930s, Carlo Levi argued that nothing had changed in the interval; Italy was still 'two civilizations [which] could have no communication except by a miracle'.[81] One civilization, that of the North, was 'the world of creative activity and cultural values'.[82] The other civilization, that of the South, was a world not of industry and culture, but of the land; a peasant world, that is, in which men 'live submerged in a world that rolls on independent of their will . . . where there can be neither happiness, as literary devotees

179

of the land conceive of it, nor hope, because those two are adjuncts of personality, whilst here there is only the grim passivity of a sorrowful Nature'.[83] It was over the uncomprehending heads of the occupants of this rural world that Mussolini's regime ruled. 'Whether this regime was tyrannical or paternalistic, dictatorial or democratic,' Levi observed, 'it remained to them monolithic, centralized and remote. This', he explained, 'was why the political leaders and many peasants could never understand one another. The politicians oversimplified things, even while they clothed them in philosophical exaggerations.' The Fascists' solution to the problem of the South, Levi acidly remarks, was simple: they ignored it, so far as they possibly could.[84] Alongside Levi's work, we may set the similar portraits of the South and of the 'two Italies' problem which it had created given earlier by Ignazio Silone in his autobiographical novel, *Fontamara*,[85] and more recently by Luigi Barzini in his book *The Italians*.[86]

The three most striking differences between Nazism and Italian Fascism have now been considered. It may well be objected at this point, however, that a fourth difference requires attention. This is the fact that the Nazi movement occurred in an advanced industrial society whilst the Italian one occurred in an extremely backward one. This point, however, has already been dealt with, in the course of the earlier critique of Marxist and developmental theory. All that need be repeated here is that the activist style of politics is not dependent upon industrialization and advanced technology; as C.W. Cassinelli observed, in a recent study of revolutionary ideologies, 'Devices for rapid communication have been the only necessities, and radios, telephones, and aircraft can be imported by very "undeveloped" countries. Technological sophistication is also not required in order to bring rudimentary literacy to a large population, in case revolutionary education is to depend on the written word.'[87] So far as the activist aspirations of Mussolini's regime are concerned, then, the important point is that they were restricted (especially during the first decades of its existence) by the relatively primitive condition of the technological developments upon which the regime had to rely for propaganda purposes. It was only in the mid-1930s, for example, that the radio superseded the printed word as the chief instrument of Fascist propaganda.[88] Until its development, the illiteracy of large sections of the population precluded any serious attempt to create the all-embracing Fascist 'ethical state', based upon the direct relationship between the leader and the mass which is the essence of this type of regime.

One final matter requires consideration. It is sometimes said that in spite of the major differences just mentioned, Italy and Germany share a vital characteristic which explains why both experienced fascism. This is the fact that both countries only achieved political unification at a relatively late stage. This view, however, is misleading: it was not the lateness of unification but rather the *kind* of unification aimed at that aided the fascist cause. In both countries the ideal of unification was shaped and moulded within the framework of a new activist style of politics which tended naturally towards demagogic extremism. The fact that unification itself was the work of politicians who despised activism is beside the point; what matters is the fact that they themselves encouraged activist dreams for their own purposes. It was not so much late unification, then, that gave Mussolini and Hitler their opportunity as a well-established style of politics which promised utopia tomorrow in return for gullibility today.

The general conclusion to emerge from this analysis of the fascist *Weltanschauung* is that the intellectual appeal of fascism derived principally from the skill with which it exploited the oldest and most potent of human dreams – the dream, that is, of creating spiritual unity and purity within societies whose institutions had come to appear divisive and corrupt. The trouble with idealism of this kind, however, is that it always leads men to concentrate upon ends and ignore means. Indifference to means meant, in particular, outright hostility to every manifestation of a limited style of politics, since that style appeared to incarnate everything most likely to destroy the ideal of spiritual unity. It was their mutual hostility to limited politics which held together the otherwise disparate intellectuals who wittingly and unwittingly supported the two principal fascist movements. Intellectual support for fascism, in sum, derived less from direct fanatical commitment than from self-deception, from an arrogant contempt for constitutional forms, from naive ideas about cleaning the Augean stables, and from a susceptibility to the various kinds of flattery by which both regimes were careful to court the intellectuals. If we move from history to theory for a moment, however, then the enduring interest of fascist ideology is to be found in the light it throws upon the inner logic and structure of the new activist style of politics which has shaped all the movement regimes of the twentieth century. In other versions of the activist ideology, such as communism, vestiges of an older European cosmopolitan and constitutional political tradition sometimes continue to survive. In fascist ideology, however, these older values are openly swept away, and the goal of totalitarian despotism is at length frankly proclaimed as the activist political ideal. With this sombre thought in mind one may turn, finally, to consider the relevance of fascism for the future course of twentieth-century political life.

6 Fascism and the Future

To speculate about the significance of fascism for the future will inevitably create the suspicion that the narrow confines of intellectual analysis are about to be abandoned for the expansive dubieties of crystal balls and prophecy. The main purpose of this final chapter, however, is not to indulge in flights of journalistic fancy but to examine briefly the two most influential interpretations of the relevance of fascism for the contemporary world to be found in current literature on the subject.*

According to the first interpretation, fascism is essentially an inter-war phenomenon which has very little relevance for the changed conditions of the post-war world. The most erudite formulation of this first view is Ernst Nolte's theory of the 'epochal' nature of fascism. Since Nolte's work was considered in detail in an earlier chapter it is only the relevance of his theory for predicting a recurrence of fascism which need concern us here. In Nolte's opinion, fascism would never have occurred without the widespread fear of a 'red peril', intensified as this was by the uncertainties attendant upon post-war social dislocation and economic recession. During the decades since the Second World War, Nolte maintains, the spectre of a 'red peril' has disappeared from western politics, largely because increasing prosperity, the Welfare State, and redistributive taxation have helped to integrate and stabilize the structure of modern European political life. Although a variety of fascist and neo-fascist movements have persisted into the post-war period, these are dismissed as the rumblings of an extinct volcano. It might be added (although Nolte himself does not make this

* The Marxist interpretation is of course still influential, but even the most refined forms of it fail to eliminate the insuperable difficulties created by the ultimate denial of the autonomy of politics. Since these were examined in an earlier chapter, I have not returned to the subject in this one.

183

point) that the post-war period has been marked by the unification of nationalism with socialism at which fascism aimed – albeit by gradualist and constitutional methods which were rejected by fascist ideology itself, of course. During the past three or four decades, in short, the ground would seem to have been completely cut from under the feet of fascism. Our first task is obviously to consider how justified this optimism is.

This view is plausible to the extent that the inter-war fear of a red peril which fascism exploited so skilfully is no longer a significant factor in European political life. In other respects, however, it is unsatisfactory, for a reason which has already been elaborated in sufficient detail for it to require no further comment. This is that thinkers who treat fascism in this way are generally too superficial in their handling of its deeper roots in modern European intellectual and political life, and especially in their analysis of its relationship to both democracy and socialism.

According to a second currently influential view fascism, far from being an inter-war phenomenon, is a precursor of the future course of twentieth-century political life at large. Prominent amongst proponents of this pessimistic outlook are thinkers who argue that the original causes of fascism were spiritual rather than socio-economic or political. Depending upon the ideological commitment of the thinker concerned, these spiritual causes are variously identified as the Death of God, a world without love, a ubiquitous consumer mentality, a sense of alienation and rootlessness, a general lack of moral discipline, and a petty, self-pitying egoism. Since these symptoms of spiritual malaise may plausibly be said to have intensified rather than abated during the past three decades, fascism is naturally held to be of even more significance today than it was during the inter-war era. For present purposes, the most obvious group of thinkers in this stable consists of the latter-day fascists themselves.

To Maurice Bardèche, for example, it is daily becoming more urgent that fascism should re-emerge to carry out the spiritual regeneration of a European order which is threatened with elimination from the stage of world history. Far from being pessimistic about the prospects for this re-emergence, Bardèche believes that the last war actually prepared the way for the final victory of the movement. Before the war, he maintains, fascism was an immature, narrowly nationalistic movement, with no clear conception of the supra-national character of its mission. The war, however, purified fascist ideology in this respect and also benefited fascism by creating a situation in which the threat of 'colonization' by America and Russia eventually made the whole western world aware of the need for a supra-national drive for unification.[1]

In order to make his advocacy of fascism plausible, Bardèche obviously has to emphasize that fascism as he understands it – that is, 'true fascism' – does not mean a renewal of Nazi-type atrocities. In common with most other leading post-war fascists, he handles the problem by treating Nazism as a betrayal of the fascist revolution partly through its exclusive nationalism and racialism, and partly through its perversion of the leader principle. According to Bardèche, the leader principle is indeed a fundamental tenet of true fascism, but is grossly misunderstood and abused when it is identified, as it was by Hitler, with the uncritical worship of one man, instead of with collective leadership by an elite. But it is not only Nazism which Bardèche criticizes; he also dismisses Italian Fascism as a betrayal of 'true fascism', on the ground that Mussolini sacrificed the interests of Italy to his personal dream of dictatorship. Bardèche qualifies his rejection of Mussolini, however, by adding that the programme which the Duce adopted in 1944, at the time of the Salo Republic, was the closest approximation there has yet been to true fascism. Indeed, Bardèche concludes, the tragedy of fascism consists precisely in the fact that the man who came nearest to understanding it did so only when it was too late.[2] For Bardèche, then, the story of historical fascism is a story of the revolution betrayed. Like every true believer, he keeps his utopia so completely insulated from life that nothing can ever dent his faith; to argue with him would merely be to beat one's head against a brick wall. The same is true of Sir Oswald Mosley, the British fascist leader, who has also assiduously defended the continuing relevance of the movement for the spiritual life of post-war western society.

According to Mosley, fascism may claim pre-eminence

amongst modern ideologies because it alone recognizes that the principal threat to western civilization now comes not from any external enemy but from the prospect of internal spiritual disintegration. This prospect arises partly from the gradual paralysis of our spiritual life by the divorce between intelligence and will which lies at the heart of modern morality, and partly from the economic anarchy created by the survival of outdated liberal-capitalist values.[3] For Mosley, as for Bardèche, the answer lies in the supra-national ideal of a spiritually regenerated and politically united Europe. Like Bardèche, he accordingly criticizes the inter-war fascist movements for excessive nationalism. The true fascist ideal is expressed in his slogan, 'Europe one nation', which in practice amounts to the demand for a new European drive for empire: having lost a western empire in America and an eastern empire in Asia, the European world must now pool its possessions and resources in order to develop a third empire in Africa.[4] In addition, Europe must follow the Soviet example and utilize its most spectacular achievement, scientific research, in order to increase its military capacity. Finally, full adaptation to the communist threat and to the internal problems of modern industrial society demands a system of state control over the economy.

To find latter-day fascists like Bardèche and Mosley insisting upon the continuing relevance of their movement is hardly surprising, but to discover that leading political publicists in the academic sphere also envisage a fascist future is more disturbing. Since none of them has any obvious ideological axe to grind, it is their views, rather than those of the latter-day fascists themselves, that deserve careful attention. According to some of these thinkers, fascism is of continuing relevance mainly because it anticipated the corporatist social order towards which all western societies are now said to be moving with increasing rapidity. Members of this group suggest, more specifically, that in countries like Britain we already have 'fascism with a human face', by which they mean a socio-economic order that resembles the corporatist one which fascism aimed to create, but without the ideological trappings and coercive machinery associated with the fascist regimes.[5] Even if we ignore the fact that the concept of corporatism still remains as vague today as it was during the fascist era itself, another objection seems unanswerable. This is that it is absurd to treat the ideological features of the Italian and German regimes as incidental accoutrements of fascism when they were, on the contrary, its very essence, as an earlier chapter on the new activist style of politics sought to show. To strip away features such as the frenzied cult of will, the theatricality, the leader principle, and the coercive machinery in the hope of exposing a corporatist 'hard core' at the centre, then, is intellectually indefensible.

There is, however, a further group of political scientists whose members are less concerned with specific aspects of fascist ideology (like corporatist doctrine) than with fascism as a style of politics which is likely to dominate the course of political life during the remainder of the twentieth century. The leading representative of this group is the American scholar, A. J. Gregor, who maintains that we have now entered an era of 'universal fascism' in which fascism has moved beyond the West to Asia, Africa, and the Middle East. To that extent, he observes, 'Mussolini, in insisting that the twentieth century would be the century of fascism, appears to have been prescient. The twentieth century seems destined to suffer fascism, in one or another political community.'[6] It is Italian Fascism, rather than Nazism, that Gregor regards as the key to universal fascism in the emerging nations. In these countries, 'Mussolini's "citizen-militiaman" has become the model for political development' and Italian Fascism provides, more generally, 'not only the style and the institutions but the rationale for the radical politics of the twentieth century'.[7] Another member of this group of scholars, John Weiss, warns in similar vein that 'the greatest potential for fascism lies not in the liberal West, but in the dialectical polarities even now increasing in non-Western or underdeveloped societies'.[8]

This ambitious thesis naturally gives rise to major problems, all of which may be illustrated by considering in particular Gregor's treatment of Black Africa as one of the most important arenas for Third World fascism. Consider first the seven characteristics which provide the basis for Gregor's theory of universal fascism. These are: (1) an ideology of intense nationalism; (2) the institutions of an authoritarian and anti-liberal state; (3) a 'charismatic' leader mobilizing the masses; (4) the control of labour and consumption in the interests of a state-managed and productionist economy; (5) differential access to resources and power by a managerial bureaucracy under the control of a single party; (6) totalitarian control over political aggregation, communication and socialization, and (7) the creation of an autarkic (i.e. self-sufficient) industrial state.[9] It is with these characteristics in mind that Gregor labels Ghana, Guinea, Mali, Tanzania, Ivory Coast and Senegal as 'developmental dictatorships' which resemble Fascist Italy. This resemblance is especially marked, he believes, at the ideological level, where pronounced parallels exist between Mussolini's national syndicalism, on the one hand, and the phenomenon of so-called 'African Socialism', on the other. The relevant features of African Socialism, Gregor argues, are, 'The recurrent and systematic appeal to political myths and faiths, to national sentiment, national values, and national solidarity, to discipline, sacrifice, and responsibility, coupled with the rejection of class as a theoretical unit of analysis.'[10] Gregor lays especial emphasis on the writings of Leopold Senghor, the Senegalese head-of-state, whom he regards as the leading intellectual representative of African Socialism.[11]

Moving beyond ideology, Gregor finds that further parallels exist between the institutions and politics of the new African states and the Italian Fascist regime. At the institutional level, two important points of resemblance are the tendency of African states towards heroic personal leadership and towards a mass-mobilizing single-party system.[12] And at the policy level, Gregor maintains, there is widespread commitment in these states to rapid industrialization, just as he believes there was in Fascist Italy.

Gregor's critics have not been slow to question the parallels upon which he relies for the concept of universal fascism.[13] At the ideological level, the analogy with Italian Fascism is difficult to sustain, mainly because the whole social and cultural context in which African political ideologies have developed is entirely different from the European one within which fascism appeared. So far as institutional parallels are concerned, Gregor's analogy is no more easy to sustain. The development of

African states is by no means exclusively towards heroic leadership of the fascist type: Arnold Hughes and Martin Kolinsky, for example, point out that of the forty-two independent mainland states existing in 1976, no fewer than twenty were under some form of military rule.[14] Nor can it be said that there is a tendency towards totalitarian one-party systems, as Gregor maintains. On the contrary, in the period after independence the tendency has been for parties to decline in significance.[15] It may be added that, in the African context, the very concept of party itself may be infelicitous.[16] Finally, Gregor's assumption that both Mussolini's regime and contemporary African ones can properly be characterized as 'developmental' is itself totally implausible. Even amongst the African states which Gregor regards as 'developmental dictatorships', both policies and overt ideological goals are far too eclectic to permit an unequivocal classification of this kind. The same is true, as has already been noticed, of Mussolini's regime itself. Not only has Gregor been rightly criticized for imparting an exaggerated degree of consistency to Fascist thinking in Italy by presenting it in predominantly 'modernizing' terms,[17] but (as has already been pointed out) he completely ignores the fact that the actual effect of Fascist policies was to hinder rather than to facilitate modernization.

The relevance of fascism for the future, then, is not adequately analysed in the existing literature: neither the theory which relegates it to the past, nor that which elevates it into a 'universal' concept which holds the key to the future, is satisfactory. There is a third view, however, which avoids the defects of the two prevailing ones. Since this third position is implied throughout the present study, it can most easily be stated by briefly reformulating the argument which has been put forward.

According to this argument, what must now be contemplated is the possibility that whilst fascism itself belongs to the past, the new activist style of politics which gave rise to it is still alive. Unfortunately, the post-war era has been marked by a general disinclination to take this possibility seriously, largely perhaps because of widespread acquiescence in the dream of an impending era of social harmony, characterized above all by the 'end of

189

ideology'. That dream has now been badly dented by economic recession and high levels of unemployment, but even before these developments a shadow had already fallen across the great hopes surrounding the future. This was the appearance of terrorist movements like the Baader-Meinhof Group in Germany and the Red Brigades in Italy.

The growth of terrorism during this period illustrates once again that the modern enemies of limited politics never appear in that role but always present themselves as champions of 'the people', of 'true liberty', and of 'true democracy'; but in the present context the main problem is to decide whether members of the various terrorist groups are properly described as 'The New Fascists',[18] or as 'Hitler's Children',[19] to use the titles of two well-known studies. Instead of implying a direct link between fascism and terrorism, as such titles do, it would be less misleading to accept, in accordance with the analysis offered here, that fascism and terrorism are linked *indirectly*, by virtue of the fact that both share the same parent – the new activist style of politics. As has been seen, the activist style is a protean one, containing as it does several ingredients which may be assembled in a variety of different 'mixes', to yield different species of modern radical ideology. The earliest of these mixes was radical democratic theory. A subsequent mix was socialism. This was followed by the most overtly destructive mix we have yet experienced, which was fascism. Most recently, there have been the various activist mixes offered by the terrorist groups. All these mixes are offspring of the same activist parent, but – and this is the important point – the common parentage does not mean that the children themselves can properly be described as fascist, neo-fascist, or quasi-fascist. To use the word fascist in this way is not only a piece of intellectual confusion, it is also to risk fixing one's eyes so firmly upon that past that the distinctive features of the new activist siblings are never noticed. Likewise, to engage in the current debate about whether particular extremist groups belong to the 'left' or the 'right' is completely to ignore the fact that the whole of the modern European political tradition is so ambiguous that labels like left and right illuminate nothing but, on the contrary, merely obscure the sources of the dangers we confront. For the moment, however, what matters is that the post-war upsurge of terrorism lends powerful support to the view that whilst fascism itself may be dead, the activist style which gave rise to it is still very much with us.

We may end by speculating about whether the inter-war Italian and German experiences shed any light upon the kind of circumstances in which a small, fanatical movement of the terrorist type might succeed in winning mass support. The most sober guide here is Ignazio Silone's *The School for Dictators* (1938). In that work, Silone attempted to schematize the sequence of events which facilitated the triumph of Mussolini and Hitler in a series of generalizations which are suggestive of the vulnerability of the liberal-democratic state. The first generalization made by Silone is that the advent of dictatorship in modern democracy initially requires the existence of a situation in which the state is threatened by dislocation so severe that it faces the prospect of complete political paralysis, with the attendant prospect of civil war. But political paralysis, Silone adds, must be accompanied by a second condition, which is that the political crisis should initially benefit the main opposition party by enabling it to pose as the only one capable of establishing a new order. A third condition is that this opposition party should then prove unable to live up to the expectations which it has aroused. As a result, its blunders intensify distress, and the general mood of disillusionment rapidly increases public willingness to give credence to the desperate extra-constitutional remedies proposed by peripheral extremist parties. Against this background, an enterprising revolutionary party will express profound concern about the chaotic state of the nation's political life, whilst at the same time assiduously exacerbating the very crisis which created its opportunity. In order for it to advance, there must be a large *déclassé* element in the population upon which it can draw directly in order (so it will always claim) to root out the corruption which parliamentary government appears only to entrench more deeply. Finally, much depends upon the timing and ingenuity of the revolutionary leader, although, in Silone's view, the revolutionary party stands a good chance of success provided only that the leader is not a complete imbecile. Unfortunately there is no

191

reason to believe that contemporary social and political life is so secure that these conditions could not recur. There is therefore no reason to believe that activist movements of the fascist type could no longer succeed in acquiring power in the post-war period.

There will, of course, be those who hasten to assure us that the activist style is either long defunct, or is rapidly becoming so; but so long as the doctrine of popular sovereignty and the ideal of self-determination continue to provide the principal legitimating myths of the modern world, only a very rash man would venture to conclude that the great secret of activism revealed by Rousseau and first fully implemented by the fascists will not be seized upon once more in times of mass confusion and distress by more Pied Pipers. That secret, as Rousseau stressed, is of embarrassing simplicity: teach them children's games. Whether men will remember next time how bloody and ill-fated these games can be is a moot point. Probably they will not, since the philosopher was no doubt right when he remarked that men do indeed learn from experience, but always too late.

Appendix

The Italian Province of Carnaro

Outline of a New Constitution for the Free State of Fiume

Quis Contra Nos?

STATUTUM ET ORDINA
TUM EST
JURO EGO
SI SPIRITUS PRO NOBIS
QUIS CONTRA NOS?

FIUME OF ITALY
27 August 1920

The Enduring Will of the People

Fiume, for centuries a free commune of ancient Italy, declared her full and complete surrender to the mother-country on October 10, 1918.

Her claim is threefold, like the impenetrable armour of Roman legend.

Fiume is warden of the Italian marches, the furthest stronghold of Italian culture, the most distant land that bears the imprint of Dante. From century to century through all vicissitudes, through strife and anguish, Dante's Carnaro has done faithful service to Italy. From her as from a centre the spiritual life of Italy has shone forth and still shines forth over shores and islands, from Volosca to Laurana, from Moschiena to Albona, from Veglio to Lussino, from Cherso to Arbe.

This is her claim from history.

Fiume, as of old Tarsatica, placed at the southern end of the Liburnian rampart, stretches thence along the Julian Alps and is contained entirely within that boundary which science, tradition, and history alike confirm as the sacred confines of Italy.

This is her claim from position.

Fiume, with will unwavering and heroic courage, overcoming every attack whether of force or fraud, vindicated her right, two years ago, to choose her own destiny, her own allegiance on the strength of that just principle declared to the world by some of her unjust adversaries themselves.

This is her claim founded on Roman right.

193

In contrast to this threefold claim stands the threefold wrong, iniquity, cupidity, and force to which Italy submits in sorrow, leaving unrecognized and unclaimed the victory that she, herself, has won.

Thus it comes to pass that the inhabitants of the free city of Fiume, faithful to their Latin origin and determined to carry out their lawful decision, are framing a new model for their constitution to suit the spirit of their new life, not intending to limit that constitution to the territory which, under the title 'corpus separatum' – was assigned to the crown of Hungary, but offering it as a free alternative to any of those communities of the Adriatic which desire to break through all hindrances and rise to freedom in the name of a new Italy.

Thus, in the name of a new Italy, the people of Fiume, taking their stand on justice and on liberty, swear that they will fight to the utmost with their whole strength against any attempt to separate their land from the mother-country, and that they will defend for ever the mountain boundary of their country assigned to it by God and by Rome.

The Basis

1. The sovereign people of Fiume, in the strength of their unassailable sovereignty, take as the centre of their Free State the 'corpus separatum', with all its railways and its harbour.

But, as on the west they are determined to maintain contact with the mother-country, so, on the east, they are not prepared to renounce their claim to a frontier more just and more secure than might be assigned to them by the next happening in the give-and-take of politics or by any future treaties which they might be able to conclude with the rural and maritime communes after the proclamation of an open port and of generous statutes.

2. The Italian province of Carnaro is made up of the district of Fiume, of the islands, traditionally Venetian, which have declared by vote that they will share her fortunes; and of any neighbouring communities, which, after making a genuine application for admission, have been welcomed fraternally and in due legal form.

3. The Italian province of Carnaro is a State chosen by the people which has for basis the power of productive labour and for constitution the widest and most varied forms of autonomy such as were in use during the four centuries of our glorious communal period.

4. The province recognizes and confirms the sovereignty of all citizens without distinction of sex, race, language, class, or religion.

But above and beyond every other right she maintains the right of the producer; abolishes or reduces excessive centralization and constitutional powers, and subdivides offices and powers so that by their harmonious interplay communal life may grow more vigorous and abundant.

5. The province protects, defends, preserves, all popular rights and liberties; insuring international order by justice and discipline, seeks to bring back a time of well-ordered happiness which should bring new life to a people

delivered at last from a Government of lies and oppression; her constant aim is to raise the status of her citizens and to increase their prosperity; so that the citizenship shall be recognized by foreigners as a title of high honour just as it was in former days under the law of Rome.

6. All citizens of the State, of both sexes, are equal, and feel themselves equal in the eye of the law.

The exercise of their constitutional rights can be neither diminished nor suppressed except by public trial and solemn condemnation.

7. Fundamental liberties, freedom of thought and of the Press, the right to hold meetings and to form associations are guaranteed to all citizens by the Constitution.

Every form of religion is permitted and respected, and allowed to erect its own places of worship; but no citizen may allege his creed or the rites of his religion as a reason for withdrawing from the fulfilment of duties prescribed by the law.

Misuse of statutory liberty, when its purpose is illegal and when it disturbs the public peace may be punished, as provided by the law; but the law must in no way transgress the principle of liberty.

8. The Constitution guarantees to all citizens of both sexes: primary instruction in well-lighted and healthy schools; physical training in open-air gymnasiums, well-equipped; paid work with a fair minimum living wage; assistance in sickness, infirmity, and involuntary unemployment; old age pensions; the enjoyment of property legitimately obtained; inviolability of the home; 'habeas corpus'; compensation for injuries in case of judicial errors or abuse of power.

9. The State does not recognize the ownership of property as an absolute and personal right, but regards it as one of the most useful and responsible of social functions.

No property can be reserved to anyone in unrestricted ownership; nor can it be permitted that an indolent owner should leave his property unused or should dispose of it badly, to the exclusion of anyone else.

The only legitimate title to the possession of the means of production and exchange is labour.

Labour alone is the custodian of that which is by far the most fruitful and profitable to the general well-being.

10. The harbour, station, railway lines comprised in the territory of Fiume are the inalienable and incontestable property of the State in perpetuity.

By a statute of the Free Port, the full and free use of the harbour for commerce, industry, and navigation is guaranteed to foreigners as to natives, in perfect equality of good treatment and immunity from exorbitant harbour dues and from any injury to person or goods.

11. A National Bank of Carnaro, under State supervision, is entrusted with the issue of paper money and with all operations concerning credit.

A law for this purpose will decide methods and regulations to be followed and will point out the rights, functions, and responsibilities of the banks already in operation in the territory and of those that may be hereafter founded there.

12. All the citizens of both sexes have the full right to choose and carry on any industry, profession, art, or craft.

Industries started or supported by foreign capital and all concessions to foreigners will be regulated by liberal legislation.

13. Three elements unite to inspire and control the regulation, progress, and growth of the Community: the Citizens; the Corporations; the Communes.

14. There are three articles of belief which take precedence of all others in the Province and the federated communes:

Life is a good thing, it is fit and right that man, reborn to freedom, should lead a life that is noble and serious; a true man is he who, day by day, renews the dedication of his manhood to his fellowmen; labour, however humble and obscure, if well done adds to the beauty of the world.

The Citizens

15. The following persons have the rank of citizens of Carnaro: all citizens now on the register of the free city of Fiume; all citizens of the federated communes; all persons who have made application for citizenship and who have obtained it by legal decree.

16. Citizens are invested with all civil and political rights as soon as they reach the age of twenty.

Without distinction of sex they become electors and eligible for all careers.

17. Those citizens shall be deprived of political rights by formal sentence, who are: condemned by the law; defaulters with regard to military service for the defence of the territory; defaulters in the payment of taxes; incorrigible parasites on the community if they are not incapacitated from labour by age or sickness.

The Corporations

18. The State represents the aspiration and effort of the people, as a community, towards material and spiritual advancement.

Those only are full citizens who give their best endeavour to add to the wealth and strength of the State; these truly are one with her in her growth and development.

Whatever be the kind of work a man does, whether of hand or brain, art or industry, design or execution, he must be a member of one of the ten Corporations who receive from the commune a general direction as to the scope of their activities, but are free to develop them in their own way and to decide among themselves as to their mutual duties and responsibilities.

19. The first Corporation comprises the wage-earners of industry, agriculture

and commerce, small artisans, and small landholders who work their own farms, employing little other labour and that only occasionally.

The second Corporation includes all members of the technical or managerial staff in any private business, industrial or rural, with the exception of the proprietors or partners in the business.

In the third, are united all persons employed in commercial undertakings who are not actually operatives. Here again proprietors are excluded.

In the fourth, are associated together all employers engaged in industrial, agricultural, or commercial undertakings, so long as they are not merely owners of the business but – according to the spirit of the new constitution – prudent and sagacious masters of industry.

The fifth comprises all public servants, State and Communal employees of every rank.

In the sixth are to be found the intellectual section of the people; studious youth and its leaders; teachers in the public schools and students in colleges and polytechnics; sculptors, painters, decorators, architects, musicians, all those who practise the Arts, scenic or ornamental.

The seventh includes all persons belonging to the liberal professions who are not included in the former categories.

The eighth is made up of the Co-operative Societies of production and consumption, industrial and agricultural, and can only be represented by the self-chosen administrators of the Societies.

The ninth comprises all workers on the sea.

The tenth has no special trade or register or title. It is reserved for the mysterious forces of progress and adventure. It is a sort of votive offering to the genius of the unknown, to the man of the future, to the hoped-for idealization of daily work, to the liberation of the spirit of man beyond the panting effort and bloody sweat of to-day.

It is represented in the civic sanctuary by a kindled lamp bearing an ancient Tuscan inscription of the epoch of the communes, that calls up an ideal vision of human labour:

'Fatica senza fatica.'

20. Each Corporation is a legal entity and is so recognized by the State.

Chooses its own consuls; makes known its decisions in an assembly of its own; dictates its own terms, its own decrees and rules; exercises autonomy under the guidance of its own wisdom and experience; provides for its own needs and for the management of its own funds, collecting from its members a contribution in proportion to their wages, salary, business profits, or professional income; defends in every way its own special interest and strives to improve its status; aims at bringing to perfection the technique of its own art or calling; seeks to improve the quality of the work carried out and to raise the standard of excellence and beauty; enrols the humblest workers, endeavouring to encourage them to do the best work; recognizes the duty of mutual help; decides as to pensions for sick and infirm members; chooses for itself symbols, emblems, music, songs, and prayers; founds its own rules and ceremonies;

197

assists, as handsomely as it can, in providing enjoyment for the commune for its anniversary, fetes, and sports by land and sea; venerates its dead, honours its elders, and celebrates its heroes.

21. The relations between the Government of the province and the corporations and between the different Corporations are regulated by the methods defined in the statutes which regulate the relations between the central province and the affiliated communes and between the several communes.

The members of each Corporation form a free electoral body for choosing representatives on the Council of Governors (Provvisori).

The first place in public ceremonies is assigned to the consuls of the Corporations and their banners.

The Communes

22. The ancient 'potere normativo' will be re-established for all communes – the right of making laws subject to the Common Law.

They exercise all powers not specially assigned by the Constitution to the judicial, legislative and executive departments of the province.

23. Each commune has full sanction to draw up its own code of municipal laws, derived from its own special customs, character, and inherited energy and from its new national life.

But each commune must apply to the province for ratification of its statutes which the commune will give.

When these statutes have been approved, accepted, and voted on by the people they can be amended only by the will of a real majority of the citizens.

24. The communes have the acknowledged right to make settlements, agreements, and treaties between themselves, administrative and legislative.

But they are required to submit them to be examined by the Central Executive Power.

If the Central Power considers that such settlements, agreements, or treaties controvert the spirit of the Constitution, it sends them up for final decision to the Court of Administration.

If the Court declares them to be illegal and invalid, the Central Executive of the province makes provision for their cancellation.

25. If order, within a commune, should be disturbed by faction, rebellion, or plot, or by any other form of craft or violence, if the dignity or integrity of a commune should be injured or menaced by the transgression of another, the Executive of the province would intervene as mediator or peacemaker, if the communal authorities agreed in requesting it to do so, if a third of the citizens exercising political rights in the commune itself should make the request.

26. The following functions belong especially to the communes: to provide for primary instruction, according to the regulations laid down by the Central Education Authority; to nominate the communal judges; to appoint and maintain the communal police; to levy taxes; to contract loans within the

territory of the province, or even outside it, provided that the sanction of the Central Government shall have been obtained, but this will not be granted except in case of absolute necessity.

Legislation

27. Two elected bodies will exercise legislative power: the Council of Senators; the Council of 'Provvisori'.

28. The Senate is elected by means of direct and secret universal suffrage, by all citizens throughout the province, who have attained the age of twenty-one years and have been invested with political rights.

Any citizen who has a vote is eligible as a member of the Senate.

29. Senators remain in office ten years.

They are elected in the proportion of one to every thousand electors, but in no case can their number be under thirty.

All electors form a single constituency.

The election is to be by universal suffrage and proportional representation.

30. The Senate has authority to make ordinances and laws with reference to the penal and civil code, the police, national defence, public secondary instruction, art, relations between the communes and the State.

The Senate meets, as a rule, only once a year, in the month of October, for a short definite sitting.

31. The Council of the Provvisori is composed of sixty delegates, elected by universal secret suffrage and proportional representation.

Ten provvisori are elected by industrial workers and agricultural labourers; ten by seamen of all kinds; ten by employers; five by rural and industrial technicians; five by the managerial staffs in private firms; five by the teachers in the public schools, by the students in the higher schools, and by other members of the sixth Corporation; five by the liberal professions; five by public servants; five by Co-operative Societies of production, of labour and of consumption.

32. The provvisori remain in office two years.

They are not eligible unless they belong to the Corporation represented.

33. The Council of the Provvisori meets usually twice in the year, in the months of May and November, and uses the laconic method of debate.

It has authority to make ordinances and laws with reference to the commercial and Maritime code; to the control of labour; to transport; to public works; to treaties of commerce, customs, tariffs, and similar matters; to technical and professional instruction; to industry and banking; to arts and crafts.

34. The Senate and the Council of Provvisori unite together once a year as a single body on the first of December, as a Grand National Council under the title of Arengo del Carnaro.

The Arengo discusses and deliberates on relations with other States; on finance and the Treasury; on the higher studies; on reforms of the constitution; on extensions of liberty.

The Executive

35. Executive power in the province is exercised by seven ministers elected jointly by the National Assembly, the Senate, and the Council of Provvisori.

The Minister for Foreign Affairs, the Minister for Finance and the Treasury, and the Minister of Public Instruction are elected by the National Assembly.

The Minister of the Interior and of Justice, the Minister of National Defence are elected by the Senate. The Council of Provvisori elects the Minister of Public Economy and the Minister of Labour.

The Minister for Foreign Affairs takes the title Prime Minister and represents the Province in intercourse with other States 'primus inter pares'.

36. The seven ministers, once elected, remain in office for their allotted time. They decide everything that does not interfere with current administration.

The Prime Minister presides over the discussions and has the deciding vote when the votes are equally balanced.

The ministers are elected for a year, and are not re-eligible except once. But, after the interval of one year, they may be nominated again.

Judiciary Power

The Judiciary Power will be held by magistrates, Labour judges, judges of the High Court, judges of the Criminal Court, the Court of Administration.

38. The magistrates, elected to inspire public confidence, by all the electors of the various communes in proportion to their number, decide all civil and commercial cases under the value of five thousand lire and questions of crime where the penalty of imprisonment does not last more than one year.

39. The Labour judges decide cases of controversy between employers and workers, whether wage-earners or salaried staff.

The Labour judges are grouped in 'colleges', the members of each 'college' being nominated by one of those 'Corporations' which elect the Council of the Provvisori.

According to the following scale: two by industrial workers and agricultural labourers; two by all workers connected with the sea; two by employers; one by technical workers, industrial or agricultural; one by the liberal professions; one by members of the administrative staff in private firms; one by public employees; one by teachers, by students of the higher institutes, and by other members of the sixth Corporation; one by the Co-operative Societies of production, of labour and of consumption.

The Labour judges have power to divide their 'colleges' into branches in order to render their proceedings more rapid, they are to dispense justice with promptitude, clearness, and expedition.

A joint assembly of the branches constitutes a Court of Appeal.

40. The judges of the High Court adjudicate on all questions civil, commercial, and penal which are not dealt with by the magistrates and the Labour judges except those which are dealt with by the judges of the Criminal Court.

The judges of the High Court constitute the Court of Appeal for sentences of magistrates.

The judges of the High Court are chosen by the Court of Administration from citizens holding the title of Doctor of Law (LL.D.).

41. Seven sworn citizens, assisted by two deputies and presided over by a judge of the High Court compose the Criminal Court; which tries all crimes of a political nature and all those misdemeanours which would be punished by imprisonment for more than three years.

42. Elected by the National Council, the Court of Administration is composed of five acting members and two supplementary.

Of the acting members, at least three, and of the supplementary members, at least one shall be chosen from Doctors of Law.

The Court of Administration deals with: acts and decrees issued by the legislative and executive authorities to ascertain that they are in conformity with the Constitution; any statutory conflict between the legislative and executive authorities, between the province and the communes, between one commune and another, between the province and the Corporations, between the province and private persons, between the communes and the Corporations, between the communes and private individuals; cases of high treason against the province on the part of citizens who hold legislative or executive power; attacks on the rights of the people; civil contests between the province and the communes or between commune and commune; questions regarding the rights of citizenship and naturalization; questions referring to the competence (function) of the various magistrates and judges.

The Court of Administration has the ultimate revision of sentences and nominates by vote the judges of the High Court.

Citizens who are members of the Court of Administration are forbidden to hold any other office either in that commune or any other.

Nor may they carry on any trade or profession during the whole period that they are in office.

The Commandant

43. When the province is in extreme peril and sees that her safety depends on the will and devotion of one man who is capable of rousing and of leading all the forces of the people in a united and victorious effort, the National Council in solemn conclave in the Arengo may, voting by word of mouth, nominate a Commandant and transmit to him supreme authority without appeal.

The Council decides the period, long or short, during which he is to rule, not forgetting that in the Roman Republic the dictatorship lasted six months.

44. During the period of his rule, the Commandant holds all powers –

political and military, legislative and executive.

The holders of executive power assume the office of commissaries and secretaries under him.

45. On the expiration of the period of rule, the National Council again assembles and decides: to confirm the Commandant in his office, or else to substitute another citizen in his place, or else to depose him, or even to banish him.

46. Any citizen holding political rights, whether he have any office in the province or not, may be elected to the supreme office.

National Defence

47. In the province of Carnaro, all the citizens of both sexes, from seventeen to fifty-five years of age, are liable for military service for the defence of the country.

After selection has been made, men in sound health will serve in the forces of land and sea, men who are not so strong and women will serve in ambulances, hospitals, in administration, in ammunition factories, and in any other auxiliary work according to the capacity and skill of each.

48. State assistance on an ample scale is granted to all citizens who, during military service, have contracted any incurable infirmity, and to their families, if in need.

The State adopts the children of all citizens who are killed in defence of their country, assists their families in distress, and commends to the memory of future generations the names of the fallen.

49. In time of peace and security, the State will not maintain a standing army; but all the nation will remain armed, as prescribed by law, and its forces by land and sea well and duly trained.

Strict military service is confined to the period of instruction or to periods when war is either actually being waged or when there is immediate danger of war.

During periods of instruction or of war, the citizen will lose none of his civil and political rights; and will be able to exercise them whenever the necessities of active service permit.

Public Instruction

50. For any race of noble origin, culture is the best of all weapons.

For the Adriatic race, harassed for centuries by a ceaseless struggle with an unlettered usurper, culture is more than a weapon; like faith and justice, it is an unconquerable force.

For the people of Fiume at the moment of her rebirth to liberty, it becomes the instrument more helpful than any other against the insidious plots that have encircled her for centuries.

Culture is the preservative against corruption; the buttress against ruin.

In Dante's Carnaro the culture of the language of Dante is the custodian of that which has ever been reckoned as the most precious treasure of the people, the highest testimony to the nobility of their origin, the chief sign of their moral right of rule.

That moral right is what the new State must fight for. On its will to victory is founded the exaltation of the human ideal.

The new State, with unity completed, liberty achieved, justice enthroned, must make it her first duty to defend, preserve, and fight for unity, liberty, justice in the spirit of man.

The culture of Rome must be here in our midst and the culture of Italy.

For this cause the Italian province of Carnaro makes education – the culture of her people – the crown and summit of her Constitution, esteems the treasure of Latin culture as the foundation of her welfare.

51. The city of Fiume will have a free University, housed in a spacious building, capable of accommodating a great number of students and ruled by its own special ordinances.

There will be in the city of Fiume, a School of Painting, a School of Decorative Art, a School of Music free from any legal interference, conducted in a candid and open spirit under the guidance of a judgment acute enough to get rid of the incumbrance of the inefficient, to choose the best students from among the good and to assist the best in the discovery of new possibilities in the rendering of human sentiment.

52. The secondary schools will be under the supervision of the Senate; the technical and professional schools under that of the Council of the Provvisori; higher education, under that of the National Council.

In every school and in every commune the Italian language will have the first place.

In secondary schools the teaching of the various dialects spoken in the Italian province of Carnaro will be obligatory.

Primary instruction will be given in the language spoken by the majority of the inhabitants of each commune and also in parallel classes in that spoken by the minority.

If any commune tries to evade the obligation of providing those double courses of instruction the Central Government of the province reserves its right to provide them at the cost of the commune.

53. An Educational Council decides upon the nature and method of primary instruction which is compulsory in the schools of all communes.

The teaching of choral singing based on the genuine poetry of the people (folk songs) and the teaching of decorative art based on examples of indigenous popular art will hold a first place.

The Council will consist of: a representative of each commune; two representatives of secondary schools; two, of technical and professional schools; two, of institutions of higher education (to be elected by professors and students); two, by the Schools of Music; two, by the School of Decorative Art.

54. Schools, well lighted and ventilated, must not have on their walls any emblems of religion or of political parties.

The public schools welcome the followers of every religious profession, the believers in every creed and those, too, who are able to live without an altar and without a God.

Liberty of conscience receives entire respect. Each one may offer up his silent prayers.

But there will be inscribed on the walls inspiring words that, like an heroic symphony, will never lose their power to raise and animate the soul.

And there will be representations of those masterpieces of the painter's art which interpret most nobly the endless longings and aspirations of mankind.

Reforms of the Constitutions
55. Every seven years the Great National Council will meet in a special conference to consider constitutional reforms.

But the Constitution can be altered at any time, when a third of the citizen electors make a request for the alteration.

The following bodies have the right to propose amendments of the Constitution: the members of the National Council; the representatives of the communes; the Court of Administration; the Corporations.

The Right of Initiative
56. All citizens belonging to electoral bodies have the right of initiating legislative proposals with regard to questions which fall within the sphere of action of one or other Council; but the initiative will not take effect unless at least one-fourth of the electors of the Council in question are unanimous in moving and supporting it.

The Power of Appeal
57. All laws that have received the sanction of the two legislative bodies may be subjected to public reconsideration with the possibility of repeal provided that such reconsideration be asked for by a number of electors equal to at least a fourth of the enfranchised citizens.

The Right of Petition
58. All citizens have the right of petition towards those bodies which they have helped to elect.

Reduplication of Offices
59. No citizen may fill more than one official post nor take part in two legislative bodies at the same time.

Recall
60. Any official appointment may be revoked: when the official in question loses his political rights through a sentence confirmed by the Court of Law;

when the decree of revocation is voted for by more than half of the members of the electoral body.

Responsibility

61. All holders of power and all public officials of the province are legally responsible for any injury caused to State, commune, Corporation, or single citizen by any transgression of theirs, whether through misdoing, carelessness, cowardice, or inaccuracy.

Remuneration

62. All public officials, enumerated in the Statutes and appointed in the new Constitution, will receive suitable remuneration, in accordance with the decision of the National Council annually revised.

The Aediles

63. There will be in the province a College of Aediles, wisely selected from men of taste, skill, and a liberal education.

This 'College' will be a revival not so much of the Roman Aediles, as of the 'Office for the adornment of the City' which, in our fourteenth century, arranged a new road or a new piazza with the same sense of rhythm and proportion which guided them in the conduct of a Republican triumph or a carnival display.

It will provide for the decorum of life; secure the safety, decency, sanitation of public edifices, and private dwellings; prevent the disfigurement of roads by awkward or ill-placed buildings; enliven civic festivals by sea and land with graceful ornament, recalling our forefathers for whom the glory of the sunshine and a few fair garlands of flowers with human beauty of pageant and motion sufficed to frame a miracle of joy; convince the workers that to add beauty, some sign of joy in the building, to the humblest habitation is an act of piety, that a sense of religion, of human mystery, of the profundity of Nature may be passed on from generation to generation in the simplest symbol, carved or painted on the kneading trough or the cradle, on the loom or the distaff, on the linen chest or the cottage beam; it will try to reawaken in our people the love of beautiful line and colour in the things that are used in their daily life, showing them how much, in the old days, could be achieved by a slight geometrical design, by a star, a flower, a heart, a serpent or a dove on a pitcher or oil jar or jug, on a bench or chest or platter; it will serve to show our people how the ancient spirit of communal liberty manifested itself even in the utensils that received the imprint of man's life; finally, convinced that a people cannot attain to strength and nobility without noble architecture it will endeavour to make modern architects realize that the new materials – iron and glass and concrete – must be raised to the level of harmonious life by the invention of a new architecture.

Music

64. In the Italian province of Carnaro, music is a social and religious institution.

Once in a thousand or two thousand years music springs from the soul of a people and flows on for ever.

A noble race is not one that creates a God in its own image but one that creates also the song wherewith to do Him homage.

Every rebirth of a noble race is a lyric force, every sentiment that is common to the whole race, a potential lyric; music, the language of ritual, has power, above all else, to exalt the achievement and the life of man.

Does it not seem that great music has power to bring spiritual peace to the strained and anxious multitude?

The reign of the human spirit is not yet.

'When matter acting on matter shall be able to replace man's physical strength, then will the spirit of man begin to see the dawn of liberty': so said a man of Dalmatia of our own Adriatic, the blind seer of Sebenico.

As cock-crow heralds the dawn, so music is the herald of the soul's awakening.

Meanwhile, in the instruments of labour, of profit, and of sport, in the noisy machines which, even they, fall into a poetical rhythm, music can find her motives and her harmonies.

In the pauses of music is heard the silence of the tenth corporation.

65. In every commune of the province there will be a choral society and an orchestra subsidized by the State.

In the city of Fiume, the College of Aediles will be commissioned to erect a great concert hall, accommodating an audience of at least ten thousand with tiers of seats and ample space for choir and orchestra.

The great orchestral and choral celebrations will be entirely free – in the language of the Church – a gift of God.

STATUTUM ET ORDINATUM EST.
JURO EGO.

Notes

Introduction

1. *Fascism in Italy: Its Development and Influence* (London, 1969), p.100.
2. P. Hayes, *Fascism* (London, 1973), p.63.
3. R.J. Soucy, 'The Nature of Fascism in France', in *J. of Cont. History*, vol.1, no.1 (1966), p.53.
4. ibid.

1 A Bolt from the Blue

1. The origin of the word 'fascism' is noteworthy for two reasons: it did not derive from Mussolini's movement, and it was for long without any specific ideological or theoretical significance.

   In ancient Rome the *fasces* was a bundle of rods carried by the lictors in front of the consuls, as a symbol of authority. During the nineteenth century, however, the bundle of rods came to symbolize strength through unity: the point being that, whilst each independent rod was fragile, as a bundle they were strong. By extension, the word *fascio* came in modern Italian political usage to mean a group. It was first used in this sense in the 1890s by groups of revolutionary socialists in Sicily, to describe themselves. Thereafter, the word retained revolutionary connotations. It was these connotations which made it attractive, for example, to the young men of the left who demanded Italian intervention in the First World War. The *fasci* they formed were scattered over Italy, and it was to one of these spontaneously created groups, devoid of party affiliations, that Mussolini belonged. This was the Milan *fascio*, of which he was leader. January 24, 1915 was a turning point in the history of the *fasci*, since it was in that year that their leaders met in Milan and formed a national organization, after naming themselves *Fasci d'Azione rivoluzionaria* (bands for revolutionary action).

   In 1919, after the war had ended, Mussolini reconstituted the Milan *fascio*, using the new name *fasci di combattimento*. Other *fasci* of the same name were created, with the common goal of opposing all those – including the monarch and the government – whose pacific interests were deemed to be depriving Italy of the fruits of victory in the war. Apart from the new name and the new objective, the Milan *fascio* 'represented much the same lot who had formed the *fascio* in 1915' (H.W. Schneider, *Making the Fascist State*, N.Y., 1928, p.56).

2. Hans Kohn, *The Twentieth Century: The Challenge to the West and Its Response* (N.Y., 1959; 1st ed., 1949), p.56.

3. *The New Leviathan* (O.U.P., 1942).

4. 'Understanding and Politics', in *Partisan Review*, vol.20 (1953), p.379.

5. *Origins of Totalitarianism* (Cleveland, 1962; 1st ed. in German, 1951), p.ix.

6. A. Bullock, *Hitler: A Study in Tyranny* (London, 1954), p.25.

7. The series was published by Jonathan Cape (London), under the general editorship of George Steiner.

8. *The Destruction of Reason* (Eng. trans., London, 1980), pp.5 and 12.

9. *The Course of German History* (London, 1948), p.248.

10. *Encounter*, Sept. 1979, p.58.

11. References are to the Mentor ed. (N.Y., 1969). The original German title was *Der Faschismus in Seiner Epoche: Die Action francaise, Der italienische Faschismus, Der Nationalsocializmus* (Munich, 1963).

12. op cit., p.18.

13. ibid., p.553.

14. ibid., p.24.

15. ibid., p.567.

16. ibid., p.460.

17. ibid., p.505.

18. ibid., p.504.

19. ibid., p.563 et seq.

20. ibid., p.539.

21. ibid.

22. ibid., p.40.

23. Quoted by M. Kitchen, *Fascism* (London, 1976), p.7.

24. This quotation, and the references to Laqueur and Gerth, are from Peter Loewenberg, 'The Psychohistorical Origins of the Nazi Youth Cohort', in *Amer. Hist. Review* 75 (1971). The relevant pages are reprinted in *The Youth Revolution*, ed. A. Esher (London, 1974). The reference here is to p.90 of the latter work.

25. Cited by Hans Rogger in *Reappraisals of Fascism*, ed. H.A. Turner Jr. (N.Y., 1975), p.172.

26. See his Foreword to R.A. Brady's *The Spirit and Structure of German Fascism* (N.Y., 1971; first published 1937), p.xiv. See p.332 for Brady's own attack on the New Deal.

27. M. Matossian, 'Ideologies of Delayed Industrialization; Some Tensions and Ambiguities', in J.A. Kautsky, ed., *Political Change in Underdeveloped Countries* (Wiley, 1962), p.254.

28. E. Kedourie, *Nationalism in Asia and Africa* (London, 1971), p.20.

29. Knopf, N.Y., 1969.

30. *Fascism: The Contemporary Interpretations* (Univ. Programs Studies, General Learning Press, N.J., 1973), pp.34–5.

31. A.J. Gregor, 'Fascism and Modernization', in *World Politics*, XXVI/3 (1974), p.378.

32. Shephard B. Clough and Salvatore Saladino, *A History of Modern Italy* (N.Y., 1968), pp.460–1; see also Clough, *The Economic History of Modern Italy* (N.Y., 1964), p.238. Similarly sceptical estimates of growth are given by S. Lombardini, 'Italian Fascism and the Economy', in S.J. Woolf (ed.), *The Nature of Fascism* (London, 1968), p.162.

33. G.H. Hildebrand, *Growth and Structure in the Economy of Modern Italy* (N.Y., 1964), p.144.

34. A. Hughes and M. Kolinsky, ' "Paradigmatic Fascism" and Modernization: A Critique', in *Political Studies*, vol.24 (Dec. 1976), no. 4, p.376. See also Roland Sarti, *Fascism and the Industrial Leadership in Italy, 1919–1940* (Berkeley, 1971), pp.118–25.

35. See A. Shonfield, *Modern Capitalism* (London, 1965), pp.177–9; and M.M. Postan, *An Economic History of Western Europe, 1945–1964* (London, 1967), pp.220–1.

36. *The Twilight of Civilization* (London, 1946), p.19.

37. W. Reich, *Mass Psychology of Fascism* (3rd ed., N.Y., 1946). Quoted by R. de Felice, *Interpretations of Fascism* (Eng. trans., U.S.A., 1977), p.79.

38. In de Felice, op. cit., p.79.

39. G.H. Lasswell, 'The Psychology of Hitlerism', in *The Political Quarterly*, 1933; E. Fromm, *The Fear of Freedom* (1941); T. Parsons, 'Some Sociological Aspects of the Fascist Movements' (1942), reprinted in T. Parsons, *Essays in Sociological Theory* (N.Y., 1954).

40. See E. Fromm, *Essays for Freedom* (1941); and especially *The Authoritarian Personality* (N.Y., 1950), by T.W. Adorno, E. Frenkel-Brunswik, D.J. Levinson and R.N. Sanford.

41. E. Fromm, quoted by de Felice, op.cit., pp.83–4.

42. cf. J.F. Kirsht and R.C. Dillehay, *Dimensions of Authoritarianism: A Review of Research and Theory* (Univ. of Kentucky Press, 1967); Roger Brown, *Social Psychology* (Free Press, 1965); R. Christie and M. Jahoda, eds., *Studies in the Scope and Method of the Authoritarian Personality* (Free Press, 1954).

43. P. Loewenberg, 'The Psychohistorical Origins of the Nazi Youth Cohort', op. cit.; reprinted in *The Youth Revolution*, op. cit., pp.99 and 104.

44. Cited by Loewenberg, op. cit., p.96. Wangh's book appeared in 1964.

45. P. Hayes, *Fascism*, op. cit., pp.9 and 13.

46. *Fascism: The Contemporary Interpretations*, op. cit., pp.52–3.

47. C. Small, *Ariel Like a Harpy: Shelley, Mary and Frankenstein* (London, 1972).

48. *The Collected Essays, Journalism and Letters of George Orwell* (Penguin Bks, 1970), vol.2, p.29.

49. ibid., pp.166–73.

50. *The Letters of Jacob Burckhardt*, ed. A. Dru (N.Y., 1975), p.107.

51. ibid., p.202.

52. ibid., p.207.

2 Fascism and the New Activist Style of Politics

1. H.W. Schneider, *Making the Fascist State*, op. cit., pp.82–3.
2. See ch. 1, above, pp.13–14.
3. In E. Weber, *Varieties of Fascism* (N.Y., 1964), p.168.
4. Schneider, op. cit., p.352.
5. Quoted by N. Cohn in *The Pursuit of the Millennium* (N.Y., 1961; first published 1957), pp.73–4.
6. A. Sorel, *Europe and the French Revolution* (Eng. trans., London, 1970; first published 1885), pp.73–4.
7. E. Kedourie, *Nationalism* (London, 1960), p.92.
8. *Lettre à un soldat de la classe 60* (Les Sept Couleurs, Paris, 1960).
9. Quoted by Peter Campbell, in his introduction to Sieyès' *What Is the Third Estate?* (Eng. trans., London, 1963), pp.11–12.
10. G. Lowes Dickinson, *Revolution and Reaction in Modern France* (second ed., 1952; first published 1892), p.30; Sieyès' italics.
11. ibid., p.33.
12. A. Fried and R. Sanders, eds., *Socialist Thought* (N.Y., 1964), p.53.
13. Quoted in Kedourie, *Nationalism in Asia and Africa*, op. cit., p.565.
14. ibid., p.145.
15. ibid., p.146.
16. *The Second Sex* (Eng. trans., London, 1975), p.19.
17. *Medusa*, no. 1, Nov. 1978. No publisher is mentioned.
18. A. Cobban and J.W. Hunt, in their introd. to Sorel, *Europe and the French Revolution*, op. cit., p.29.
19. Kedourie, *Nationalism*, op. cit., p.18.
20. Cited in D. Mack Smith, ed., *Garibaldi* (N.J., 1969), p.42.
21. The words are those of Don Fabrizio, in Giuseppi di Lampedusa's *The Leopard* (Fontana ed., 1963; first published in Milan, 1958), p.145.
22. In Mack Smith, *Garibaldi*, op. cit., p.48.
23. ibid., p. 171.
24. ibid., p.132.
25. ibid., p.18.
26. ibid., p.112; italics in the original.
27. In A.W. Salomone, *Italy from the Risorgimento to Fascism* (Newton Abbot, 1971), p.230.
28. Quoted by Sir Ernest Barker, *Reflections on Government* (London, 1942), p.298.
29. Leon Degrelle, 'The Message of Rex'; quoted by Jacques Saint-Germain in *La Bataille de Rex* (Paris, 1937), pp.210–14.
30. N.H. Baynes, ed., *The Speeches of Adolf Hitler* (London, 1942), vol.2, pp.1166–7.
31. *Behemoth: The Structure and Practice of National Socialism, 1933–1944* (N.Y., 1966; first published 1942), pp.42–3.
32. *Genesis and Structure of Society*, trans. H.S. Harris from the posthumous ed. published in Florence, 1946 (Illinois, 1960), p.179.

33. J.H. Hallowell, *The Decline of Liberalism as an Ideology* (London, 1946), p.ix.
34. In *Varieties of Fascism*, op. cit., p.139.
35. C. Hibbert, *Mussolini* (Penguin Bks, 1975; first published 1962), p.156.
36. Quoted by Kedourie, *Nationalism in Asia and Africa*, op. cit., p.603; the emphasis is Robespierre's own.
37. Kedourie, *Nationalism*, op. cit., p.18.
38. *Commandant of Auschwitz* (Eng. trans., London, 1974; first published in Polish, 1951), p.201.
39. ibid., p.143.
40. In *Documents on Nazism, 1919–1945*, introd. and ed. J. Noakes and G. Pridham (London, 1974), pp.492–3.
41. Hibbert, *Mussolini*, op. cit., p.144.
42. H. Trevor-Roper, *The Last Days of Hitler* (London, 1976; first published 1947), p.118.
43. B. King, *The Life of Mazzini* (London, 1912); quoted in *The Youth Revolution*, ed. Esher, op. cit., p.41.
44. ibid., p.46.
45. *Mein Kampf*, trans. J. Murphy (London, 1939), p.340.
46. Baynes, *Speeches of Adolf Hitler*, op. cit., vol.1, p.548.
47. Noakes and Pridham, *Documents*, op. cit., pp.359–60.
48. N. Stone in the *T.L.S.* (16 Oct. 1981), p.1200.
49. Kedourie, *Nationalism*, op. cit., p.94.
50. ibid., p. 92.
51. A. de Musset, *La Confession d'un enfant du siècle* (1836), Eng. trans., *A Modern Man's Confession*, by G.F. Monkshood (London, 1906), pp.9 and 16.
52. Quoted by Sir Lewis Namier in *Vanished Supremacies* (London, 1958), p.25.
53. Hibbert, *Mussolini*, op. cit., p.156.
54. Trevor-Roper, *The Last Days of Hitler*, op. cit., p.126.
55. B.D. Wolfe, *An Ideology in Power* (London, 1966), p.347.
56. Quoted by D. Settembrini, 'Mussolini and the Legacy of Revolutionary Socialism', in *J. of Cont. History*, vol.11 (Oct. 1976), p.261.
57. G.L. Mosse, *The Culture of Western Europe* (Chicago, 1961), p.343.
58. D. Mack Smith, *Italy* (Michigan, 1959), p.327.

3 Fascism as Theatrical Politics

1. Eng. trans. (Harvard Univ. Press, 1950). The German ed. first appeared in 1946.
2. ibid., p.75.
3. ibid., p.72.
4. *Popolo d'Italia*, 5 March 1919; quoted in Schneider, op. cit., p.57.
5. *Mein Kampf*, op. cit., p.278.

6. I am indebted in the following paragraph to an unpublished paper by Mr David George, of Newcastle University.
7. In Weber, *Varieties of Fascism*, op. cit., p.157.
8. ibid., p.139.
9. In S.W. Halperin, *Mussolini and Italian Fascism* (N.Y., 1964), p.99.
10. Weber, *Varieties of Fascism*, op. cit., p.62.
11. *Mein Kampf*, op. cit., p.113.
12. In *Italian Fascisms*, ed. A. Lyttelton (London, 1973), p.147.
13. *Mein Kampf*, op. cit., p.111.
14. ibid., p.283.
15. In Salomone, *Italy*, op. cit., pp.231–3.
16. ibid., pp.250–5.
17. See, in particular, his *Mussolini's Roman Empire* (Peregrine Bks, 1979).
18. See, for example, A.J. Gregor, *The Fascist Persuasion in Radical Politics* (N.J., 1974), pp.412–13.
19. *Varieties of Fascism*, op. cit., p.62.
20. 'Discourse on Political Economy', in *The Social Contract and Discourses*, trans. and ed. G.D.H. Cole (revised ed., J.M. Dent, 1973), p.127.
21. 'Government of Poland', in *Political Writings*, ed. F.M. Watkins (London, 1953), p.244.
22. ibid., p.171.
23. ibid., p.176.
24. ibid., p.178.
25. ibid., p.179.
26. ibid., pp.179–80.
27. ibid., p.169.
28. ibid., pp.162–7.
29. cf. Judith Shklar, *Men and Citizens* (C.U.P., 1969), ch. 1.
30. Nolte, *Three Faces*, op. cit., p.344.
31. Quoted in *The Youth Revolution*, ed. A. Esher, op. cit., p.33.
32. G. Mosse, 'Mass Politics in the Political Liturgy of Nationalism', in *Nationalism*, ed. E. Kamenka (London, 1976), p.40.
33. ibid., p.42.
34. ibid., p. 40.
35 ibid.
36. *Behemoth: The Structure and Practice of National Socialism, 1933–1944* (N.Y., 1966; first published 1942), p.465.
37. Mosse, op. cit., p.40.
38. M. Maschmann, *Account Rendered* (Eng. trans., London, 1964), p.35.
39. Mack Smith, *Italy*, op. cit., p.336.
40. ibid., p.334.
41. Quoted by Nolte, *Three Faces*, op. cit., p.243.
42. ibid., p.244.
43. ibid.
44. M.A. Ledeen, *The First Duce: D'Annunzio at Fiume* (Eng. trans., London, 1977; first published in Italy, 1975 as *D'Annunzio a Fiume*), p.10.

45. cf. O. Sitwell, *Noble Essences* (London, 1950), p.123.
46. ibid.
47. Nolte, *Three Faces*, op. cit., p.243; italics in the original.
48. Sitwell, op. cit., p.125.
49. Ledeen, *The First Duce*, op. cit., pp.9–10.
50. ibid., p.202.
51. ibid., p.201.
52. ibid.
53. The Constitution of Fiume is reprinted in full, in an English translation, in the Appendix.
54. Quoted by A.G. Rabinbach in 'The Aesthetics of Production in the Third Reich', in *J. of Cont. History*, vol.11, no.4 (Oct. 1976), p.43.
55. Burton, 1938, p.17; quoted by Rabinbach, op. cit., p.63.
56. Rabinbach, op. cit., p.49.
57. Mack Smith, *Italy*, op. cit., p.336.

4 The Fascist Revision of the New Activist Style

1. Namier, 'The First Mountebank Dictator', in *Vanished Supremacies*, op. cit., pp.54–5.
2. In Salomone, *Italy*, op. cit., p.214.
3. *The Crowd*, Eng. trans. (London, 1896), p.231.
4. ibid., p. 15.
5. ibid., p.80.
6. ibid.
7. ibid., p.81.
8. ibid., p.35.
9. ibid.
10. ibid., p.141.
11. ibid.
12. ibid., p.142.
13. ibid., pp.143–6.
14. J.L. Stanley, *From Georges Sorel* (N.Y., 1976), p.205.
15. ibid.
16. ibid.
17. ibid.
18. ibid.
19. ibid.
20. ibid.
21. ibid.
22. ibid.
23. ibid.
24. ibid.
25. 'The Legacy of Georges Sorel', *Encounter*, Feb. 1970.
26. *Mein Kampf*, op. cit., p.385.

213

27. ibid., p.375.
28. ibid., p.346.
29. See M. Oakeshott, ed., *The Social and Political Doctrines of Contemporary Europe* (C.U.P., 1938), p.179.
30. *Mein Kampf*, op. cit., p.383.
31. London, 1930 (revised edition; first published 1916), pp.235–6.
32. *The Storm of Steel* (Eng. trans., London, 1929), p.xii.
33. ibid., p.316.
34. Quoted by R.D'O. Butler, *The Roots of National Socialism, 1783–1933*, (London, 1941), p.207.
35. ibid., p.206.
36. *Alfred Rosenberg: Selected Writings*, ed. by R. Pois (London, 1970), pp.161–2. The italics are Rosenberg's.

5 The Fascist Weltanschauung

1. *Mein Kampf*, op. cit., p.492.
2. In Mack Smith, *Italy*, op. cit., p.395.
3. In Noakes and Pridham, eds., *Documents*, op. cit., p.433.
4. See Barker, *Reflections*, op. cit., pp.348–9.
5. ibid., p.349.
6. ibid., p.350.
7. ibid., pp.354–5.
8. Mack Smith, *Italy*, op. cit., p.396.
9. Quoted G. Salvemini, *Under the Axe of Fascism* (London, 1936), p.418.
10. Mack Smith, *Italy*, op. cit., p.411.
11. Matteotti: a wealthy socialist landowner who was an outspoken critic of Fascism. On 13 June 1924, shortly before it was believed he was going to publish documents revealing the bloodthirsty activities of leading Fascist figures, his body was discovered buried in a shallow grave twenty kilometres outside Rome. Both liberals and socialists were outraged, and for some months opposition to Mussolini appeared strong and united enough to bring down his regime. On 3 January 1925, however, Mussolini declared in a speech to the assembly that, 'I and I alone assume the political, moral and historic responsibility for everything that has happened.' In face of this challenge, the opposition proved weak and disorganized and thereafter Mussolini was able to proceed without encountering significant resistance. See, for example, C. Hibbert, *Benito Mussolini* (Penguin Bks, 1975; first published 1962), pp.65–8.
12. H. Rauschning, *Hitler Speaks* (London, 1939), pp.175–6.
13. The way in which the alienation theme helped the Nazi cause is explored in detail by F. Stern, in *The Politics of Cultural Despair* (U.S.A., 1965; first published 1961).
14. J.M. Ritchie, *Gottfried Benn* (London, 1972), pp.100–1.
15. ibid.
16. ibid., p.102.

17. Quoted by A. Hamilton, *The Appeal of Fascism: a Study of Intellectuals and Fascism 1919–1945* (London, 1971), p.147.
18. Lukács, *The Destruction of Reason*, op. cit., p.832.
19. Hamilton, op. cit., p.165.
20. E. David, *Italian Food*, Penguin Bks, 1977, pp.93–4.
21. Hamilton, op. cit., pp.125–6.
22. *Germany's Third Empire* (Eng. trans. by E.O. Lorimer, 1971; first published 1934).
23. ibid., p.193.
24. ibid.
25. ibid., p.238.
26. ibid., p.239.
27. ibid., p.220.
28. See, for example, J.P. Stern, *Ernst Jünger* (Cambridge, 1953).
29. Hamilton, op. cit., p.123.
30. Stern, *Ernst Jünger*, op. cit., p.12.
31. Quoted by I. Silone in *Emergency Exit* (Eng. trans., London, 1969), p.115.
32. G.L. Mosse, *The Nationalization of the Masses* (N.Y., 1975), p.201.
33. ibid.
34. Noakes and Pridham, *Documents*, op. cit., p.98.
35. Barker, *Reflections*, op. cit., p. 298.
36. Noakes and Pridham, *Documents*, op. cit., p.85.
37. La Mazière, *The Captive Dreamer* (U.S.A., 1974), p.31.
38. ibid., p.32.
39. Noakes and Pridham, *Documents*, op. cit., pp.331–2.
40. Barker, *Reflections*, op. cit., p.298.
41. ibid.
42. Quoted by A. Lyttelton, 'Fascism in Italy: The Second Wave', in *J. of Cont. Hist.*, vol. 1, no. 1 (1966), p.77.
43. Quoted by Lukács in *The Destruction of Reason*, op. cit., p.660.
44. Quoted by Barker (from Schmitt's *Staat, Bewegung, Volk*) in *Reflections*, op. cit., p.375.
45. K. Larenz, 'Die rechts-und staatsphilosophie des deutschen Idealismus und ihre gegenwarts Bedeutung', (in *Staatsphilosophie*, a part of *Abt. IV des Handbuchs der Philosophie*), p.168. Quoted in Barker, *Reflections*, op. cit., p.134, note 2.
46. Hitler's speech at Lustgarten, Berlin, 30 Jan. 1936.
47. *Mein Kampf*, op.cit., p.290.
48. Quoted by Salomone in *Italy*, op. cit., p.251.
49. *Staat, Bewegung, Volk* (1933); quoted by Barker in *Reflections*, op. cit., p.291.
50. Schmitt, op. cit., quoted by Barker, ibid.
51. Quoted by Lukács in *The Destruction of Reason*, op. cit., p.659.
52. Kedourie, *Nationalism*, op. cit., p.58.
53. ibid., p.56.

54. In Butler, *The Roots of National Socialism, 1783–1933* (London, 1941), p.24.

55. In J.G. von Herder, *Reflections on the Philosophy of the History of Mankind* (Eng. trans., Chicago, 1968), p.7.

56. Namier, *Vanished Supremacies*, op. cit., p.42.

57. ibid., p.40.

58. ibid., p.47.

59. Kedourie, *Nationalism*, op. cit., p.114.

60. Quoted by E. Halévy in *The Era of Tyrannies* (N.Y., 1965), p.60.

61. In J. Braunthal, *Need Germany Survive?* (London, 1943), p.36.

62. Baynes, *Speeches of Adolf Hitler*, op. cit., vol.1, pp.774–5.

63. Quoted in Salomone, *Italy*, op. cit., pp.296–7.

64. Weber, *Varieties of Fascism*, op. cit., p.142.

65. In H.S. Reiss, *The Political Thought of the German Romantics* (London, 1955), pp.107–8.

66. Butler, *The Roots of National Socialism, 1783–1933*, op. cit., pp.37–8.

67. See Braunthal, *Need Germany Survive?*, op. cit., pp.34–5; also F.W. Kaufmann, 'Fichte and National Socialism', in *APSR*, vol.36, pp. 460–471.

68. Mack Smith, *Italy*, op. cit., p.422.

69. *Mein Kampf*, op. cit., pp.330–1.

70. 'The Doctrine of Fascism', in *Political and Social Doctrines of Contemporary Europe*, ed. Oakeshott, op. cit., p.167.

71. In Lyttelton, ed., *Italian Fascisms*, op. cit., p.149.

72. A. J. Gregor, *The Ideology of Fascism* (N.Y., 1969), pp.252–3.

73. Printed in Gregor, op. cit., as Appendix A, pp.383–6.

74. cf. Gregor, op. cit., p.267.

75. Renzo de Felice, *Fascism: An Informal Introduction to Its Theory and Practice* (N.J., 1976), p.68.

76. Mack Smith, *Italy*, op. cit., p.121.

77. In 1923, Mussolini bombarded the island of Corfu on the pretext of responding to Greek aggression. His real aim was to achieve domestic popularity by eclipsing D'Annunzio's Fiume exploit. In this respect he was partially successful, but the wider significance of the incident is the early indication which it provided of the likely future course of Fascist foreign policy. As Denis Mack Smith observes, 'It set an ominous example of unpunished violence, at the same time as it defied the League of Nations' (*Italy*, op. cit. p.446).

78. ibid., p.145.

79. Lyttelton, *Italian Fascisms*, op. cit., p.116.

80. Quoted in Mack Smith, *Italy*, op. cit., pp.134–5.

81. *Christ Stopped at Eboli* (Eng. trans., London, 1946), p.80.

82. ibid., p.89.

83. ibid., p.76.

84. ibid., p.250.

85. Eng. trans., London, 1959.

86. London, 1964.
87. C.W. Cassinelli, *Total Revolution* (Oxford, 1976), p.237.
88. A. Lyttelton, *The Seizure of Power* (London, 1973), p.400. Lyttelton records that by 1930 there were only 100,000 licensed radio sets in Italy.

6 Fascism and the Future

1. M. Bardèche, *Qu'est-ce que le Fascisme?* (Les Sept-Couleurs, Paris, 1961), pp.19–20.
2. ibid., p.20.
3. O. Mosley, *Mosley: The Facts* (London, 1957), p.200.
4. ibid., p.20.
5. See, for example, Pahl and Winkler, 'The Coming Corporatism', in *New Society*, 10 Oct. 1974; also S. Brittan, 'Towards a Corporate State?', *Encounter*, vol.44, no.6 (June 1975); G. Ionescu, *Centripetal Politics* (London, 1975).
6. A.J. Gregor, *The Fascist Persuasion in Radical Politics* (N.Y., 1974), p.434.
7. ibid., pp.412–13.
8. J. Weiss, *The Fascist Tradition: Radical Right-Wing Extremism in Modern Europe* (N.Y., 1967), p.129.
9. These attributes are listed by Gregor in ch. 5 of *The Fascist Persuasion*, op. cit., in the course of a comparison of Fascist Italy and Stalinist Russia. The summary here is from Hughes and Kolinsky, ' "Paradigmatic Fascism" and Modernization: A Critique', op. cit., p.372.
10. A.J. Gregor, 'African Socialism and Fascism, an Appraisal', *Review of Politics*, XXIX/3 (1967), p.399.
11. Gregor, ibid., pp.336–44.
12. Gregor, *The Fascist Persuasion in Radical Politics*, op. cit., p.399.
13. See, for example, Hughes and Kolinsky, ' "Paradigmatic Fascism" and Modernization: A Critique', op. cit., pp.371–96.
14. ibid., p.386.
15. ibid., p.387.
16. ibid.
17. ibid., p.381.
18. L.P. Wilkinson, *The New Fascists* (London, 1981).
19. G. Becker, *Hitler's Children* (London, 1977).

Select Bibliography

This short selection of works by leading authorities has been compiled mainly with a view to illustrating the variety of different interpretations of the subject.

Hannah Arendt, *The Origins of Totalitarianism* (London, 1968)

E. Barker, *Reflections on Government* (London, 1942)

A.J. Gregor, *The Fascist Persuasion in Radical Politics* (Princeton, 1974)

E. Kedourie, *Nationalism* (London, 1960)

J. Maritain, *The Twilight of Civilization* (Eng. trans., London, 1946)

F. Meinecke, *The German Catastrophe* (Eng. trans., Boston, 1950)

A.F. Organski, *The Stages of Political Development* (New York, 1969)

N. Poulantzas, *Fascism and Dictatorship* (Eng. trans., London, 1974)

H. Rauschning, *Germany's Revolution of Destruction* (Eng. trans., London, 1939)

J.L. Talmon, *The Rise of Totalitarian Democracy* (Boston, 1950)

Index